The Horseman's Way:

Leadership Skills from the Arena

SCOTT CHAMPION

Cp
PUBLISHING

First published in 2025 by Champion Performance Publishing,

62 Pamplings Road,

Peak Crossing Qld 4306

ISBN: 978-1-7644687-3-2

NATIONAL LIBRARY OF AUSTRALIA

A catalogue record for this book is available from the National Library of Australia

Disclaimer

This book is provided for informational and educational purposes only. While the author and publisher have made every effort to ensure that the information contained in this book is accurate and up to date, no representations or warranties are made regarding the completeness, accuracy, reliability, or applicability of the information to any particular individual, situation, or purpose.

The content of this book reflects the author's personal experiences, observations, and interpretations, and should not be relied upon as a substitute for independent judgment or professional advice. Any reliance you place on the information contained in this book is strictly at your own risk.

CONTENTS

DEDICATION

To my wife, Cara,

For your unwavering support, your patient encouragement, and your belief in this book even when the words wouldn't come. Your strength made this journey possible.

To my parents, Warwick and Rosemary,

For putting me in the saddle when I was young, for nurturing my love of horses, and for teaching me that true horsemanship is about far more than riding. The seeds you planted in my youth have grown into everything these pages contain.

To my sons, William and Tyrell,

You didn't know it at the time, but you were the loves of my life from the day you were born. Watching you both become the men that you have, has inspired me to keep pushing my boundaries.

Thank you to each of you!

PREFACE

Over the years I have had many roles: a student, a cattleman, a soldier, a surveyor, a pro-rodeo cowboy, and a father, to name a few. As long as I can remember, though, I have been a horse trainer. But I only became a professional horse trainer a few years ago. I chose this path because I felt a deep urge to help people communicate with horses in a better way, and I realized I couldn't fully serve that calling without committing myself completely to the work of training.

Throughout my life I have been blessed to be guided by some of the finest teachers of horsemanship in the world. Australian trainers, men of the calibre of Gordon McKinlay, Ken May, and Ian Francis, nurtured my understanding through my late teens and early twenties. Later, it was people like Robbie Hodgeman, Mark Buttsworth, Darren Palmer, and Lynda McCallum who continued my education, sanding off the rough edges, helping me develop in the cutting pen and the campdraft arena.

Two American trainers probably had the greatest influence upon me: Ray Hunt and Pat Parelli. But there were also others like Terry Clifford (an American-based Australian trainer) and Graham Amos (a retired American-based Australian trainer) who provided intimate knowledge about training cutting horses. The tradition that exists, where men and women who have assimilated knowledge over time are encouraged to pass it on to successive generations, is one of the greatest blessings we have.

I say these things not because I'm trying to beat my own drum, though I am deeply appreciative of the opportunities I've had to study under these great instructors. Rather, I want you to see that you have the opportunity to learn skills and develop talents in virtually any direction or skillset you choose. Just because your career path has taken you down a particular road doesn't mean you must always focus exclusively on the field you know.

I have written this book because horsemanship is the language I use to talk to people about becoming who they're capable of being. You might be a doctor, a lawyer, a business director, a builder, or anything else in your life away from horses. But when you step into the yard with a horse, they don't know any of that and couldn't care less. To them, you are simply who you are when you're standing in front of them. And they have a world of knowledge to teach you, if you're ready to listen.

The knowledge they offer isn't the kind you'll gain in schools and universities around the country. But it's applicable to every discipline those institutions teach, to your place of business, to your home, and to your community. Developing the feel for how another person is experiencing a situation. Seeing challenges through their eyes. Helping them achieve the tasks in front of them while enabling you to achieve your goals as a result. These are the things you can learn from these beautiful creatures.

Finally, I would like to give credit to Dr. Myron Golden for explaining a concept I had never considered before. The "Be, Do, Do, Do, Have" framework that I've heard Dr. Golden teach numerous times led me to conceive of the agricultural methodology upon which I've structured this book. Fundamentally, the concept takes the following form:

1. Be the Farmer (or in this case, the leader)

2. Do Plant the seed (establish the foundational idea)

3. Do Grow the plant (nurture the idea as it develops)

4. Do Prune the plant (remove what doesn't serve the purpose)

5. Have Enjoy the fruits of your harvest

By applying this concept to my training and coaching methodology, I've been able to see just how close I had been to success, while at the same time seeing how far away from achieving that success I continued to stay because I kept taking the pruning step for granted.

By taking that step back and refocusing upon what was important, and more importantly, removing what was not important from my focus, I was able to become freer, more relaxed, and more in tune with my horses. And with everyone else I connected with.

This book is the result of that pruning, the essential principles distilled from decades of learning, ready to be planted in new soil.

The Horseman's Way

INTRODUCTION

The Mirror That Tells the Truth

One moment I was walking into the arena, relaxed and confident after years of working with Harry. Knowing those years of preparation held the key to our success. The next, I was feeling everything I knew about horsemanship, about leadership, about myself, fall apart in a cloud in the arena dust.

Harry wasn't being deliberately mean. He wasn't trying to embarrass me in front of the judges, though that happened. Without knowing it, he was simply showing me, with the honesty that only a horse can bring, that I had been missing something fundamental. For more than three years, I'd been working on him when I should have been working with him. I'd been focused on technique, which is important, but I missed the opportunity to truly connect with him.

Tom Dorrance once said, "The horse is a mirror to your soul, and sometimes you might not like what you see in the mirror." That day, looking at Harry's anxious, high-headed performance, I saw exactly what Tom meant. The horse was showing me the truth about my leadership: I had strength, but did I have enough humility? I had ambition but was I compassionate enough? I was determined but had no understanding!

I had everything except what mattered most.

What This Book Is About

This is not another book about horse training techniques. You won't find detailed instructions on lateral flexion or collected gaits. You won't learn the "seven steps to a perfectly trained horse" or discover the "secret" that professional trainers don't want you to know.

What you will find is something far more valuable: a framework for developing the kind of competence that transcends the physical and mental, reaching into territory that Tom Dorrance struggled to articulate but that he called, for lack of a better word, "spirit."

The Horseman's Way is about learning to work with horses, and with people, at the deepest possible level. It's about developing what I call Incorporeal Competence: mastery that isn't limited by physical strength or mental cleverness because it draws on something more fundamental.

It's about creating true unity and willing communication, not just between horse and human, but between spirit and spirit.

The lessons in this book come from three sources:

From the arena: Personal stories of working with horses who have taught me more through my failures and my successes and working with them every day than any human teacher could. Horses like Harry, who showed me that competence without compassion is just sophisticated domination. Horses like Ironman, who taught me that strength without gentleness solves nothing. Horses who, by being exactly who they are, revealed who I needed to become.

From history: Leaders, warriors, and wisdom figures who demonstrated these principles long before anyone thought to apply them systematically. Alexander the Great turning Bucephalus to face the sun. Moses transforming from an angry prince into a humble shepherd-leader. Marcus Aurelius writing to himself beside the Danube about emotional regulation. Jesus demonstrating that power and gentleness aren't opposites but partners. Their stories aren't just inspiring, they're instructive.

From the wisdom of master horsemen: Particularly Tom and Bill Dorrance, the brothers who revolutionized horsemanship not through force or technique, but by learning to listen to what horses were trying to tell them. Tom could feel a fly land on a dog's tail through his hand resting on the dog's head. That level of sensitivity, that willingness to feel and honour another being's reality, is what this book is ultimately about developing.

The Framework: From Foundation to Harvest

The journey to Incorporeal Competence follows a clear path, structured like a year in the life of a farmer:

The Foundation (Chapters 1-2): Before you can build anything lasting, you need solid ground. Before you can plant you need fallow ground. We'll explore why ancient wisdom matters in our modern world, then establish Humble Strength as the fallow ground for the growth of everything that follows, looking at the paradox of possessing power while refusing to wield it carelessly.

Three Pillars, Each with Three Stages:

The book is organized around three pillars of development, Courage & Vision, Communication, and Service, each progressing through agricultural stages of planting, growing, and pruning.

Pillar One: Courage & Vision

- **Planting (Chapter 3 - Fearless Guidance):** Learning to step into uncertainty first, demonstrating that courage is possible
- **Growing (Chapter 6 - Compassionate Ambition):** Maturing courage into sustainable drive that honours others' wellbeing
- **Pruning (Chapter 9 - Peaceful Directedness):** Refining ambition into calm, clear guidance that doesn't waver with circumstances

Pillar Two: Communication

- **Planting (Chapter 4 - Emotionless Communication):** Removing emotional distortion from messages to create clarity
- **Growing (Chapter 7 - Balanced Coordination):** Aligning body, mind, and emotion into embodied congruence
- **Pruning (Chapter 10 - Centred Transcendence):** Expanding awareness from stillness to touch others spirit-to-spirit

Pillar Three: Service

- **Planting (Chapter 5 - Powerful Gentility):** Integrating strength and softness in service of others
- **Growing (Chapter 8 - Determined Understanding):** Persisting in the pursuit of truth even when it's uncomfortable
- **Pruning (Chapter 11 - Creative Destruction):** Developing wisdom to know what must be released so new growth can emerge

The Harvest (Chapter 12 - Incorporeal Competence): When all three pillars are fully developed, something extraordinary becomes possible: the ability to work at the level of spirit with skill, sensitivity, and wisdom.

But Why the Agricultural Metaphor?

Working with horses, and with people, isn't a mechanical process. You can't simply apply technique A to problem B and expect result C. Living beings don't work that way.

But they do respond to the same principles that govern all growth in the natural world:

- Seeds must be planted before anything can grow. You establish fundamental principles and practices.
- Plants require a growing season where development happens gradually, sometimes invisibly. You tend the qualities you've planted with consistent practice.
- Mature plants need pruning to reach their full potential. You refine what you've developed, letting go of what no longer serves.
- Only after this cycle is complete can you harvest. The qualities you've developed culminate in mature competence.

This isn't a "90-day transformation" or a "seven-step program." This is the work of years, practiced daily, refined continuously, matured patiently. Just as Tom and Bill Dorrance spent ninety-three years each developing their understanding, this framework acknowledges that real mastery takes time.

How to Read This Book

Each chapter can be read independently, but the framework is designed to be progressive. The foundation enables the pillars. Each planting enables its growing season. Each growing season makes pruning possible. And the harvest only comes when all three pillars are developed.

You might read straight through to understand the complete framework, then return to specific chapters for deeper study. You might work through one pillar at a time, spending months developing each stage before moving to the next. You might recognize yourself at different stages in different pillars and focus your attention where it's most needed.

However you approach it, remember this: the horse will tell you if you're getting it right. Not through perfect performance, but through willing partnership. Through trust that grows deeper with each session. Through the willingness to try difficult things because they know you won't sacrifice them to your ambition.

A Word About Spirit

Throughout this book, I use words like "spirit" and "spiritual" frequently. If these terms make you uncomfortable, if they feel too mystical or religious or vague, I understand. Tom Dorrance wrestled with this same discomfort. "For lack of a better word," he said, "I've taken to calling this the horse's spirit."

What I mean by spirit isn't mystical or supernatural. I mean the innermost part of a being, the part that experiences consciousness, that makes choices, that feels and responds and connects. It's what makes you you and not just a collection of thoughts and behaviours. It's what makes a horse a sentient being and not just a four-legged vehicle.

When I talk about working at the level of spirit, I mean working with the deepest, most authentic part of another being. Not manipulating their behaviour. Not even just understanding their psychology. But genuinely honouring their reality as fully valid, fully real, fully deserving of respect.

This is what Incorporeal Competence is ultimately about: developing the ability to recognize spirit, in yourself, in horses, in every person you encounter, and to work with it as skilfully as you might work with physical bodies or mental patterns.

An Invitation

The journey ahead is challenging. It will require you to question assumptions you've held for years. To practice disciplines that feel awkward at first. To persist through plateaus where nothing seems to change. To let go of patterns that no longer serve you, even when they're comfortable.

But it's worth it. Not just for what you'll accomplish with horses, though that alone would justify the effort. It's worth it for who you'll become in the process.

Because here's what I've discovered: when you develop the competence to work with horses at the level of spirit, something remarkable happens. That competence transfers. It changes how you lead teams. How you raise children. How you navigate conflict. How you show up in every relationship and interaction.

The arena becomes a laboratory for developing qualities that transform your entire life.

Tom and Bill Dorrance discovered this. Ray Hunt demonstrated it. And now, through the pages ahead, I'm inviting you to discover it for yourself.

Not because I've mastered it, I'm still learning, still making mistakes, still being humbled by horses who see through my pretensions and argue with my best efforts. But because the journey itself is transformative... Because even the early stages of development Incorporeal Competence changes everything.

So let's begin. Let's start with a man named Ray Hunt standing in a dusty Australian yard, facing a mare who came in like hell on four legs. Let's watch him demonstrate what Humble Strength looks like when it's embodied so fully that it doesn't even look like strength at all.

Let's see what horses can teach us about becoming fully human.

"The horse is a mirror to your soul, and sometimes you might not like what you see in the mirror. But if you're willing to look—really look—the horse will show you not just who you are, but who you're capable of becoming."

- Tom Dorrance

PART I

PREPARING THE GROUND

CHAPTER 1

ANTIQUATED INTELLIGENCE

"To the dull mind all nature is leaden. To the illumined mind the whole world burns and sparkles with light."

- Emerson, *Journals*, 1831

The Old Horseman

The old man stood calmly in the middle of the large dusty yard.

It was the early nineteen eighties, at a week-long clinic in Gracemere, central Queensland. Ray Hunt, the master horseman from Wyoming, had been working his way through a group of young horses all morning. We fence-sitters watched, mesmerized, as he worked each animal with a quiet authority that seemed to come from somewhere deeper than technique.

Ray was in his fifties then, lean and weathered from decades of ranch work and traveling clinics. Born in Idaho in 1929, he'd spent his entire life around horses and cattle. But it was his apprenticeship under Tom Dorrance in the 1960s that transformed him from a good hand into something more, a horseman who understood that the horse's mind mattered as much as his body.

"The horse is a mirror to your soul," Ray would later tell people, echoing Tom's wisdom. "Sometimes you might not like what you see in the mirror." This wasn't just a saying. Ray lived it. Every horse was a teacher. Every session was an opportunity to learn something about himself as much as about the animal.

There was something about the way Ray moved, economical, deliberate, never wasted, that told you this man had spent his life learning from horses rather than trying to dominate them. His hands were scarred from rope work, but they held the braided nylon line with surprising gentleness. He never raised his voice. Never rushed. Never seemed to take anything personally when a horse struggled or resisted.

All morning, he'd been using a fifty-foot nylon rope, slightly thinner than most, with an aluminum hondo on the end. Unlike the normal hondo that stays tight when you rope something, this aluminum one would release with a flick. Ray used it to teach horses about pressure and release, about giving to the rope rather than fighting it. He'd rope a hind leg, maybe any leg or part of the horse, patiently explaining the intricacies of teaching the horse to find softness in pressure.

"The horse is always looking for the comfortable place," Ray would say in that quiet Wyoming drawl, a phrase he'd learned from Tom. "Your job is to make the wrong thing difficult and the right thing easy. Then get out of his way and let him find it himself."

After he had worked with the horses for a while, the owners would come into the yard, saddle their horses while Ray held a back leg, and climb aboard for the first ride. By mid-morning, six nervous riders were milling around on freshly started colts in the adjacent yard, each of them wondering how they'd ended up riding a green horse with nothing but a halter for control.

But Ray was patient with them too. Never rushing. Never criticizing. Just quietly adjusting a hand position here, suggesting a slight shift in weight there. "Feel of him," he'd say, using Tom's language. "He's trying to tell you something. Are you listening?" ... Then they let the next horse into the yard.

This mare came in like hell on four legs. Teeth and hooves going everywhere, eyes rolling white with rage or fear or both. Ray got himself and his horse out of the way without injury, moving with the same economic precision he'd shown all morning. Not panicked. Not angry. Just clear-eyed assessment of danger and appropriate response.

Over the microphone, his voice came through steady as steel: "I'd appreciate it if we could leave this mare till last today. She and I need to have a different conversation than the one I've been having with these other horses."

The words were polite, almost apologetic. But there was no question in them. This was what needed to happen. He went on with the remaining horses, never referring to the mare again, never building drama around what was coming. Just finished the work at hand first.

When all the other horses had been started, we crowded up to the fence for the final demonstration. The afternoon sun was slanting across the dusty yard as they opened the gate.

The mare exploded into that big yard, ears flat against her skull, racing straight at Ray with her mouth open to attack. We watched, transfixed, as the old horseman stood his ground. He was seventy feet from the fence. There was no way he could reach safety if he wanted to.

He dropped the loop of rope he'd been holding lightly in his hand. With a deft flick of his wrist, he closed the loop and swung the rope in a circle. Back, up, and down as the mare charged.

At the precise moment when we were certain he was about to be trampled, when the mare was three strides away and closing fast, the aluminum hondo flashed from the sky.

It struck her between the ears as she reared to strike.

The mare wheeled away, shocked. Not hurt, Ray's timing was too precise for that, just enough force to interrupt her momentum, but her entire belief system had shattered in that instant. She'd been certain of her dominance, certain she could intimidate this human like she'd apparently intimidated others. And in one perfectly timed moment, that certainty was gone.

She retreated to the fence, as far from Ray as she could get, sides heaving.

What happened next revealed the real mastery.

Ray didn't chase her. Didn't press his advantage. Didn't use her fear to dominate her further. Instead, he stood quiet for a moment, letting her process. Then he began to work her, but with different language than he'd used with the other horses.

He asked her to move. When she moved, he released pressure. He roped a hind leg, gently now, teaching rather than restraining. When she pulled against it, he simply held steady until she found the release in softness. When she gave, even a little, he immediately rewarded that try by letting the rope slacken.

"She's looking for the answer now," Ray said quietly into the microphone. "Before, she thought she had all the answers. Thought the answer was to fight. Now she's asking the question instead. That's when learning can happen."

For the next hour, we watched Ray rebuild what that single strike had deconstructed. He established boundaries, clear, firm, non-negotiable. But within those boundaries, he offered partnership. The mare learned she couldn't attack, couldn't dominate. But she also learned that she didn't need to. That there was another way.

When it came time for the saddle, the mare that had come in like a demon stood quietly. Not defeated, that's the crucial distinction. Her spirit was intact. Her fire was still there. But it was now directed by understanding rather than scattered in blind aggression.

The owner, watching from outside the yard, finally spoke: "I don't think I see much point in going on with this horse."

Ray just nodded. No judgment. No convincing. The man had looked into his own psyche, saw his fear and found it larger than his ambition. Sometimes discretion is the better part of valor.

But those of us watching had seen something profound. We'd seen strength, real strength, the kind that comes from decades of quiet competence, expressed without arrogance. We'd seen a man assert dominance over a half-ton animal without cruelty, without anger, without any need to prove he was superior. The boundary he set was absolute, but the moment after setting it, he became gentle again.

This was humble strength in its purest form.

Ray would often tell people, "I'm still learning from every horse I meet." This from a man who had started thousands of horses, who traveled the world teaching clinics, who was sought out by horsemen who wanted to learn from the best. But he meant it. There was no false modesty in it. He genuinely saw himself as a perpetual student, just as Tom Dorrance had taught him to be.

Tom Dorrance was the quiet genius who revolutionized American horsemanship, teaching that you worked with the horse's nature rather than against it. Ray had sought Tom out after watching him work, recognizing immediately that this man understood something profound. For years, Ray followed Tom from ranch to ranch, absorbing not just techniques but a completely different philosophy about horses and leadership.

"The horse is always honest with you," he'd say. "If you're willing to hear what he's saying, he'll teach you everything you need to know. But most people are too busy trying to teach the horse to let the horse teach them."

That combination, absolute confidence in his ability combined with genuine humility about his understanding, was what made Ray Hunt exceptional. He possessed tremendous skill but never wielded it carelessly. He demonstrated authority that invited rather than demanded. He had power but refused to use it except in service of the horse's learning.

Watching him work was like watching a master class in leadership itself.

Why Antiquated Intelligence

This book is about the lessons that horses can teach us about making meaningful connections - connections that carry over into our daily lives, at home, at work, and in the wider community.

Antiquated intelligence introduces the possibility that we can remember valuable lessons long forgotten. Lessons that our grandfathers learned from their grandmothers, passed down through countless years, but have been lost with the industrial revolution, and have evaporated in the information age.

Ray Hunt demonstrated something in that dusty cattle yard that our modern world has largely forgotten: that true mastery comes not from dominating but from understanding, not from force but from partnership. What looked like horse training was actually a masterclass in ancient wisdom - wisdom passed from Tom Dorrance to Ray Hunt, and from Ray to those of us watching from the fence.

We've lost sight of something fundamental: the people around us are not machines that can be plugged in and switched on and off at will. When employees struggle to keep up with modern processes, it's easy for managers to consider replacing them with newer, more 'intelligent' models - regardless of the cost to society, our businesses, and our own wellbeing.

In an age of Artificial Intelligence, what can we offer that machines cannot? The answer lies not in competing with computers at what they do best, but in cultivating what makes us distinctly human: wisdom, presence, and the ability to see potential in others that they cannot yet see in themselves.

This book explores Antiquated Intelligence - not outdated intelligence, but rather ancient wisdom. The wisdom of spirit and soul. The understanding that makes us valuable partners to both people and machines. The knowledge that will keep us valuable to our families as we navigate this changing world.

This is what Ray Hunt offered that mare: not superior force (though he had it), but understanding, boundaries, and an invitation to partnership. This is what The Horseman's Way offers you.

The Foundation of the Three Pillars

What I witnessed in that dusty yard, and what I'd spend the next forty years getting a deeper understanding of, wasn't just a horsemanship technique. It was something more fundamental. Something that would become the bedrock of everything in this book.

In the Incorporeal Competence framework, which we'll explore throughout this book, Humble Strength isn't one of the three pillars. It's not part of Courage and Vision, though it enables fearless guidance. It's not part of Communication, though it makes emotionless communication possible. It's not part of Service, though it's essential to powerful gentility.

Humble Strength - the foundation beneath each pillar.

It's the soil in which every seed must be planted. It's the bedrock upon which the entire structure rests. Without this foundation, the three pillars cannot stand. They might appear to function for a time, but they'll be built on sand rather than stone. Eventually, pressure will reveal their instability.

Let me be specific about how Humble Strength enables each pillar:

First: How Humble Strength Enables Courage and Vision

Without Humble Strength, Fearless Guidance becomes reckless bravado. You step into uncertainty not because the destination is worth reaching, but because you need to prove you're not afraid. Your courage serves your ego rather than those you're leading. You take risks that endanger others because you're more concerned with appearing brave than with reaching the destination safely.

Strength gives you capacity to act. But humility ensures that action serves a purpose beyond self-promotion.

Moses as a prince had courage, he killed the Egyptian overseer. But without humility, that courage was just violence. It accomplished nothing except his own exile. Only after forty years as a shepherd, when strength had been tempered by humility, could his courage be directed toward actually freeing his people.

Similarly, without Humble Strength, Compassionate Ambition becomes impossible to sustain. You can't maintain ambitious vision while honoring others' wellbeing if you're driven by ego. Your ambition becomes about proving yourself rather than achieving something worth achieving. You'll sacrifice people to reach your goals because deep down, the goals are really about you.

Strength provides the drive to push toward difficult objectives. But humility ensures you don't destroy what matters while getting there.

And Peaceful Directedness, the refined state where courage matures into calm, clear guidance, is utterly impossible without Humble Strength as its foundation. You can't provide direction that others trust if you're directing from ego. They'll sense the self-interest beneath your words. They'll question whether your decisions serve the mission or serve your need to be seen as decisive.

Strength gives you the capacity to make difficult calls and hold to them. But humility ensures those calls are made from wisdom rather than pride. This is what Ray demonstrated when he courageously established the boundary with the mare, immediately returning to gentleness - strength and humility working together, not alternating between the two as she showed her willingness to work with him.

Second: How Humble Strength Enables Communication

Without Humble Strength, Emotionless Communication becomes cold manipulation. You remove emotion from your messages not to create clarity, but to control how others respond. You wield neutrality like a weapon rather than offering it as a gift. Your words are technically clear but spiritually empty because there's no genuine care beneath them.

Strength gives you capacity to regulate your emotional responses, to deliver difficult messages without being derailed by others' reactions. But humility ensures you're regulating emotion in service of understanding rather than in service of control.

Ray's voice remained calm and clear when that mare charged him, but the calmness wasn't about looking unflappable. It was about ensuring his response served the mare's learning. That's emotionless communication rooted in humble strength.

Similarly, without Humble Strength, Balanced Coordination, where mind, body, and emotion move in synchronization, becomes performance rather than authenticity. You coordinate yourself to appear trustworthy, to project confidence, to manage others' perceptions. But there's a gap between your surface and your depths, and people feel it even if they can't name it.

Strength gives you capacity to align your various aspects. But humility ensures that alignment serves truth rather than image management.

And Centred Transcendence, that state of grounded awareness where you maintain inner stillness while reaching out to guide others, cannot exist without Humble Strength. You can't be genuinely centred if your centre is ego-based. You can't maintain stillness if you're constantly proving something. You can't expand your awareness beyond yourself if yourself is what you're primarily concerned with.

Strength gives you the capacity to remain grounded under pressure. But humility ensures your grounded-ness serves others rather than serving your need to appear unshakeable. This same resolve is what Ray Hunt showed each of us as we watched him work through that long hot day.

Third: How Humble Strength Enables Service

Without Humble Strength, Powerful Gentility becomes calculated niceness. You're gentle not because you respect the other's autonomy and development, but because you're trying to get what you want without appearing demanding. It's dominance wearing a velvet glove. It's manipulation dressed as care. Strength gives you capacity to set boundaries, to say hard things, to be firm when firmness serves. But humility ensures you're gentle whenever gentleness will work, that you never use force simply because you can.

Ray could have struck that mare harder. Could have dominated her more thoroughly. Could have broken her spirit entirely. He had the strength to do it. But his humility meant he used only the force necessary to establish the boundary, then immediately returned to gentleness. That's powerful gentility rooted in humble strength.

Similarly, without Humble Strength, Determined Understanding becomes impossible to maintain. True understanding requires you to question your own assumptions, to stay curious even when certainty would be more comfortable, to keep exploring even when you think you already know the answer. This level of intellectual humility only works if it's grounded in genuine humility about your own limitations.

Strength gives you confidence to keep seeking truth even when it's difficult or unpopular. But humility ensures you're actually seeking truth rather than seeking validation for what you already believe.

And Creative Destruction, knowing when to dismantle what no longer serves so something better can be built, requires tremendous Humble Strength. You need strength to tear down established structures, to release what's familiar, to let go of what once worked but no longer does. And you need humility to admit that what you built might need to be rebuilt, that your previous understanding might be incomplete, that growth sometimes requires loss.

Strength gives you capacity to make hard decisions about what must end. But humility ensures you're destroying in service of renewal rather than in service of ego or novelty. This is what Ray demonstrated when he used only the force necessary to establish the boundary with the mare, then immediately returned to teaching - service through the precise calibration of strength and gentleness.

This is why Humble Strength must be established first, before you attempt to develop any of the three pillars. Without this foundation, your best efforts will be compromised by ego. Your courage will be reckless. Your communication will be manipulative. Your service will be self-serving.

But when Humble Strength is firmly established as your foundation, everything you build upon it has integrity. Your Fearless Guidance actually serves those you're leading. Your Emotionless Communication actually creates clarity. Your Powerful Gentility actually facilitates growth.

The foundation determines everything that comes after.

The Prince Who Became a Shepherd

Thirty-three centuries before Ray Hunt stood in that dusty Australian cattle yard, another man was learning the same lesson about strength and humility. But his education took eighty years and cost him everything he thought he was.

Moses grew up as Egyptian royalty. Educated by the finest teachers in the known world. Trained in warfare, strategy, and leadership. He learned to read Egyptian hieroglyphs, to speak multiple languages, to move with confidence through the corridors of power.

He possessed tremendous strength. What he lacked was the humility to use it wisely. And that lack would cost him forty years in the wilderness before he could become the leader his people needed. In the next chapter, we'll explore his journey from strength without humility to Humble Strength fully realized - a transformation that teaches us how this foundation is built in the crucible of lived experience.

"A great part of courage is the courage of having done the thing before."

- Emerson (1860)

CHAPTER 2

HUMBLE STRENGTH

"For those who exalt themselves will be humbled, and those who humble themselves will be exalted."

- Matthew 23:12

Two Kinds of Strength

There are two kinds of strength that shape who we are and how we lead. Understanding the distinction between them is fundamental to developing Humble Strength.

The first is Strength of Character. This represents our internal virtues, the lens through which we view the world. It's who we are when no one is watching. The values we hold. The principles we won't compromise. The integrity that holds us steady when external pressures would push us to bend.

The second is Strength of Will. This speaks to how we act upon the world. It's our determination to pursue goals. Our perseverance through difficulty. Our ability to make decisions and follow through on them regardless of obstacles or opposition. These two strengths are like two sides of the same coin. Both are essential. Both feed each other, for better or worse. And both, without the tempering force of humility, can become destructive.

A person with strong character but weak will knows what's right but can't bring themselves to act on it. They see injustice but remain silent. They recognize opportunity but lack the courage to pursue it. They understand what needs to be done but can't muster the determination to do it.

A person with strong will but weak character acts decisively but toward wrong ends. They pursue their goals without regard for ethics. They achieve their objectives while trampling others. They demonstrate impressive determination in service of questionable purposes.

Humble Strength requires both character and will, integrated and balanced. Strong character provides the foundation, the 'why' behind your actions. Strong will provides the execution, the 'how' you bring that character into the world. And humility ensures that both remain in proper proportion, that your strength serves purposes larger than yourself.

The Character Strengths That Shape Us

Psychologists Christopher Peterson and Martin Seligman identified 24 character strengths that contribute to human flourishing. But when we're talking about developing Humble Strength, six stand out as particularly essential:

Judgment—the ability to think things through and examine them from all sides. This isn't about being judgmental toward others. It's about having the wisdom to see situations clearly, to weigh evidence carefully, to distinguish truth from deception. The leader with strong judgment doesn't jump to conclusions or make decisions based on incomplete information. They take the time to understand fully before acting decisively.

Bravery—not shrinking from threat, challenge, difficulty, or pain. This isn't recklessness. It's the capacity to feel fear fully and then act anyway because the situation requires it. The brave person doesn't pretend danger doesn't exist. They acknowledge it, respect it, and move forward through it when necessary.

Perseverance—finishing what one starts despite obstacles, boredom, or discouragement. This is the strength that gets you up when you've been knocked down. The quality that keeps you moving forward when progress feels impossible. The determination that says 'I may not succeed today, but I'll try again tomorrow.'

Kindness—doing favours and good deeds for others from genuine care, not from duty or desire for recognition. This is compassion in action. The person with this strength sees others' struggles and responds with help freely given. They create environments where people can flourish because they genuinely want others to succeed.

Fairness—treating people according to notions of justice and equity. This means giving each person what they've earned, not what benefits you. It means maintaining standards consistently, not bending rules for favourites. It means making decisions based on merit and circumstance, not on prejudice or preference.

Self-Regulation—controlling what one feels and does; being disciplined. This is perhaps the most challenging strength to develop because it operates in every moment. It's the capacity to feel anger without acting from anger. To experience desire without being controlled by it. To have impulses without being ruled by them.

These six character strengths work together to create the foundation of Humble Strength. But character alone isn't enough. You also need the will to express that character through action. And that's where humility becomes essential.

Humility: The Great Tempering Force

Humility is not thinking less of yourself. It's thinking of yourself less. This distinction matters enormously. False humility diminishes your actual capabilities, pretends you don't know what you clearly know, plays small to make others comfortable. That's not humility. That's self-deception dressed as virtue.

True humility acknowledges your strengths honestly while recognizing they exist to serve purposes beyond yourself. It accepts your limitations without being limited by them. It holds capabilities and weaknesses with equal honesty, using both to serve others and grow personally.

Living in the truth of things means seeing yourself accurately, neither inflated by ego nor deflated by false modesty. It means understanding that your strengths are gifts to be stewarded, not achievements to be hoarded. It means recognizing that your weaknesses are opportunities for growth and connection, not shameful secrets to hide.

Humility tempers Strength of Will. Without humility, strong will becomes domination. You use your determination to impose your agenda regardless of cost to others. You achieve your goals by trampling anyone in your path. You demonstrate resolve at the expense of relationships.

But when humility shapes your will, strength becomes service. You pursue goals that benefit more than just yourself. You demonstrate determination while honouring others' dignity. You persevere through difficulty while remaining open to feedback that might redirect your efforts.

Humility also shapes Strength of Character. Without humility, strong character becomes self-righteousness. You know what's right and wrong, and you're convinced everyone should see things your way. You hold high standards and judge others harshly for failing to meet them. You maintain integrity while demonstrating contempt for those who struggle.

But when humility shapes character, strength becomes wisdom. You know your values while respecting that others may arrive at different conclusions. You maintain standards while extending grace to those who fall short. You hold convictions while remaining open to learning from those who disagree.

This is why humility is called the great tempering force. It takes raw strength, both of character and will, and refines it into something more useful. Less brittle. More flexible without losing integrity. Stronger precisely because it knows its limits.

Running for His Life

The sun hung low and brutal over the Egyptian desert. Moses urged his horse Barak forward with what little strength remained, both rider and mount reduced to desperation by a full day without water. Barak's steps had become mechanical, unthinking, driven only by Moses' will and the ingrained obedience of a well-trained cavalry mount.

Moses had killed a man. Not in battle, where death carried honour. Not in defence, where necessity justified action. He had killed in anger, watching an Egyptian overseer beat a Hebrew slave, and something inside him had snapped. The violence of his response had shocked even him, the way his training had taken over, the way the overseer had crumpled under his hands, the terrible realization that he'd just murdered one of Pharaoh's officials.

He'd hidden the body. Thought he'd hidden the crime. But the next day, when he'd tried to stop two Hebrews from fighting, one had sneered: 'Who made you ruler and judge over us? Are you thinking of killing me as you killed the Egyptian?'

The news had reached Pharaoh within hours. Moses, the princess's adopted son, the prince of Egypt, the commander of cavalry, had fled the palace with only his horse, his sword, and the growing certainty that his strength had betrayed him.

Because that's what it had been. Strength without wisdom. Will without character. Power unleashed in service of momentary rage rather than measured justice. The overseer had deserved punishment, yes. But execution? Without trial? Without authority? Moses had been a vigilante, not a judge. A murderer, not a liberator.

Now, dying of thirst in the wilderness, Moses understood something he'd never grasped in all his years of military training and palace education: strength alone solves nothing. It can only destroy. Real change, real justice, requires something more. Something he didn't possess.

At the Well

Barak's ears pricked forward. Moses, half-dead himself, almost missed the change in the horse's bearing. Then he saw it, a cluster of trees in the distance. Where there were trees, there was water.

The well sat in a depression between low hills, stone-lined and ancient. A wooden trough beside it suggested this was a watering place for flocks. Moses dismounted slowly, his legs barely holding him. Barak waited with the patience of exhaustion while Moses drew water, his hands shaking as he lifted the bucket.

The horse drank first. Moses made sure of that. Barak had carried him faithfully through terrain that would have killed a lesser mount. The least Moses could do was ensure the horse's survival before seeing to his own. This small act of service, putting another's need before his own desperate thirst, was perhaps the first genuine humility Moses had shown in years.

He was drinking his third handful when he heard voices. Female voices, young and cheerful. Moses moved into the shadows of the trees, instinct from years of military training making him invisible. He watched as seven young women approached the well, shepherding a small flock of sheep before them.

They worked efficiently, these daughters of the desert. Two drew water while the others managed the flock. Their movements spoke of long practice, of daily routine performed with competence. There was laughter among them, the easy familiarity of sisters comfortable with each other and their work.

Moses watched, fascinated despite his exhaustion. These women were nothing like the court ladies of Egypt. No cosmetics. No elaborate dress. Just practical clothing and capable hands. Yet there was a grace to their movements, a dignity to their bearing that made them beautiful in a way that transcended ornamentation.

Then he saw the shepherds approaching. A dozen men, rough and loud, driving a larger flock toward the well. Moses recognized trouble immediately, these men moved with the swagger of bullies who'd found easy prey.

'Move along, girls,' one of the shepherds called out. 'This well belongs to those strong enough to hold it. And you seven aren't strong enough.'

The oldest of the sisters stepped forward. 'Our father is Jethro, priest of Midian. We have as much right to this well as anyone.'

'Your father isn't here, is he?' The lead shepherd grinned. 'Just seven soft girls who should be home grinding grain, not wasting time playing at shepherd work.'

Moses watched the oldest sister's hands clench. Saw her jaw tighten. Recognized the exact moment when she made the decision to stand her ground despite the odds. And he saw what she couldn't see, how the shepherds were positioning themselves, cutting off escape routes, preparing to use force if necessary.

Three days ago, Moses would have charged in without thought. Would have scattered these bullies with the same unthinking violence he'd used on the Egyptian overseer. Would have demonstrated his strength without considering wisdom.

But three days of dying in the desert had changed something. As Moses stepped out of the shadows, he found himself thinking rather than reacting. Calculating rather than charging.

'Perhaps,' Moses said quietly, 'we can share the well. There's water enough for all the flocks.'

The lead shepherd turned, his sneer faltering slightly as he took in Moses's size, his bearing, the sword at his hip. But bravado won over caution. 'Perhaps you should mind your business, stranger. Unless you want trouble.'

'I want water for my horse,' Moses said, his voice still quiet. 'And I'd prefer to get it without violence. But I'm prepared for either outcome.'

There was something in Moses's eyes, something in his absolute calm, that made the shepherd recalculate. This wasn't a man who threatened. This was a man who stated facts. And the fact being stated was simple: if this came to violence, the shepherd would lose.

The tense moment stretched. Then the lead shepherd spat in the dust. 'Keep your well. We'll water our flocks downstream.'

Moses remained still, watching until the shepherds and their flock disappeared over the rise. Only then did he turn to the seven sisters.

The oldest approached carefully. 'Thank you. They've been harassing us for weeks.'

'You defended your right to be here,' Moses said. 'I just made the cost of taking that right too high for them to want to pay it.'

'Still. We're grateful.' She hesitated. 'I'm Zipporah. These are my sisters.'

Moses introduced himself simply, leaving out the parts about being a prince of Egypt or a wanted murderer. 'Your sheep need water. Let me help you draw it.'

'You don't have to—'

'I know,' Moses interrupted gently. 'But my horse is already watered. I'm stronger than you. And it's the least I can do for the hospitality of sharing your well.'

For the next hour, Moses drew water while the seven sisters watered their flock. It was servant's work, the kind of labour that would have been beneath a prince of Egypt. But Moses found something settling in his soul as he worked. Something that felt more right than anything he'd done in years of commanding troops and administering provinces.

This was strength in service. Not strength to dominate. Not strength to impress. Just strength used quietly to help others accomplish their work. And in that quiet service, the first seeds of true humility began to take root in Moses's soul.

Strength Has Two Sides

I learned about the two sides of strength from a mare we called Smarty. She came to us as a yearling, not full of herself in the way that some young horses often are. Athletic, but lacking in confidence. As a two year old she was unaware that she was one of the most capable horses in the paddock.

By the time she was three, the shy yearling had transformed. We'd started her on cattle and she was showing that she had real talent for cutting. Quick, intelligent, with a rare combination of caution and calculation that makes for a great cow horse. She loved the work. Loved the challenge. Loved showing what she could do.

And as she matured she began to understand she was good.

As her confidence grew, it was wonderful. When I needed her to power through a difficult situation, to hold a particularly aggressive cow, to make a bold move that a less confident horse might hesitate over, Smarty's strength of will began to carry us through. I believed she could do it, so she began to believe she could do it, and that belief made the difference.

But that strength, that certainty could become problematic. Sometimes Smarty would decide she knew better than I did what needed to happen. She'd commit to a cow before I asked. She'd make a move before I cued it. She'd use that strength and confidence to override my judgment with hers.

One day we were in the arena, practicing on cattle in preparation for the futurity, as we had been for months. I asked her to turn while the cow stood there, just to work on her head position a little, a simple request she'd done hundreds of times. But in that moment, Smarty decided she didn't need to.

She had the cow in front of her. She was comfortable in the knowledge that she was doing the job she was trained to do. Why listen when I was trying to take her away from her job? I asked again, more clearly. She ignored me.

I insisted. She locked up, stopped moving entirely, stood there almost radiating resentment that I was making her do something she didn't want to do. The slightest pull on the reins caused her to raise her front end off the ground.

This was strength without humility. Smarty's confidence in her own ability had crossed the line into refusal to submit to guidance. Her strength of will, unchecked by any tempering force, had become massive resistance.

I had to make a choice in that moment. I could force the issue, use my strength to override hers, prove that I was stronger and she had to comply. And run the risk of making the problem worse. Of causing her to rear more. Or I could find another way.

I chose something different. I pushed her sideway, away from the cow, making her bend around my leg, not as punishment, but as a reset. To break that connection that she had with the cow. To bring her thoughts back to asking what it was that I wanted. Then I asked her to turn, to follow my guidance. To do the dry work I had set out to do.

Moving sideways like that required the horse to think, to coordinate all four feet in an action, to break out of whatever mental pattern they're stuck in. When I asked for the turn again, after I had put her back on the cow, this time I prepared her better, gave her a clearer requesting, made sure she understood exactly what I was asking. She listened to me perfectly.

The difference was that I'd used my strength not to dominate her but to create conditions where she could choose to do what I asked. I'd demonstrated that I was capable of making her do it, the moving sideways had made that clear. But I'd also given her the opportunity to comply willingly rather than being forced into submission.

Over the following months, Smarty learned a better balance. She continued to grow in confidence and boldness, I never wanted to stop that growth. That was what was going to make her exceptional. It wasn't always perfect, but she gradually developed humility in her relationship with me.

She learned that my guidance was worth following because it served both of us. That using her strength in partnership was more effective than using it in resistance.

This is what Humble Strength looks like with horses. You maintain your capability to enforce boundaries, the horse needs to know you're strong enough to insist when necessary. But you use that capability primarily to create partnership, not to demonstrate dominance. You're strong enough to force compliance but humble enough to prefer cooperation.

This is the power of Humble Strength: knowing you're capable of force but choosing service. Maintaining the capacity to insist while preferring to invite. Being strong enough to demand compliance but humble enough to seek cooperation.

The Wilderness Years

Moses camped near the home of Zipporah and her sisters, uncertain whether he was welcome, unsure what came next. But Jethro, their father, came looking for him the following day. 'My daughters tell me you drove off the shepherds who've been harassing them,' Jethro said. 'And that you helped water our flock without being asked.'

Moses shrugged. 'They needed help. I was able to provide it.'

'Most men would have demanded payment. Or tried to impress the girls. Or at minimum expected gratitude and recognition.' Jethro studied him carefully. 'You did none of those things. You just helped and then tried to disappear. Why?'

It was a good question. Why had Moses helped? Not for recognition, he was a fugitive trying to stay invisible. Not for reward, he had nothing to offer in trade and wanted no debts. Not to impress, though he'd noticed Zipporah was beautiful, his immediate motivation hadn't been courtship.

'I've spent my life using strength to take,' Moses said slowly. 'I think I need to learn how to use it to give.'

Jethro smiled. 'Then come work for me. I need a shepherd. And I suspect you need time to learn some things you can't learn in palaces or on battlefields.'

Moses worked for Jethro for forty years. Forty years of tending sheep in the wilderness. Forty years of learning that leadership is patience. Forty years of discovering that strength is often quietest when it's most effective.

Sheep taught him humility in ways no human instructor could. They're not like horses, who can be trained and directed. Sheep are fundamentally foolish creatures who make terrible decisions and need constant guidance. You can't force sheep to go anywhere they don't want to go, try it and they scatter in every direction. You have to lead them, patiently, persistently, one step at a time.

Moses learned to be the first into danger and the last to rest. Learned to put the flock's needs before his own comfort. Learned that authority comes not from position but from consistent care. The sheep followed him because he'd proven, day after day, year after year, that following him led to safety, food, water, and protection.

He learned to use just enough force and no more. When a sheep wandered toward danger, Moses would intercept it, but gently, redirecting rather than dominating. When predators threatened, he would fight, but only to protect, never to prove his strength. When the flock was tired, he would find rest, but only after ensuring their safety.

This was completely different from his training in Egypt. There, he'd learned to command. To impose his will. To demonstrate power. To achieve objectives regardless of cost. Now he was learning something more subtle and far more difficult: how to guide without dominating. How to protect without controlling. How to serve while leading.

The wilderness years transformed Moses from a prince into a servant. From a commander into a shepherd. From a man who used strength to take into a man who used strength to give. The change wasn't dramatic. It happened slowly, one day at a time, through countless small acts of patient care.

When God finally met Moses at the burning bush and called him to return to Egypt, Moses was no longer the confident prince who'd fled forty years earlier. He was hesitant, uncertain, aware of his limitations in ways his younger self never could have been.

'Who am I that I should go to Pharaoh?' Moses asked. The question revealed everything about how the wilderness had changed him. Once he would have said, 'I am Moses, prince of Egypt, commander of cavalry, trained in the finest schools.' Now he asked, 'Who am I?' as though he genuinely didn't know.

That question, that humility, that awareness of his own inadequacy, was exactly what qualified him to lead. The strength was still there, forty years of shepherding had kept him physically capable, and his military training hadn't been forgotten. But now that strength was tempered by humility. Now he understood that leadership wasn't about imposing his will but about serving a purpose larger than himself.

Confronting Pharaoh

When Moses returned to Egypt and confronted Pharaoh, he demonstrated what Humble Strength looks like in practice.

He didn't storm into the throne room making demands. He made a request: 'The God of the Hebrews asks that you let His people go into the wilderness to worship.' Not a threat. Not an ultimatum. A request backed by divine authority but delivered with respect for Pharaoh's position.

When Pharaoh refused, Moses didn't respond with rage the way his younger self would have. He didn't attempt a coup. Didn't try to assassinate Pharaoh. Didn't marshal the Hebrews into premature rebellion. He simply delivered the consequence: 'If you refuse, this is what will happen.' Then he let God demonstrate the truth of that statement through the plagues.

After each plague, Moses returned to Pharaoh. Each time giving the same message: 'Let my people go.' Each time maintaining the same calm determination. Never gloating. Never enjoying Pharaoh's suffering. Never using the power God had given him for anything beyond the specific purpose of liberating the Hebrews.

This was strength without arrogance. Moses knew he had divine authority. He'd watched plagues devastate Egypt. He'd seen Pharaoh's magicians unable to match God's power. But he never used that strength to humiliate Pharaoh or to elevate himself. He used it solely to accomplish the mission he'd been given.

Even after the Exodus, when the freed Hebrews complained constantly, questioned his leadership, threatened rebellion, Moses demonstrated Humble Strength. He could have destroyed them, God offered more than once. He could have walked away, who would have blamed him for abandoning such difficult people? But he stayed. Interceded for them. Led them through wilderness toward a land he knew he'd never personally enter.

This is Humble Strength matured: possessing power but using it only in service of others. Having the capacity to dominate but choosing to guide. Being strong enough to force compliance but humble enough to seek cooperation. Maintaining authority while remaining accountable to purposes larger than self.

What Humble Strength Is NOT

Not Self-Effacement

Humble Strength is not constantly putting yourself down or diminishing your capabilities. I've watched people who are genuinely skilled pretend they're not, who understand situations clearly but act confused, who have valuable contributions to make but hold back because they think humility means making themselves small.

That's not humility. That's self-deception. Or worse, it's manipulation, making yourself appear weak so others will underestimate you, then revealing your strength at strategic moments to maximum effect.

True Humble Strength acknowledges capabilities honestly. 'Yes, I'm good at this. Yes, I understand this situation. Yes, I have something valuable to contribute.' The humility comes not in denying these truths but in recognizing they're gifts to be used in service of others, not achievements to be hoarded for self-aggrandizement.

Moses didn't pretend he wasn't a trained military commander. He didn't act like he didn't understand strategy or leadership. He acknowledged his capabilities while remaining humble about their source and purpose. 'This isn't about me being impressive. This is about accomplishing what God has called me to do.'

Not False Modesty

Humble Strength is not the performance of humility that is actually dishonest. I've encountered leaders who practice false modesty, 'Oh, I'm not really that skilled, I just got lucky, anyone could have done what I did', while clearly expecting to be contradicted and reassured of their excellence.

This false modesty is actually a form of pride. It's fishing for compliments while appearing humble. It's seeking validation while maintaining plausible deniability about seeking validation. It's dishonest in a way that genuine humility never is.

Humble Strength requires honesty about both strengths and limitations. 'I'm good at strategy but weak at patience. I understand leadership but struggle with details. I can inspire others but sometimes fail to notice when they're struggling.' This honest assessment serves others by helping them know what they can rely on you for and where they'll need to compensate for your weaknesses.

Not Weakness Disguised as Virtue

Perhaps the most common misunderstanding is that Humble Strength means being passive, accepting mistreatment, avoiding conflict, never standing up for yourself or others. This confuses gentleness with weakness, humility with cowardice, service with servility. Moses demonstrated the falseness of this belief when he drove off the shepherds harassing Jethro's daughters. He didn't accept their bullying in the name of being humble. He didn't avoid conflict because that would have been 'the gentle thing to do.'

He confronted the situation directly, using exactly as much force as necessary and no more. Humble Strength recognizes when strength is needed. When boundaries must be enforced. When injustice must be opposed. When people must be protected. The humility comes in using strength proportionally, in service of others, and without seeking glory for having done so.

Being strong enough to protect others while remaining humble enough to not seek recognition for it, that's Humble Strength. Being capable of force while preferring invitation, that's Humble Strength. Having the capacity to dominate while choosing to serve, that's Humble Strength.

Not Switching Between Two Modes

Finally, Humble Strength is not about having two separate modes, 'strong mode' and 'humble mode', that you switch between depending on circumstances. I've watched leaders who are humble when they're in positions of weakness but arrogant when they're in positions of power. Or leaders who are strong in public but servile in private. Or leaders who are humble with superiors but domineering with subordinates.

That's not integration. That's compartmentalization. It's having strength and humility as separate, competing qualities rather than as integrated aspects of your character.

True Humble Strength is being simultaneously strong and humble in the same moment. Not alternating between them. Not being strong in some contexts and humble in others. But expressing both strength and humility through every action.

When Moses stood before Pharaoh, he was both strong (backed by divine authority, unwavering in his demand) and humble (speaking respectfully, not seeking personal glory, serving a purpose beyond himself) in the same moment. When he led the Hebrews through the wilderness, he was both strong (decisive in crisis, firm in maintaining standards) and humble (interceding for those who complained, acknowledging his dependence on God) simultaneously.

This integration is what makes Humble Strength so powerful. You're not weakened by humility or made arrogant by strength. Both qualities enhance each other, creating leadership that others trust because it's both capable and safe.

The Foundation of All Leadership

Humble Strength isn't just one quality among many. It's the foundation that makes all other leadership qualities possible.

- *Without* Humble Strength, courage becomes recklessness. You're willing to take risks, but you don't count the cost to others. You're bold, but your boldness serves your ego rather than your mission. You step into danger, but you drag others into danger with you unnecessarily.

- *With* Humble Strength, courage becomes purposeful. You still take risks, but you calculate them carefully. You're bold when boldness serves others, cautious when caution protects them. You step into danger when necessary, but you don't ask others to take risks you wouldn't take yourself.

- *Without* Humble Strength, communication becomes manipulation. You're skilled at persuasion, but you use it to serve your agenda. You understand how to influence others, but you influence them toward your benefit rather than theirs. You speak clearly, but your clarity serves deception rather than truth.

- *With* Humble Strength, communication becomes service. You use your persuasive ability to help others see what's true. You influence them toward their own growth rather than your gain. You speak clearly to illuminate rather than to impress.

- *Without* Humble Strength, service becomes either domination or enabling. You either 'serve' by controlling (making yourself indispensable so others remain dependent) or you 'serve' by rescuing (protecting others from all difficulty, preventing their growth). Both are ultimately self-serving.

- *With* Humble Strength, service becomes empowerment. You help others while promoting their independence. You support them through difficulty while letting them do the work of growing. You provide what they need while respecting their agency.

This is why Humble Strength must be developed first, before attempting to develop other leadership qualities. It's the foundation. Everything else builds on it. Without it, every other strength becomes distorted, turned toward self rather than service.

What It Looks Like in the Arena

When you work with horses from a foundation of Humble Strength, several things change:

- **First**, you stop needing to prove yourself. The young trainer, insecure in their abilities, often needs the horse to comply quickly so they can demonstrate their skill. They rush training. They use more force than necessary. They treat resistance as a personal affront that must be crushed to maintain their authority.

  But when you're secure in your strength while humble about its purpose, you can take your time. You can let the horse learn at their pace rather than yours. You can use the minimum force necessary because you're not trying to prove you're strong, you're just trying to accomplish the actual training goal.

- **Second**, you can acknowledge your mistakes without losing authority. I've made countless errors in training, asked for something before the horse was ready, misread their signals, pushed when I should have paused. Humble Strength allows me to recognize these mistakes, adjust my approach, and maintain the horse's trust because they see I'm learning alongside them rather than pretending to be infallible.

- **Third**, you can celebrate the horse's successes without making it about you. When Smarty finally learned to control her boldness enough to wait for my cues, I didn't congratulate myself on being a brilliant trainer. I celebrated her growth, her learning, her development. The humility recognized that I was facilitating her development, not creating it.

- **Fourth**, you can maintain boundaries without becoming harsh. Horses need clear limits. They need to know what's acceptable and what isn't. But Humble Strength allows you to enforce those limits matter-of-factly rather than angrily. 'This behaviour isn't acceptable' delivered calmly is far more effective than 'How dare you!' delivered with rage.

- **Fifth**, you can adapt your approach to each individual horse. The insecure rider applies the same method to every horse because it's the one they know. But Humble Strength provides the security to experiment, to try different approaches, to acknowledge when your preferred method isn't working for this particular horse and try something else.

- **Finally**, you can prioritize the relationship over immediate results. Sometimes the best thing to do is end a session early, even if you haven't accomplished what you planned, because the horse is overwhelmed or exhausted. Humble Strength makes this possible because you're secure enough to not need today's breakthrough to validate your capability.

What It Looks Like Outside the Arena

The same principles that create Humble Strength in horsemanship create it in all forms of leadership:

- In professional settings, Humble Strength manifests as confidence without arrogance. You know your capabilities and contribute them fully without needing to dominate every conversation or decision. You can support others' ideas without feeling diminished. You can acknowledge others' expertise in areas where they know more than you without feeling threatened.

- You can make difficult decisions and deliver hard feedback without cruelty. You can maintain high standards without contempt for those who fall short. You can be the final decision-maker while genuinely seeking input from others.

- In family relationships, Humble Strength looks like parents who can provide structure and boundaries while respecting their children's growing autonomy. Who can say 'no' firmly while explaining the 'why' behind the limit. Who can admit when they've made parenting mistakes while maintaining their authority as guides.

- It looks like partners who can be strong when strength is needed and vulnerable when vulnerability serves the relationship. Who can lead in their areas of strength while following in their partner's. Who can insist on boundaries while remaining open to feedback about how their behaviour affects the other.

- In community leadership, Humble Strength creates leaders people actually want to follow. Leaders who are confident enough to make decisions but humble enough to admit when they're wrong. Who are strong enough to weather criticism but humble enough to learn from it. Who are capable enough to lead but humble enough to recognize that leadership is service, not privilege.

When the Balance Tips

Understanding what Humble Strength looks like when it's working also means recognizing what happens when the balance tips too far in one direction.

When strength dominates and humility fades, you see leaders who are effective but ultimately destructive. They achieve their objectives, but they leave damaged relationships and burned-out people in their wake. They demonstrate impressive capability, but they use that capability to elevate themselves rather than serve others. They're confident to the point of arrogance, certain to the point of close-mindedness.

I've worked with riders like this. They can get horses to perform, but the horses don't enjoy working for them. Compliance comes from fear or overwhelming pressure rather than from willing partnership. Results are achieved, but the horse's spirit is diminished in the process.

When humility dominates and strength fades, you see leaders who are kind but ultimately ineffective. They care deeply about not hurting anyone, but this prevents them from making necessary decisions. They want everyone to be happy, so they avoid difficult conversations until small problems become large crises. They're so afraid of being seen as domineering that they fail to provide clear direction when people desperately need it.

I've watched riders like this too. They're gentle with horses, but they never develop those horses' full capability because they won't push through the discomfort required for growth. They care about the horse's feelings, but this prevents them from creating the challenges that would develop the horse's confidence and skill.

Humble Strength requires both qualities in balance. Strong enough to accomplish what needs accomplishing. Humble enough to do it in service of others. Capable enough to provide clear direction. Humble enough to remain open to feedback about that direction.

Developing This Quality

So how do you develop Humble Strength? How do you integrate these seemingly opposite qualities into a coherent foundation for leadership?

1. Honestly assess both your strengths and weaknesses. Not to diminish yourself. Not to inflate yourself. Just to see yourself accurately. What are you genuinely good at? Where do you consistently struggle? What do people rely on you for? Where do you need to rely on others?

    This honest self-assessment is the beginning of both strength and humility. You can't be strong in areas where you pretend weakness, and you can't be humble about capabilities you won't acknowledge. Accurate self-knowledge is the foundation.

2. Before any important interaction, before entering the arena, before a difficult conversation, before a significant decision, check your intention. Ask yourself: Am I doing this from ego or from true purpose? Am I trying to prove something about myself, or am I trying to serve something beyond myself?

29

This question cuts through self-deception quickly. You'll know, if you're honest, whether your primary motivation is self-serving or service-oriented. And that awareness gives you the opportunity to adjust your approach before you act.

3. Practice being fully present. Right here. Right now. Not thinking about how this interaction will make you look. Not worrying about outcomes beyond your control. Just fully attentive to what this moment requires. Presence is a form of humility.

    It says, 'This moment, this person, this horse matters more than my concerns about past or future.' When you're genuinely present, your natural strength emerges in service of what's actually needed rather than in service of your ego.

4. Cultivate the strength to say what needs to be said. From clarity, not from anger. From purpose, not from pride. From service, not from self-protection. This is harder than it sounds.

    We often convince ourselves we're being humble by avoiding difficult conversations when we're actually being cowardly. True Humble Strength speaks truth even when it's uncomfortable, but it speaks that truth in ways designed to serve the other person's growth, not to prove ourselves right.

5. Cultivate the humility to admit when you're wrong. To ask for help when you need it. To acknowledge others' expertise in areas where they know more than you. To learn from anyone, regardless of their status or position. This is equally difficult.

    Our egos resist admitting error, asking for help, or learning from those we perceive as beneath us. But humility recognizes that truth and wisdom can come from anywhere, and that growing in understanding matters more than protecting our image of expertise.

6. Serve others without needing recognition for that service. The most powerful form of Humble Strength is strength used so quietly, so naturally in service of others, that it doesn't even register as remarkable. Moses drawing water for Jethro's daughters didn't announce that he was a prince of Egypt serving beneath his station.

    He just drew water because it needed doing and he was capable of doing it. That's the kind of service that builds Humble Strength, the kind that happens when no one's watching, when no reward is forthcoming, when the only motivation is that someone needs help and you can provide it.

7. Find mentors who embody this quality and study how they operate. Watch leaders who are both strong and humble. Notice how they make decisions. Observe how they handle criticism. Pay attention to how they use their strength in service of others rather than in service of themselves.

   You can't develop Humble Strength in isolation. You need models. You need people who can show you what integration looks like, who can call you out when you tip too far toward either strength without humility or humility without strength. Who can help you find and maintain the balance.

The Journey Continues

Moses never entered the Promised Land. After forty years leading the Hebrews through wilderness, after confronting Pharaoh and parting the Red Sea, after receiving the Law at Sinai and interceding countless times to keep God from destroying His stubborn people, Moses died within sight of the land he'd spent four decades helping others reach.

Some see this as tragedy. I see it as the ultimate expression of Humble Strength.

Moses's purpose was never to reach the Promised Land himself. His purpose was to lead others there. And he accomplished that purpose faithfully, even knowing from the beginning that he personally wouldn't receive the reward. That's service. That's strength used not for personal benefit but for others' good. That's humility demonstrated through decades of patient, persistent leadership that served a purpose beyond himself.

This is what Humble Strength ultimately creates: leaders whose legacy outlives them because they built something larger than themselves. Whose influence continues because they empowered others rather than creating dependence. Whose strength served purposes that transcended their own limited lifetimes.

In the arena and outside it, this is the foundation we're building. Not impressive demonstrations of capability. Not humble self-effacement that diminishes genuine strength. But the integration of both, strength and humility working together to serve purposes beyond ourselves.

Every day offers opportunities to practice this integration. Every horse you work with teaches lessons about when to be strong and when to be gentle, when to insist and when to invite, when to demonstrate capability and when to simply serve.

Every person you lead presents the same questions. When does this situation require strength? When does it require humility? How do I use my capabilities in service of their growth rather than in service of my ego? How do I maintain authority while remaining accountable to purposes larger than myself?

The answers won't always be clear. You'll make mistakes. You'll tip too far toward strength and need to recover humility. You'll tip too far toward humility and need to recover strength. That's normal. That's how growth happens.

What matters is that you keep pursuing the integration. Keep working to be simultaneously strong and humble. Keep using your capabilities in service of others. Keep learning from horses and people and circumstances how to balance these seemingly opposite qualities into a coherent foundation for everything else you'll build.

Because without Humble Strength as your foundation, everything else will be unstable. Your courage will become recklessness. Your communication will become manipulation. Your service will become control. But with Humble Strength as your foundation, every other quality can develop properly. Can serve its intended purpose. Can contribute to leadership that others trust because it's both capable and safe.

That's the foundation. That's where we begin. And everything that follows, all the courage and communication and service we'll explore in the chapters ahead, builds on this.

Be strong enough to accomplish what needs accomplishing. Be humble enough to do it in service of others. And trust that this integration, practiced faithfully over time, will create something far more powerful than either quality could create alone.

"I think I saw it, once or twice, this lowly thing called humility."

- Robert F. Morneau

PART II

PLANTING THE SEED

CHAPTER 3

FEARLESS GUIDANCE

"Through every generation of the human race there has been a constant war, a war with fear. Those who have the courage to conquer it are made free and those who are conquered by it are made to suffer until they have the courage to defeat it, or death takes them."

— Alexander the Great

The horse dealer had come a long way to reach the Macedonian court where King Philip II reigned. Philonicus was a Thessalian, from the region that bred the finest cavalry horses in all of Greece, and the animal he brought with him that day in 344 BCE was magnificent. Black as polished obsidian, with a coat that seemed to absorb the sunlight. A white star blazed on his forehead, and his head was massive, so large they called him Bucephalus, "ox-head."

The price Philonicus asked reflected the horse's quality: thirteen talents. Three times what a normal cavalry horse cost, even in Macedonia where King Philip II was building the greatest military force Greece had ever seen.

Philip watched from the reviewing stand as his best handlers approached the stallion. The first man barely got within ten feet before Bucephalus reared, screaming, his front hooves pawing the air. The second handler tried from the other side. Same result. A third handler, one of Philip's most experienced horsemen, managed to get hold of the lead rope before the horse wheeled violently, knocking him to the ground.

Each handler thought they knew what they were dealing with. A difficult horse, yes. High-strung, certainly. But manageable with the right approach, the right amount of pressure, the right show of dominance. Each man was wrong.

The horse's eyes rolled white with terror. His nostrils flared. When anyone approached, he would explode into violence, not aggression, but panic. Pure, desperate panic.

Philip had seen enough. He raised his hand. "Take him away. The beast is wholly useless and intractable. We'll have no use for such a horse."

From the crowd of courtiers and officers watching the spectacle, a young voice called out. "What an excellent horse do they lose, for want of address and boldness to manage him!"

Philip turned to see his twelve-year-old son Alexander standing at the rail, his eyes not on the king but on the horse being led away.

"Do you reproach those who are older than yourself," Philip said, his voice carrying the edge of a father's irritation, "as if you knew more and were better able to manage him than they?"

"I could manage this horse better than others do."

Laughter rippled through the assembled nobles. The audacity of this boy, challenging men who had been handling horses since before he was born.

Philip's eyes narrowed. "And if you do not, what will you forfeit for your rashness?"

"I will pay the whole price of the horse."

The laughter grew louder. Thirteen talents. More money than most men would see in a lifetime. But Alexander was already moving, walking down from the stands toward where the handlers held the terrified stallion.

He had been watching. Not the way the adults watched, seeing only the horse's violence and interpreting it as vice or poor breeding. Alexander had been watching the horse's eyes, the direction of his movement, the pattern of his fear. And he had seen something they all missed.

The horse wasn't reacting to the handlers. He was reacting to something else.

Alexander took the bridle from the surprised handler and began turning Bucephalus. Gently, with no force, just steady pressure. He turned him to face directly into the sun, so the horse's shadow fell behind him, invisible, forgotten.

Then he did something extraordinary. He stood there. Just stood, one hand on the horse's neck, speaking quietly, words no one else could hear. The courtiers fell silent, watching this strange tableau. A twelve-year-old boy and a terrified warhorse, facing the sun together.

Bucephalus's breathing began to slow. The rigid tension in his neck softened. His ear swivelled toward the boy who stood beside him with such calm certainty.

Alexander stroked the horse's neck one more time. Then, in a single fluid motion, he dropped his cloak, grabbed the saddle, and vaulted onto Bucephalus's back.

The crowd held its breath.

Alexander urged the horse forward. Not roughly, not with force, but with clear intention. And Bucephalus responded. They moved from a walk to a trot, then to a canter, then to a full gallop across the practice field. The black stallion stretched out, powerful and free, no longer running from fear but running toward something, partnership, perhaps, or simply the joy of movement with someone who understood him.

When they returned, Alexander's face was flushed with triumph and exertion. Philip was weeping.

The king stepped down from the reviewing stand, pulled his son into an embrace, and kissed his forehead. According to Plutarch, Philip said: "O my son, look thee out a kingdom equal to and worthy of thyself, for Macedonia is too little for thee."

Twenty years later, when Bucephalus finally died of wounds and exhaustion on the banks of the Hydaspes River in India, having carried Alexander through every major battle from the Granicus to Gaugamela, Alexander founded a city in his honour. Alexandria Bucephalous stands to this day in modern Pakistan, a monument to the partnership between a fearless leader and the horse who taught him his first lesson in guidance.

The Nature of Fear

Bucephalus wasn't afraid of humans. He was afraid of his own shadow.

Every time he moved, the dark shape beneath him shifted, and his instinct told him something was pursuing him. The more he tried to escape, the more the shadow followed. The harder the handlers pushed, the more desperate his flight became. They saw stubbornness. Alexander saw terror.

The handlers tried to solve the wrong problem. They attempted to dominate the horse, to force him to accept what he feared. Alexander solved the actual problem. He changed the horse's relationship with his own shadow by changing where the horse faced.

This is the essence of Fearless Guidance. It's not about having no fear. It's about understanding fear, your own and others', well enough to find a way forward despite it.

But more fundamentally, Fearless Guidance is about the decision to step into uncertainty first. It's the planted seed of courage that allows others to find their own. When Alexander turned Bucephalus to face the sun, he didn't eliminate the horse's fear, he gave him a new perspective that made courage possible. This is what leaders do: they go first into the unknown, demonstrating that the journey is survivable, showing others that what seemed impossible is merely difficult.

The seed of Fearless Guidance is planted the moment a leader decides that their destination is more important than their fear, and then takes that first step while others are still hesitating. Everything that grows after, sustained courage, mature judgment, refined wisdom, begins with this single act: choosing to move forward when every instinct says to wait.

I've watched this same dynamic play out in lessons countless times. A horse refuses to cross a water crossing, or to step over a track in the newly dragged arena. To approach a flag flapping in the breeze, or a pipe laying on the ground. Some riders interpret this as disobedience and apply more pressure. The horse becomes more frightened. The rider becomes more frustrated. The partnership dissolves into a battle of wills that no one wins.

But when the rider understands that the horse is just scared, everything changes. You can help a scared horse. You can show them that the terrifying object is actually harmless. You can be the steady presence that gives them courage to face what frightens them, but you can't help a horse you believe is defying you.

The same principle applies to leading people. Some team members who appear resistant to change aren't being difficult, they're terrified of the unknown. Some employees who seem to lack initiative aren't lazy, they're afraid of making mistakes. Some leaders who appear autocratic aren't power-hungry, they're scared of losing control.

When you misdiagnose fear as something else, as weakness, or stubbornness, or malice, you are trying to solve the wrong problem. And you fail, time and again, wondering why force isn't working.

Fearless Guidance begins with seeing the problem clearly. Then it requires the courage to step toward that problem first, before anyone else, demonstrating that it can be faced.

Leading Into the Unknown

"I accept this land as a gift from the gods!" stated Alexander, throwing his spear into the sand of the beach.

Persian soil... Asian soil!

Standing in the bow of the boat as it ran onto the beach, surrounded by the leaders of the various parts of his army, this statement signified the start of his campaign to take Persia. The assembled leadership of his army, some inspired by what they had just seen, some perplexed, and some thinking it foolish.

All kept their thoughts to themselves that day; but all would recount the story to their men, many times over through the months and years of the campaign that followed.

A decade after Alexander tamed Bucephalus, he stood on that shore, the doorstep of Persia, with an army of thirty-five thousand men. The year was 334 BC. He was twenty-two years old.

His father Philip had been assassinated. Some of the Greek city-states were plotting rebellion. His treasury was nearly empty. That was what was behind him.

Ahead of him lay the Persian Empire, the largest, richest, most powerful empire the world had ever known.

The Persian king Darius III commanded resources that dwarfed Macedonia's. The Persian navy controlled the seas, threatening Alexander's supply lines back to Greece. No one knew how or when the Persian army would deploy. Where they would make their stand.

Alexander was gambling on rapid conquest. Believing he would succeed before the money ran out. Every advisor who counselled him saw prudence as the right course of action. When he threw that spear into the Asian soil and declared that he accepted Asia as "a gift from the gods," he was planting something essential in the minds of his men.

He wasn't expressing certainty about the outcome, he was creating belief. He was drawing his people into the vision his father had given him when Philip said, "O my son, look thee out a kingdom equal to and worthy of thyself, for Macedonia is too little for thee."

This is what Fearless Guidance looks like in practice. Not the absence of doubt or danger, but the willingness to move forward into uncertainty as if the outcome were already decided. Not because you're deluded about the risks, but because you understand that your people need to see confidence in order to find their own courage.

Just as the twelve-year-old Alexander saw what seasoned handlers couldn't see in Bucephalus, leaders see possibilities in people that they can't yet see in themselves. In his book "Developing the Leader Within You 2.0", John C. Maxwell writes about leadership and vision, particularly addressing the question, "What you can see determines what you can be." He identifies four kinds of people that leaders encounter based on how they respond to vision:

- People who never see it—they are wanderers.
- People who see it but never pursue it on their own—they are the followers.
- People who see it and pursue it—they are achievers.
- People who see it, pursue it, and help others to see and pursue it—they are leaders.

This is precisely what Alexander understood about Fearless Guidance. When he threw that spear and declared Asia a gift from the gods, he was doing more than making a bold statement. He was inviting his army to see what he saw, a future where the impossible became possible.

Some of his men were wanderers, unable or unwilling to see beyond their immediate circumstances. Others were followers, capable of seeing the vision but needing someone to lead them toward it. A few were achievers who would pursue the vision with him. And from this group, leaders would emerge who would help others see and pursue the same destination.

Fearless Guidance plants the seed of vision in such a way that wanderers can become followers, followers can become achievers, and achievers can become leaders themselves. It doesn't demand that everyone see the vision immediately or perfectly. It simply requires that the leader step forward first, making the invisible visible, demonstrating that what seems impossible is merely difficult.

The seed is planted through action, not words alone. Alexander didn't just talk about conquering Persia. He threw his spear into Persian soil. He stepped off the boat first. He made the future he envisioned tangible in the present moment. This is how Fearless Guidance transforms people: by giving them something concrete to follow, a visible path into the unknown.

Three months later, Alexander faced his first major test at the Granicus River. The Persian army waiting on the eastern bank, cavalry positioned in front of infantry. Ready to repel any crossing. His second-in-command, Parmenion, experienced, cautious, wise; counselled waiting until morning. The army had marched all day. Attacking across a river with steep banks was dangerous. Better to rest and cross at dawn when they were fresh.

Alexander's response captures everything about his approach to uncertainty: "It would disgrace the Hellespont should he fear the Granicus." If he had already crossed the greater danger, the strait between Europe and Asia, why hesitate before this lesser river?

He personally led the Companion cavalry across.

During the chaotic melee on the far bank, a Persian noble named Rhoesaces struck Alexander on the head with his scimitar. The blow cracked his helmet and sliced off part of the tall white plume that made him so recognizable.

Alexander thrust his lance through Rhoesaces' chest. But as he did, another Persian appeared behind him, sword raised for what should have been a fatal strike. At the last moment, one of Alexander's officers, Cleitus the Black, severed the Persian's raised arm, saving Alexander's life.

The cracked helmet became proof of something essential to Fearless Guidance. Alexander didn't lead from safety. He didn't ask his men to take risks he wouldn't take himself. He fought not from the rear, giving orders, but from the thickest part of the combat where the danger was greatest.

And he nearly died doing it.

Over the next eleven years, Alexander would be wounded at least nine times. An arrow through the thigh at Issus. A catapult bolt through the shoulder at Gaza. A stone to the head causing temporary blindness at Cyropolis. An arrow that fractured his leg at Maracanda.

The worst came at the siege of a Mallian fortress in 326 BCE. Frustrated by the slow pace of the siege, Alexander grabbed a ladder and began climbing the wall himself. When the ladders collapsed under the weight of soldiers rushing to protect him, Alexander faced a choice. He could retreat to safety, or he could advance into the enemy.

He leaped into the citadel. Into the midst of hundreds of enemies. Alone.

During the desperate fighting that followed, an arrow from a heavy bow penetrated his breastplate and lodged in his lung. When it was extracted, his lung collapsed. Rumors of his death quickly spread through the army. His men, believing him dead, tore down the city gates with their bare hands in their rage, and killed every inhabitant.

When Alexander recovered enough to address his troops, to those concerned about the danger he constantly put himself in, he spoke about his wounds:

"Come now! Whoever of you has wounds, let him strip and show them, and I will show mine in turn; for there is no part of my body, in front at any rate, remaining free from wounds, nor is there any kind of weapon used either for close combat or for hurling at the enemy, the traces of which I do not bear on my person."

His scars were his credentials. They gave him moral authority to ask for sacrifice from others. This is the price of Fearless Guidance. The leader must be willing to go first into the danger.

The Weight of an Impossible Inheritance

A thousand years before Alexander set about conquering the known world, another leader had stepped into an impossible inheritance on the other side of the ancient Near East.

For forty years Moses led the Israelites through the wilderness. They were wanderers. He had spoken with God, but the people couldn't see the vision. He had performed miracles that freed the nation from slavery, but he couldn't free their minds from the bonds of slavery. Finally, together with that whole generation, Moses, the "servant of the LORD", died. They never made it to the "Promised Land".

Joshua, the assistant who stood in Moses' shadow for decades, was tasked to lead the next generation. But now with more purpose. Now into the promised land.

God's first words to Joshua reveal how he was feeling. "Be strong and courageous, because you will lead these people to inherit the land I swore to their ancestors to give them." Then, "Be strong and very courageous." And again: "Have I not commanded you? Be strong and courageous. Do not be afraid; do not be discouraged, for the LORD your God will be with you wherever you go."

Joshua was terrified.

Moses had just died and Joshua was suddenly leading two million people. A people in mourning. A people grieving. A people without focus. And the way to the promised land lies across a river in flood.

Joshua was to learn that courage wasn't the absence of fear. It was finding strength beyond himself when fear was overwhelming. The primary aspect of Fearless Guidance that Joshua grew to understand, and Alexander knew, is that courage isn't a feeling you have. It's a decision you make.

Faith Before Evidence

Joshua's first challenge after Moses's death was leading approximately two million people across the swollen Jordan River. A river in flood, when the waters were most dangerous and treacherous. There were no bridges. No boats. No engineering solution available.

God's instructions required something extraordinary from the priests carrying the Ark of the Covenant. They had to step into the flooded water before God acted.

Not after the waters parted. Before. They had to act on faith.

The miracle didn't come first. Obedience preceded evidence. The priests had to walk into a raging river, trusting that somehow their next step would find dry ground rather than drowning them.

When they did, when those priests stepped into water that should have swept them away, the river stopped flowing. Twenty miles upstream at a town called Adam, the water piled up in a visible heap. All of Israel crossed on dry ground while the priests stood in the middle of the riverbed, holding the Ark, holding the line, until every single person had crossed safely.

I think about faith sometimes, the same faith those priests showed, when I'm asking a horse to do something that terrifies them or me. I'm not asking them to trust that it's safe, rather asking them to trust me enough to find out if it's safe. There's a difference.

A few years ago, we bred our top mare to a stallion that was one of the best cutting horses in Australia at the time. When the foal was born, a filly foal, I was still in the army and we were living on only two and a half acres. She was smart and friendly, a real pleasure to have around, but maybe a little spoilt. We called her Possum.

At that time, we had just enough land to get yourself into trouble when you're trying to train horses. When it came time to wean the foal, we took her to an agistment paddock to get her away from her mother. A day or so later I went over to the paddock to check on her, and it looked like she may not have had a drink at the dam, even though I had made a point of showing her where the water was when I dropped her there.

Just to be sure, I led her to the water to see if she would drink. When we got to the dam, I became convinced that she hadn't been to the dam, as there was no way that she could have drunk from the dam without getting her feet muddy. But despite being obviously tucked up and consequently very thirsty, there was no way that she would step into the mud to get a drink.

All her life to that point she had only ever drunk milk from her mother, or water from a trough. Did I mention spoilt, and precious?

So after some time standing on the water's edge, trying to drive her into the water, while she explained to me that she was sure that there were alligators and crocodiles sitting under the surface, just waiting to get her. I explained that there wouldn't actually be crocodiles in southern Queensland, and alligators are just like little goannas, so pretty harmless.

While I believe that she saw my logic, she said it wasn't worth the risk in any case, so I decided that the only answer to this problem would be for me to lead her into the water. Boots and all, I led her into the water. The photo on my Instagram page shows the filly drinking thirstily, with me standing in the middle of the dam holding her.

This contrast between Possum's refusal and the priests' obedience illustrates something profound about vision and faith. Possum represents those who cannot or will not see beyond their immediate fear, even when the path forward is clear and the leader is willing to go first. She had never learned to trust beyond her own limited experience.

But the priests at the Jordan, and the people of Israel who followed them, represent something different. Years later, when Joshua was an old man, he gathered all Israel and recounted their history in Joshua 24:2-10. He reminded them of how Abraham had followed God's call, leaving everything familiar to travel throughout Canaan toward an unseen promise.

He spoke of how Moses and Aaron had confronted Pharaoh and led the people out of Egypt through the Red Sea. He described their own crossing of the flooded Jordan.

The difference between wanderers and followers, between those who refuse the vision and those who embrace it, often comes down to this: the willingness to step forward when the leader goes first. Possum had a leader standing in the water, demonstrating it was safe, yet still refused. The Israelites watched the priests step into the flood and found the courage to follow.

Fearless Guidance plants a seed that requires faith to germinate. The leader can step into the unknown first, can demonstrate that the journey is survivable, but ultimately each person must choose whether to trust the vision enough to follow. This is not an example of faith in the leader alone, but faith in the destination the leader has articulated, and the willingness to move toward it despite fear.

When Possum finally took that first step into the water, she felt it only come up to her ankles and realized she wasn't going to die. She stood there drinking for a long moment. From that day forward, water has no longer been her enemy, and she has gone on to realise that she can trust me, to go where I ask her to go.

That's what the priests at the Jordan did. They stepped into their fear on behalf of two million people who needed to see that it was possible. And when those people watched the priests stand firm as the waters stopped, they learned something essential about following leadership into the unknown.

"That day the LORD exalted Joshua in the sight of all Israel; and they stood in awe of him all the days of his life, just as they had stood in awe of Moses." Fearless Guidance doesn't mean you never ask people to step into uncertainty. It means you step in first, and you stand firm while they make the crossing.

When Strategy Defies Logic

Seven days after crossing the Jordan, Joshua stood outside the walls of Jericho. It was one of the oldest, most fortified cities in Canaan. Archaeological evidence suggests walls six feet thick at the base and twelve feet high, built above a smooth stone slope angling upward at thirty-five degrees for thirty-five feet. Cities like this fell only to months-long sieges or elaborate engineering.

In the leadup to the battle for Jericho, God gave Joshua instructions that defied every principle of military science. He was told, "March around the city once a day for six days. Have seven priests carry trumpets before the Ark. On the seventh day, march around seven times. When the trumpets sound, have all the people shout. The walls will collapse."

Imagine being Joshua in that moment. You've just earned your people's trust by leading them across the impossible river. Now God is asking you to execute a strategy that makes no military sense whatsoever. You risk looking like a fool to your own people and to the Canaanites watching from the walls.

For six days, the Israelites marched in silence. The people of Jericho watched with confusion, then contempt. What kind of army marches in circles?

But Joshua had learned something in those forty years following Moses through the wilderness. He had learned that Fearless Guidance sometimes means executing a strategy that makes no human sense, trusting the source of the command rather than your own understanding. Following that vision.

On the seventh day, when the trumpets sounded and the people shouted, the walls collapsed outward. Archaeological evidence confirms this unusual detail, the walls fell outward, creating a ramp that allowed attackers to climb directly into the city. Israel won an overwhelming victory.

Less experienced clients sometimes ask me why I use certain training methods with particular horses. Methods that seem counterintuitive, even risky, to them. Why would you ask a horse to move toward something that scares them? Why would you sometimes use less pressure instead of more? Why would you reward a try even when the horse didn't complete the task?

The answer is because I've learned what works through years of making big mistakes and winning small victories. From watching and learning from other horsemen who knew, and still know, more than I did. Learning from the horses that I was training, these are the best teachers. Seeing that strategies that makes sense to a novice aren't necessarily the strategies that work.

Learning to trust the process even when you can't see how it affects the outcome, and learning to read between the lines to hear what is not being said. From having a plan and following through to completion, then looking back I sense the unseen thread of continuous learning that has guided me on my horsemanship journey.

There is a critical distinction between blind faith and Fearless Guidance. Joshua didn't follow God's strategy at Jericho because he was incapable of thinking for himself. He followed it because he had a relationship built over decades. He had seen God's guidance prove faithful again and again. He had earned the right to trust instructions that seemed illogical because the source had proven trustworthy.

In the same way, a horse doesn't follow you blindly into danger just because you ask. They follow you into danger because you've built a relationship where your judgment has proven more reliable than their instinct. That relationship takes time to build. It requires consistency. And it absolutely requires that you never ask them to trust you into something that will actually harm them.

Trust, once broken, is almost impossible to fully restore.

The Unexpected Mutiny

Eight years into his Asian campaign, Alexander's army finally reached its limit. They were eleven thousand miles from home. They'd been marching and fighting continuously. Monsoon rains had delayed them for months in India. Rumours spread of even larger armies ahead, the Nanda Empire reportedly fielded forces five times Alexander's size.

When Alexander announced plans to continue eastward to the Ganges, his men refused. Not individually. Not quietly. As a unified force, his army told their king, "No. We're not going." An officer named Coenus spoke for the exhausted soldiers, "The men long to again see their parents, their wives and children, their homeland."

Alexander reacted with fury. He declared he would continue with or without them. Then he withdrew to his tent and refused to see anyone for three days.

He expected the mutiny to collapse, for his men to come crawling back with apologies. They did not.

The seed of Fearless Guidance that Alexander had planted eleven years earlier, when he threw his spear into Persian soil, had grown into sustained courage that carried his army across the known world. But even the strongest plant has limits to its growth. Knowing when to stop pushing forward is itself a form of wisdom, though it belongs to a later stage of development than the initial planting we're discussing here.

Joshua faced a similar moment late in his leadership. The Israelites had been fighting for years. They'd conquered most of Canaan, but some territories remained. And at a certain point, Joshua essentially said: "We've done enough. The rest is for you to finish." He divided the remaining land among the tribes and released them to complete what he'd started.

That's not failure. That's understanding that Fearless Guidance doesn't mean leading until you collapse. It means leading until you've brought people far enough that they can complete the journey themselves. The seed is planted.

Three Kinds of Courage

Working with horses has given me an understanding of three distinct kinds of courage. Fearless Guidance needs a leader willing to call on the right one at any given moment, though primarily, it plants the seed of trusting courage as the foundation from which all other courage grows.

1. **Reactive courage**. The courage in response to the imminent threat, the desperate defence in the face of danger. Powerful, explosive, and unsustainable. It's the opposite to the flight response. It's the courage that sees the simple soldier transformed into a fighting machine like Keith Payne, who though wounded, went behind enemy lines to rescue fellow soldiers; or the rodeo clown, who puts himself between the bull and the bull-rider down in the chute.

   This courage serves a purpose, but it's not the seed we're planting with Fearless Guidance. It's reactive, not directive.

2. **Obedient courage**. The courage that sees the soldier follow orders, despite knowing that he will probably be wounded or worse; or sees the soldier suffer for months, enduring the hardships of the trenches; or sees the soldier line up with his mates to charge the enemy position although it means almost certain death.

It is when a horse does something frightening simply because you've asked them to. They push themselves alongside of the path of the mob that rushes in the middle of the night, as the stockmen struggle to wheel them. This works, in a limited sense, but it is partnership built on compliance rather than trust. It's useful, but it's not the ideal we're planting.

3. **Trusting courage.** This is the act of acting despite fear by believing in your own abilities, the process, or the guidance of a higher power. It involves stepping into the unknown, letting go of the need for complete control, and trusting that you have the inner strength to navigate challenges as they arise.

   Trusting courage is both internal, a belief in your own resourcefulness, and external, a trust in others or a divine path. This is the courage Alexander inspired in his men. Not through threats or conditioning, but through a decade of keeping them alive through impossible situations.

This is the courage Joshua inspired in Israel. Not because he performed miracles himself, but because he created the conditions where God could work. And the people learned that Joshua's guidance was trustworthy.

This is the seed that Fearless Guidance plants: trusting courage. It cannot be forced or manufactured. It must be grown from the foundation of relationship, consistency, and proven reliability.

You can't create trusting courage quickly. It's built slowly, one kept promise at a time. One moment of steady presence in the face of danger. One decision that proves your judgment is sound. One small act of Fearless Guidance that leads to safety rather than harm.

And it can be destroyed in an instant. One betrayal of trust. One moment where you ask them to follow you into danger and then abandon them to face it alone. One decision made from ego rather than wisdom.

This is why Fearless Guidance carries such weight. You're not just responsible for making the right call in this moment. You're responsible for maintaining the trust that makes future guidance possible. As your courage matures into sustained ambition and eventually into peaceful direction, that trust will be tested and refined, but it all begins here, with the seed of trusting courage planted through your willingness to go first into the unknown.

Understanding the Terrain

As we develop Fearless Guidance, it's important to understand something about fear itself. Fear has a geography, zones of intensity that help us understand how to plant courage effectively.

The art of Fearless Guidance is knowing these boundaries and working within them. You want to bring the horse, or the person, to the edge of their comfort zone, not past it. You want them slightly uncomfortable but still capable of thought. That's where the seed finds purchase.

As courage grows and matures, which we'll explore in Compassionate Ambition, the leader learns through trial and error where these boundaries lie for each individual. Some horses need to be brought very carefully, very gradually, to the edge of their fear. Others can be asked for more, sooner. But this understanding of how to sustain and temper courage comes later. For now, in the planting stage, what matters is recognizing that there are boundaries, and that effective Fearless Guidance works within them rather than bulldozing through them.

Alexander understood this intuitively. He pushed his army to extraordinary lengths, but he also knew when they'd reached their limit. Joshua understood this. He led Israel into Canaan, but he didn't try to conquer every city himself. Both leaders planted the seed of courage and then created conditions where that courage could grow, a process we'll explore more fully in subsequent chapters.

What It Looks Like Outside the Arena

When you plant Fearless Guidance in professional settings, in family dynamics, in any area of leadership, the planting action looks specific and intentional:

> **You demonstrate how to take the first step into uncertainty**. Not by talking about courage or explaining why fear shouldn't matter. But by physically, visibly, stepping into the unknown while others watch. When your team faces a difficult pivot, you don't send others to test the waters, you go first. When your family confronts a challenging change, you don't just announce it, you lead the way into it, showing through your actions that it's survivable.

> This is what Alexander did throwing his spear into Persian soil. This is what Joshua's priests did stepping into the Jordan. This is what plants the seed: visible action that demonstrates courage is possible.

You establish yourself as someone worth following into the unknown. This isn't about charisma or charm. It's about reliability. When you say you'll do something, you do it. When you commit to a direction, you follow through. When you promise something is worth the difficulty, you prove it by staying the course yourself. The relationship that makes following possible is built through countless small moments of consistency.

The horse learns your judgment is reliable by watching you be right about small things before they'll trust you about large things. People do the same. Every promise kept, every moment of presence maintained under pressure, every decision that proves sound, these build the foundation of trust that makes Fearless Guidance possible.

You articulate a vision compelling enough to make courage feel worthwhile. People don't follow you into danger for the sake of danger. They follow because they believe the destination is worth the journey. When Alexander declared Asia "a gift from the gods," he wasn't just making a bold statement, he was painting a picture of possibility that transformed dangerous uncertainty into a meaningful task providing service to the nation.

The vision doesn't have to be grand or cosmic. Sometimes it's as simple as: "If we can get through this quarter, we'll have proven we can handle anything the market throws at us." Sometimes it's: "If we can teach this horse to trust us through their fear, we'll have created a partnership nothing can break." Sometimes it's: "If we can cross this flooded river, we'll finally reach the land we've been working toward for forty years."

What matters is that the vision is clear, compelling, and worth the courage it costs to pursue it. These three elements, visible demonstration, reliable character, and compelling vision, are what plant Fearless Guidance. Everything else, the sustained drive, the refined judgment, the peaceful mastery, grows from this planted seed.

The Question You Must Answer

Every horse we work with eventually asks a question. They don't ask it with words, obviously. They ask it through a test. They present us with a situation where we have to choose between being right and being trustworthy. Between our ego and their welfare. Between force and partnership.

The specific test varies. Sometimes it's a spook at something unexpected. Sometimes it's refusing to do something we've asked. Sometimes it's just a hard day where nothing seems to be working. But the underlying question is always the same: "Is your guidance worth following?"

Purpose matters. Direction matters. A horse will follow you into difficult situations if they believe in you. But if they suspect you're just exercising authority for its own sake, their compliance will be grudging at best and actively resistant at worst.

This is what made both Alexander and Joshua such effective leaders. They had a destination in mind that was bigger than themselves. Alexander wanted to unite the known world under Hellenic culture. Joshua wanted to establish Israel in the land God had promised them. These weren't just personal ambitions. They were missions that gave meaning to the suffering required to achieve them.

When Alexander's army finally mutinied, it wasn't because they didn't trust him anymore. It was because they'd achieved enough. They'd conquered Persia. They'd reached India. The destination Alexander sought, the edge of the world, seemed less compelling than the destination they longed for. Home.

When Joshua divided the remaining land among the tribes, it wasn't because he'd failed to complete the conquest. It was because he'd brought them far enough that they could finish it themselves. His mission wasn't to conquer Canaan. His mission was to lead Israel into Canaan. Once they were established, once they'd seen that it was possible, his part was done.

In the arena and in the boardroom, a similar principle applies. People will follow you through difficulty when they see tomorrow's destination is worth the pain. Horses will follow you through difficulty if they trust in you and see today's destination is worth their pain. But if you can't articulate why the journey matters, if you can't connect today's struggle with the reward, you're asking them to suffer for no purpose.

Fearless Guidance requires a destination worth the courage it takes to reach it.

The Measure of a Leader

When Bucephalus died in 326 BCE, Alexander wept. His officers were shocked by the depth of his grief. It was just a horse, after all. There would be other horses, other wars, other victories.

But Alexander understood something his officers didn't. Bucephalus wasn't just a horse. He was a partner who had carried him through every major battle of his Asian campaign. He was proof that Fearless Guidance works in both directions. Alexander had guided Bucephalus out of terror into courage. And Bucephalus had carried Alexander safely through situations where courage alone wasn't enough.

The city Alexander founded in Bucephalus's honour still stands. Alexandria Bucephalous is a minor city now, not particularly notable except for one thing: it exists because a leader valued the partnership that made his victories possible.

Joshua died at age 110, having successfully led Israel into the Promised Land. His final words to the people he'd guided for decades were simple: "Choose for yourselves this day whom you will serve... But as for me and my household, we will serve the LORD."

He didn't demand their loyalty. He didn't threaten consequences for disobedience. He simply stated his own commitment and invited them to make their own choice. That's the ultimate expression of mature leadership. Offering guidance without demanding compliance. Creating the conditions for courage without forcing it.

The measure of a leader isn't how many people follow you. It's where those people end up because they followed you. Did they become more capable, more confident, more courageous? Or did they simply become more dependent on you?

I measure my success with a horse not by how well they perform for me, but by how much confidence they've gained through our work together. A horse who needs me constantly, who falls apart when I'm not there, who can only be brave when I'm making them brave, that's not success. That's dependence.

But a horse who has learned through our partnership that they can face difficult things, who has discovered their own courage, who has developed the confidence to navigate uncertainty on their own, that's the goal. That's Fearless Guidance done right.

The same applies to leading people. If your team only functions well when you're micromanaging every decision, you haven't created Fearless Guidance. You've created dependence. But if your team has learned to navigate uncertainty on their own, to make courageous decisions without needing your constant input, to trust themselves because they first learned to trust you, that's leadership worth celebrating.

This is how you measure whether you've successfully planted the seed of Fearless Guidance: by whether those who follow you develop courage of their own, not just the ability to follow your courage.

The Truth About Fear

Here's what I've learned from years of working with horses and decades of studying leaders like Alexander and Joshua. Fear never completely goes away. You don't conquer it. You just learn to move forward despite it.

Alexander was wounded nine times. Each time, he recovered and went back into battle. You think he wasn't afraid? You think the arrow through his lung didn't make him reconsider whether this campaign was worth dying for? But he went back anyway because his men needed to see that fear wasn't the final word.

Joshua stood at the banks of a flooded river at age eighty, facing the impossible task of leading two million people into enemy territory. You think he wasn't terrified? But he gave the order to march anyway because his people needed someone to show them that faith could overcome fear.

The horse who has overcome the fear of crossing creeks sometimes still hesitates at the edge. But they've learned that the momentary discomfort of overcoming their fear is worth the freedom on the other side.

Fearless Guidance isn't about being fearless. It's about not letting fear make your decisions for you. It's about acknowledging the danger while choosing to move forward anyway. It's about being honest about your own uncertainty while maintaining the conviction your people need to find their own courage.

There's a moment every horseman recognizes. You've asked the horse to face something difficult. They're standing at the edge of their courage, every muscle tense, ready to bolt or fight. And they turn their head to look at you. Just for a moment. Just long enough to check: "Are you sure about this?"

In that moment, they're not asking if it's safe. They're asking if you believe it's worth it. They're asking if you're certain enough in your guidance that they can trust you with their fear.

How you answer that question, not with words, but with your presence, your certainty, your willingness to stand with them in their uncertainty, determines whether they bolt or step forward.

That's Fearless Guidance. Not the absence of fear. Not the denial of danger. But the willingness to go first, to stand firm, and to be worthy of the trust required to lead others into the unknown.

Alexander threw his spear into the Asian shore and declared the land a gift from the gods. Joshua commanded the priests to step into a flooded river. Neither knew for certain how things would turn out. But both understood that their people needed to see them move forward with conviction, or they'd never find the courage to follow.

Every day in the arena, we have the opportunity to practice this same principle. Every time a horse hesitates at something that frightens them, we are invited to demonstrate whether we're a leader worth following. Not through force or manipulation, but through the patient building of trust that makes courage possible.

And every time we choose to be present, to be clear, to be worthy of that trust, we understand a little better what Alexander felt when he turned Bucephalus to face the sun. What Joshua felt when he watched the priests step into the Jordan. What every leader feels when they realize that guidance isn't about having all the answers, it's about having the courage to move forward when the answers aren't clear and helping others find their courage to follow.

The horse doesn't follow your title. They follow your truth. And the truth is that fear is real, danger is real, uncertainty is real. But so is courage. So is trust. So is the possibility that by moving forward together, you and those who follow you can reach destinations that neither could reach alone.

That is the heart of Fearless Guidance. Not conquering fear but transforming it into forward motion. Not eliminating uncertainty but moving through it with clear-eyed determination. Not demanding courage from others but creating the conditions where courage becomes possible.

Every great leader I've studied, every horse that's taught me, every moment in my own life when I've had to choose between comfort and growth, they all point to the same truth.

Fearless Guidance isn't about being unafraid. It's about deciding that your destination is more important than your fear, and then helping others make that same decision.

The walls of Jericho fell. The Jordan stopped flowing. Alexander conquered the known world. And every day in arenas around the world, horses who were once terrified learn to trust enough to face their fears. Not because they stopped being afraid. But because someone showed them it was possible to be afraid and courageous at the same time.

That's the lesson. That's the gift. That's Fearless Guidance.

The seed is planted when you take that first step into the unknown. What grows from that seed, sustained ambition, refined judgment, peaceful mastery, we'll explore in the chapters ahead. But it all begins here, with the decision to go first.

In Chapter 6, we'll explore how this planted seed of Fearless Guidance grows into Compassionate Ambition - how initial courage deepens into sustainable drive, and what happens when the costs of leadership become clear. But first, the seed must be planted.

"I am not afraid of an army of lions led by a sheep; I am afraid of an army of sheep led by a lion."

- Alexander the Great

CHAPTER 4

EMOTIONLESS COMMUNICATION

"You have power over your mind — not outside events. Realize this, and you will find strength."

- Marcus Aurelius

The river Danube had never looked so cold. From his command tent on the northern bank, Marcus Aurelius stood watching the grey waters flow past, carrying with it the detritus of war. Broken shields, spent arrows, and sometimes worse. Much worse.

It was the winter of 172 AD, and the Emperor of Rome had been campaigning against the Germanic tribes for nearly three years. The Marcomanni and their allies had proven far more resilient than the Senate had anticipated. But that wasn't what troubled him as he stood in the predawn darkness.

The dispatch had arrived just after midnight. Another betrayal. One of his most trusted generals, a man he had personally elevated to command, had been discovered taking bribes from tribal leaders. Worse, he had been providing intelligence about Roman troop movements. How many legionaries had died because of this man's greed? How many families would never see their fathers again?

Marcus felt the familiar tightness in his chest, the heat rising in his throat. Anger. Righteous, justified anger. This man deserved to be executed. Publicly. Brutally. An example needed to be made.

He took a deep breath. Then another. The cold air burned his lungs.

"What does my anger accomplish?" he asked himself quietly. "Will it bring back the dead? Will it make me a better emperor? Will it help me make the right decision about what to do next?"

No. To all three.

Turning away from the river with a sigh, he let the heavy canvas flap fall. This tent, and the bearskin that he slept in, were the only concessions he ever made toward creature comforts. As long as he could remember, much to his mother's disgust, he had preferred the simple pleasures of a stoic.

Sitting down at his desk, with the bearskin wrapped around his shoulders, Marcus reached for the small leather journal he always carried. In the dim light of the oil lamp, he began to write. Not orders for execution. Not a scathing condemnation. Instead, he wrote to himself, reminding himself of what he knew to be true:

"When you wake up in the morning, tell yourself: The people I deal with today will be meddling, ungrateful, arrogant, dishonest, jealous and surly. They are like this because they cannot tell good from evil. But I have seen the beauty of good, and the ugliness of evil, and have recognized that the wrongdoer has a nature related to my own."

By the time the sun rose over the frost-covered camp, Marcus had made his decision. The general would face trial, yes. Justice would be served. But Marcus would not let his personal feelings of betrayal and anger cloud his judgment about what punishment fit the crime, or worse, about his strategy going forward. He would not give this betrayal power over his mind.

That afternoon, when he finally met with his war council to discuss the situation, his younger commanders were shocked. They had heard the reports of the treachery. They expected the emperor to be raging, perhaps even irrational in his desire for vengeance. Instead, they found him calm, measured, focused.

He asked questions of these men. The old commanders, and those, much younger, that had just replaced the few who fell on the battlefield. How did this happen? How can we ensure it does not happen again? He listened to their counsel. He made decisions based on what was best for Rome, not what would make him feel better in the moment.

One of the younger tribunes, emboldened by the emperor's composure, finally asked, "Caesar, how are you not furious? This man's betrayal cost us dearly. Does it not anger you?"

Marcus looked at him with eyes that had seen too much war, too much death, too much of humanity's capacity for both greatness and depravity. "Of course it angers me," he said quietly. "I am human. I feel everything you feel. But I do not let that anger decide my actions. My emotions are like passing clouds. I acknowledge them, I feel them, but I do not let them obscure my view of what must be done."

The Greatest Misunderstanding

When I first introduce the principle of Emotionless Communication to corporate leaders or professionals, I often see a visible reaction. Eyes narrow. Arms cross. Someone usually interrupts to say something like, "But you can't just be a robot. People need to see your passion. They need to know you care."

They are absolutely right. You are not a robot. Your people must know your passion. They must see that you care.

Emotionless Communication is perhaps the most misunderstood principle of The Horseman's Way. Emotionless Communication doesn't mean having no emotions. It doesn't mean being cold, distant, or uncaring. Just as Marcus Aurelius felt anger at his general's betrayal, Jesus wept at Lazarus's tomb. These were people with deep feelings.

You must feel your emotions fully. You need to acknowledge all of your emotions. Feel the pain, appreciate the highs. Honestly accept your feelings, but you do not let them control your communication or your decisions. Experience the anger, but do not speak from anger. Feel the fear, but you do not let fear act within you. Know the grief, but you do not let grief blind you to how you can make a difference in this world.

I have been honoured to have horses that have taught me this lesson far more clearly than any philosophy text ever could have.

Planting the Seed of Clear Communication

In the framework of The Horseman's Way, Emotionless Communication is the planting stage of what I call the Communication Pillar. Like a farmer preparing soil and setting seed, we begin here with the foundational practice of communicating without emotional distortion. This is not the end of the journey, but the essential beginning.

Just as Humble Strength provides the foundation for all leadership, Emotionless Communication plants the seed for all effective interaction. When this seed is planted well, tended carefully, it will grow into something far greater. It will mature into what I call Balanced Coordination, where your words, actions, and internal state move in perfect harmony. Eventually, with continued practice and refinement, it will be pruned into Centred Transcendence, that state of grounded awareness where you maintain inner stillness even in chaos.

But we're getting ahead of ourselves. Before we can harvest anything, we must first learn to plant properly.

The seed we're planting is simple in concept but demanding in practice, communication that is clean, neutral, and precise. Communication where we remove emotional charge before speaking. Where we convey boundaries without hostility. Where we deliver truth with steadiness.

A horse requires this absolutely. They don't respond to what you say. They respond to what you are. And what you are shows up not in your words, but in your energy, your tension, your congruence or lack thereof.

The Mirror That Never Lies

Some time ago, I had to deal with a situation that serves to help to understand the concept of Emotionless Communication. A client asked for help to deal with a horse that had become "difficult." According to the owner, the horse could no longer be caught in the paddock. She would pin her ears and turn away whenever anyone approached, and the owner was concerned because the horse kicked out at his teenage daughter.

When I went out to meet the horse, from a distance I could see the tension radiating from the mare before I even got to the gate. Her movements were quick, almost jerky. Her head was up, and her breathing shallow as she continually looked around to check her exit path was still clear. She was already frustrated before anyone even attempted to catch her.

"She's going to give me hell again," the owner muttered on the way toward the paddock. "Just watch. She's the most ignorant horse I've ever seen."

Sure enough, as soon as we opened the gate and the owner headed toward the mare with the halter, she wheeled away, ears flat, nostrils flared. The owner's frustration exploded into anger, chasing the horse, waving the halter, voice getting louder and sharper with each step.

The mare ran to the far corner of the paddock and stood there, nervously looking around, ready to take off again.

I asked the owner stop what he was doing. I had seen enough. Taking the halter, I asked him to wait outside the paddock. Once inside the paddock, I stood near the gate, not moving toward the horse, not even looking directly at her. I simply stood there and breathed. Slowly. Deeply. I wanted to let the owner's frustration float away on the breeze. I had to free my mind, to let go of any anticipation of difficulty, any agenda about what needed to happen next.

Approximately ten minutes passed. The mare's ears slowly came forward. Her head lowered slightly. She took a step toward me. I stepped away. Then the mare took another step, and another. Each time the horse stepped toward me, I stepped away. Even though the distance between us was more than twenty metres, the connection was developing between myself and the horse.

I didn't move to catch her. The mare moved to within ten metres and stopped. I took a small step toward the horse, and she stepped away. The I took another step, and the mare turned and trotted back to the corner. I followed quickly, positioning myself so that if the mare left the corner, she would have to move toward me, even if it was only a slight amount.

The mare stopped in the corner and looked back at me, daring me to come toward her. Knowing she could outrun me no matter what I tried. As I took a step toward the mare, she took off. I followed pushing her, just applying pressure with my presence. Around, and around the paddock she went at a canter. I didn't have to move much. She soon tired of the run and slowed to a trot. I stopped and backed away. The mare slowed to a walk, and I continued to back away. Matching her step for step.

The mare's path veered slightly towards me. With every step I took backwards, the mare took another step toward me. The owner later said, "It was like there was a connection somehow between you. You kept backing away and she kept coming toward you!" This is the mirror that never lies. By mirroring her every move, she learnt firstly, that I wasn't a threat, and secondly, That she couldn't run away from me.

Soon she stopped in front of me, and I just stood there, barely acknowledging her presence. I remained calm, and waited. Slowly, she walked toward me and I reached out to rub her neck. I could tell that she was thinking that maybe it was okay to trust me. Stepping in beside her, I slipped the end of the rope halter around her neck. She lowered her head into the halter I held open in front of her.

The owner was speechless. "I didn't do anything special," I told him. "I just knew not to take emotional chaos into the paddock with me. She wasn't being stubborn. She was simply responding to your emotional state, the way you were moving. The way you were acting." This is Emotionless Communication at its most basic level, creating trust by allowing the option to run away, but making this option the hard option. Allowing her to find the easy option by being with me.

When Emotionless Communication gets hard

Communicating with horses on a daily basis enables these lessons to become ingrained. Working with a mare, Sunny, a couple of years ago, tested my resolve and proved the value of this understanding.

Together with three other horses, we had purchased Sunny as a yearling from a sale in May. Our intention was to start them under saddle as soon as we could, and to train them prior to putting them back through the sale the following year as "going" two-year-olds. Our plan was to let them grow out for a couple of months on an agistment property, while we went to the NCHA futurity with a couple of others.

We had been away for a few days, at the Goondiwindi cutting, in preparation for the upcoming futurity, and I thought I had better check on the new horses when we returned. Sunny was standing peacefully at the fence, a good-old, barbed wire fence, when I drove through the gate. Leaning over the fence, I rubbed her on the neck, saying I was glad to see she had been looking after herself, before climbing through the fence in front of her.

As I straightened up, I glanced at her near-side hind leg. The skin in front of her hock joint lay open, exposing the muscle and sinews beneath in an angry looking wound about the size of a baseball. My heart sank. All of our hopes and dreams for this mare were dashed in a split second. I remember thinking, "At least she's a nice mare. She will have some nice babies." There was no hope for much else.

I left her standing at the fence as much as hated leaving her, arriving back at the paddock a couple of hours later with the gooseneck to take her back home. She had hardly moved, which was understandable given the pain she must have been in. That pain wasn't going to make loading her any easier.

The ramp on the gooseneck was quite steep, so I backed it into the table-drain so that the end of the tailgate would sit on the dirt road, a foot or so higher. It made a lot of difference, but the ramp was still kind of steep. It took over an hour and a half to convince her to walk up it as she still had to power through the pain to push herself up the ramp using her hind legs a lot more than I wanted her to.

Through the whole process of loading her, I was forced to deal with so many emotions. Both mine, and hers. The last thing that I wanted to do was to cause her any more pain, but we had to get her treated. I felt guilty about asking her walk up the ramp. Should I go and get hire or try to borrow a float that wasn't so hard to get into? This would take time, probably adding at least another four hours to the time before we could get her to the vet. I decided against it.

The only way to get her into the gooseneck was to basically force her through the pain, dragging her, one step at a time. My compassionate side hated this, but it also recognised that the sooner she got treatment, the sooner her pain would be reduced. Sunny was hating the experience also, for obvious reasons. Having decided on this course of action we had to keep going until the job was done, or one of us died trying.

Although she wanted to do what I asked, to be compliant, she would go through periods of anger and resistance because of the pain. We were both in a lather of sweat by the time she finally got to the top.

When we arrived home, it was much easier to get her off the gooseneck trailer, but there was still some pain involved. The vet arrived shortly after we got there, having been prewarned that the mare was in need of attention.

The vet expertly bandaged the mare's leg, and left instructions to replace the bandage every day for the next two weeks, the wound would be reviewed to see how it was healing. As we were not qualified to use it she didn't leave us any of the sedation she had used on the mare. Quite understandable, but as it turned out, quite inconvenient.

Late the next afternoon we set out to replace the bandage, Sunny stood there, quiet, willing to allow us to remove the bandage, but when it came time to put the fresh bandage on, she said, "No way"! With a wound of this nature, firstly, it is critical that no foreign material gets into the wound that could promote infection, and secondly, that no additional damage occurs to the injury to setback the healing process.

It was like she had built a wall around her leg in her mind, and no matter what our intentions, there was no way we were coming in. By the time we had been going around, and around, with the mare for over an hour, our patience was wearing pretty thin. I would reach down her leg with the pad to go under the bandage, and as soon as it got near the site of the injury, she would step away, or kick out, or both.

I eventually decided to put her in the vet crush, which is just a chute with a gate on each end, and big enough for a pregnant mare to stand inside. The horses usually just stand there while the vet does their thing to the horses, but I had hesitated to use it for Sunny due to the risk of her getting down and further injuring herself. But as we were well into our second hour of trying to get the treatment completed, I figured that it was time to take that risk.

It took a while, but we eventually got it done. At least in the vet crush, I could kneel down beside her hind leg with a much lower risk of her kicking me, and kick she did. Every time I touched her leg anywhere she would kick out, but she finally accepted that. Then I would place the pad on the wound, and she would kick out again, often sending the sterile pad flying, which required a fresh pad. But little by little that wall was coming down.

In this situation, my ability to continue to communicate with the mare without letting my emotions take over was sorely tested, but deep down I knew that allowing my emotions into the conversation with her would be counterproductive. This is what is meant by Emotionless Communication. It is fundamental to ensuring that you are able to stay in the fight, once the decision is made to stay, and fight.

This mare has always been the alpha mare, the leader of the herd, but the day that I found her standing beside the fence, she was asking me for help. She recognised that she was in a situation that she couldn't control. She needed help. My help.

She wanted my help right up to the time when she said, "This hurts too much". That was when the wall went up. That was when she started getting angry, started getting defensive, and then it became a fight. But it was fight that I knew

I would win. I had decided that this had to happen. There was no alternative, there could be no going back.

No matter how much she argued, how much she fought. There was no room for emotion. There was no room for doubt. We just had to keep going through the pain, her pain. And my pain. When originally loading her, after the injury, each time I walked down that ramp to talk to her, to reassure her, and then climbed back up the ramp. Each time I pulled on the lead rope, and she pulled back, the effort became a little bit harder for both of us.

Her pain became my pain as the day wore on. As she got more tired and moved from resentment to anger. From anger to just stubborn resistance, my body got more and more tired, but I knew that I could not afford to let me emotions to have any say in the way that I acted. Like Joshua's army marching around the walls of Jericho, we had to keep going around, and around that wall. Until it final fell.

The alternative would have been to tie her up, force her into submission. I never considered this course of action for an instant for one simple reason. The logical long-term result of doing this, where the horse has no choice, sees the job get done regardless of the mental and physical damage that results. From force, not from understanding. Rather than becoming a partner, she becomes a pawn!

Horses don't understand frustration or anger as emotions with reasons behind them. The sensitive ones know that it's not safe to be around people when they're broadcasting that kind of negative energy. Horses live in the present moment. At their most basic level, they are motivated by only three things. The three F's. Food, Flight or Fight.

They are extraordinarily sensitive to the emotional state of every creature around them. It's a survival mechanism developed over millions of years. In the wild, if one member of the herd suddenly becomes anxious or agitated, it might mean a predator is near. The rest of the herd needs to respond immediately.

This same sensitivity makes horses perfect teachers of Emotionless Communication. They don't care why you're angry or anxious or frustrated. They only know that your emotional state makes you unpredictable, and unpredictable creatures are dangerous. They will either flee from you, fight you, or shut down entirely.

But when you approach them with emotional composure, when you acknowledge your feelings but don't broadcast them, when you're present and grounded and clear, they can relax. They can trust. They can engage. The same principle applies to humans, though we're usually less honest about it than horses are.

Two Philosophers, One Truth

Marcus Aurelius, Stoic philosopher and Roman emperor, and Jesus of Nazareth, the Jewish rabbi and spiritual teacher, lived in completely different lives despite those lives being radically affected by the Roman empire. Marcus ruled the known world from his throne in Rome. While over a hundred years earlier, Jesus walked the dusty roads of Galilee with no home to call his own, in a land under Roman rule.

Both taught remarkably similar lessons about emotional mastery and communication.

Marcus wrote in his Meditations, "If you are distressed by anything external, the pain is not due to the thing itself, but to your estimate of it; and this you have the power to revoke at any moment." He was teaching that our suffering comes not from events themselves, but from our emotional reactions to them, and that we have the power to choose our response.

Jesus taught his followers, "Do not worry about tomorrow, for tomorrow will worry about itself. Each day has enough trouble of its own." He demonstrated this principle perfectly when he stood before Pontius Pilate, falsely accused, facing execution. The religious leaders were shouting accusations. The crowd was calling for his blood. Pilate himself was confused and conflicted.

And Jesus? He remained calm. Composed. He spoke when necessary, clearly and without defensiveness. He remained silent when words would serve no purpose. His emotional state didn't waver based on the chaos around him or the injustice being done to him.

This wasn't because he didn't care or couldn't feel. The gospels tell us he experienced the full range of emotions. He felt righteous anger when he drove the money changers from the temple. Deep sorrow when he wept over Jerusalem. He felt such anguish in the Garden of Gethsemane that his sweat became like drops of blood.

But he never let those emotions control his communication or cloud his purpose.

Marcus Aurelius faced similar challenges. As emperor, he dealt with betrayal, war, plague, political intrigue, and personal tragedy. His beloved wife died. His sons disappointed him. His generals failed him. His empire teetered on the brink of collapse.

Yet he continued to write in his journal, reminding himself: "The impediment to action advances action. What stands in the way becomes the way." He chose to see obstacles not as reasons to react emotionally, but as opportunities to practice virtue.

Both men understood a fundamental truth: emotional reactions are natural and human, but emotional control is what separates wise leadership from reactive chaos. They both taught that true strength lies not in suppressing emotions, but in experiencing them fully while choosing how to respond.

Jesus said, "You have heard that it was said, 'Eye for eye, and tooth for tooth.' But I tell you, do not resist an evil person. If anyone slaps you on the right cheek, turn to them the other cheek also." This wasn't about being passive or weak. It was about refusing to let another person's actions control your response. It was about maintaining your own emotional composure regardless of how others behave.

Marcus wrote, "The best revenge is not to be like that." When his general betrayed him, he didn't respond with the emotional vengeance that would have been expected, even justified. Instead, he responded with measured justice, guided by reason rather than rage.

Both teachers emphasized the importance of self-awareness in achieving emotional mastery. When Jesus taught, "Why do you look at the speck of sawdust in your brother's eye and pay no attention to the plank in your own eye", He was calling people to examine their own internal state before judging others.

Marcus constantly practiced this self-examination. His Meditations are essentially a journal of his own attempts to master his reactions, to remind himself of what truly matters, to stay centered amid chaos. "Look within," he wrote. "Within is the fountain of good, and it will ever bubble up, if you will ever dig."

The Three Levels of Communication

In my work with horses and with people, I've observed that communication happens on three distinct levels. Understanding these levels is crucial to developing Emotionless Communication.

Level One: The Words We Say

This is the surface level, the content of our message. It's what we think we're communicating. In business settings, it might be presenting data, outlining a strategy, or giving instructions. In the arena, it might be the verbal and non-verbal cues we give a horse.

Most people believe this is all that matters. They craft their words carefully, practice their presentations, choose their vocabulary strategically. And yes, words matter. But they're only about 7% of what we're actually communicating.

Level Two: How We Say It

This includes our tone of voice, our pace, our volume, our body language, our facial expressions. This is where our emotions start to show up whether we want them to or not.

You can say the words "I'm not angry" with gritted teeth and clenched fists, but nobody will believe you. Your body is telling a different story than your words. Horses are particularly attuned to this level. They can hear the tension in your voice, see the tightness in your shoulders, feel the rigidity in your movements.

Research suggests this accounts for about 55% of our communication. But there's an even deeper level.

Level Three: The Energy We Bring

This is the hardest level to describe because it's largely unconscious, but it's perhaps the most powerful. It's the emotional and energetic state we're in when we communicate. It's the intention behind our words and actions. It's what horses feel when they read us, even from across a paddock.

You've experienced this yourself, even if you've never named it. You walk into a room where two people have just been arguing, and even though they're not saying anything, you can feel the tension. You meet someone for the first time, and within seconds you have a gut feeling about whether they're trustworthy or not, though you couldn't explain why.

This is energy. This is presence. This is what Marcus Aurelius was working on when he took those deep breaths by the Danube. He was changing his internal state so that when he met with his council, he would bring calm clarity instead of reactive anger.

Emotionless Communication requires all three levels to be congruent. Your words, your delivery, and your internal state all need to align. When they don't, people and horses both will trust their understanding of what is going on at a deeper levels over the words that sit on our surface layer.

What It Looks Like in the Arena

When you bring Emotionless Communication into your work with horses, here's what changes:

1. You become aware of your own emotional state before you ever open the gate. Are you frustrated by the way someone has treated you, or spoken to you? Anxious about something that has nothing to do with this horse? Excited and wanting to rush through training to get to the 'good part'?

   You acknowledge these feelings. You don't judge them or try to suppress them. But you don't bring them through the gate. I teach my students to take what I call 'the three breath reset' before working with a horse.

   Three slow, deep breaths. With each exhale, you consciously release whatever emotional state you were carrying. With each inhale, you choose presence, clarity, calm.
   It's not about becoming emotionless. It's about becoming emotionally grounded.

2. You communicate clearly and consistently, without the static of emotional noise. If the horse needs correction, you provide it matter-of-factly, the way you'd state any other truth. Not with anger or frustration, but with the calm certainty that this is what needs to happen.

   The horse responds not to punishment, but to clarity. If the horse does something well, you acknowledge it with the same clear composure. Not with gushing excitement that might actually startle the horse, but with quiet but generous approval that reinforces the behaviour.

3. You stay present with what is, not what you wish it would be or what you're afraid it might become. The horse shies at a shadow? You don't get angry about it or anxious about what it means for your training timeline. You simply address it: acknowledge the concern, provide reassurance, move forward.

I've watched many students transform their relationships with horses simply by learning this principle. The horses they thought were "difficult" or "stubborn" suddenly become willing partners. Why? Because the horses finally have a leader who is emotionally reliable, predictable, safe.

Horses don't need you to be perfect. They need you to be consistent. They need to know that you won't explode in anger when they make a mistake or collapse in fear when something goes wrong. They need to know that your emotional state won't change based on their behaviour or external circumstances.

This is what Marcus Aurelius understood. This is what Jesus demonstrated. Your external circumstances don't have to dictate your internal state.

What It Looks Like Outside the Arena

The same principles that work with a five-hundred kilogram horse work remarkably well with teams, clients, and stakeholders, in families, communities, and every human relationship.

I've consulted with executives who pride themselves on being "passionate" leaders. They wear their emotions on their sleeves. When things go well, they're ebullient. When things go poorly, everyone knows it. They believe this emotional transparency makes them authentic and relatable, but what they don't see is the impact this has on their teams.

Their employees learn to manage the leader's emotions rather than focus on the work itself. People start making decisions based on what mood the boss might be in rather than what's best for the company. They withhold bad news because they're afraid of the emotional reaction. They exaggerate good news to keep the leader happy. The entire organization becomes focused on emotional management rather than strategic execution.

Contrast this with a leader who practices Emotionless Communication. When presented with bad news, they don't explode or panic. They ask clarifying questions. They work through the problem methodically. Their team learns that it's safe to bring them the truth, even when it's uncomfortable.

When things go well, they acknowledge the success without getting carried away with euphoria that might lead to poor decisions. They maintain that steady, grounded presence that allows everyone to stay focused on what matters: the work, the mission, the next right step.

This doesn't mean they're cold or uncaring. In fact, the most effective leaders I know are deeply empathetic. They care immensely about their people and their work. But they've learned to separate their care from their reactivity. They can be deeply concerned about a problem without being emotionally dysregulated by it.

Think about the best leader you've ever worked for, or the most influential person in your life. Chances are, one of their defining characteristics was their ability to remain calm under pressure. Not calm because they didn't care, but calm because they understood that their emotional state would either help or hinder their ability to respond effectively.

This same principle applies in families. The parent who can remain calm when a child is melting down doesn't add fuel to the fire. The spouse who can listen to criticism without becoming defensive creates space for honest communication. The friend who can sit with someone's pain without trying to fix it immediately provides genuine comfort.

In communities and volunteer organizations, the person who can facilitate difficult conversations without taking sides or becoming reactive becomes invaluable. They create the conditions where honest dialogue can happen, where conflicts can be resolved, where different perspectives can be heard.

This is Emotionless Communication in practice. It's what allowed Marcus Aurelius to lead the Roman Empire through plague, war, and betrayal without losing himself to reactive chaos. It's what allowed Jesus to maintain his purpose and clarity even as everything around him collapsed into violence and injustice.

The Danger of Misunderstanding

There's a shadow side to this principle that I need to address clearly. Emotionless Communication, when misunderstood or misapplied, can become emotional suppression. And emotional suppression is not only ultimately ineffective, but it can be seriously unhealthy.

I've worked with people, mostly men if I'm honest, who heard about this principle and thought it meant they should never show any emotion at all. They confused composure with coldness, regulation with repression. They believed being a good leader meant being stoic to the point of appearing inhuman. This isn't what Marcus Aurelius or Jesus taught, and it's not what horses teach us either.

Suppressed emotions don't disappear. They go underground, where they fester and eventually erupt in ways you can't control. The leader who never shows any emotion at work might find themselves exploding at their spouse over something trivial. The person who prides themselves on never getting angry might discover they've developed anxiety, depression, or physical health problems.

Horses can smell this kind of suppression a mile away. You might think you're presenting a calm exterior, but if underneath you're a roiling mass of unexpressed emotion, the horse knows. They'll either avoid you or challenge you, because suppressed emotion creates the same kind of unpredictability as expressed emotion, just more subtle and therefore more dangerous.

In reality, Emotionless Communication requires you to feel your emotions fully. Marcus Aurelius didn't write in his journal to avoid feeling anger at his general's betrayal. He wrote to process that anger, to understand it, to ensure it didn't control his decisions. Jesus didn't maintain composure before Pilate by suppressing his fear of death. He confronted that fear directly in the Garden of Gethsemane, sweating blood as he wrestled with what he was about to endure.

The path to emotional composure runs through emotional awareness, not around it.

This means you need to develop practices that allow you to feel, process, and release emotions in healthy ways. For some people, that's journaling like Marcus did. For others, it's talking with a trusted friend, a therapist, or a coach. It might be physical exercise, meditation, prayer, or creative expression.

What matters is that you're not asking yourself to be less human. You're asking yourself to be more conscious about when, where, and how you express your humanity.

Planting This Seed

So how do we plant this seed of Emotionless Communication in fertile soil? How do we ensure it takes root and begins to grow? Like any worthwhile cultivation, it requires preparation, patience, and consistent care.

1. **Self-Awareness** -You can't regulate what you don't notice. Start paying attention to your emotional state throughout the day. Not in

a judgmental way, but with genuine curiosity. What are you feeling right now? Where do you feel it in your body? What triggered it?

Keep a simple journal. Marcus Aurelius, the most powerful man in the known world at the time, took the time each day to write down his thoughts and to describe his feelings. If an emperor leading the Roman Empire during wartime could find time for this practice, perhaps you can too. Don't write for anyone else. Don't try to sound profound or wise.

Just note what you're experiencing. "Felt frustrated during the team meeting when John interrupted me for the third time. Noticed my shoulders tightening and my voice getting sharper." That's it. Just awareness.

2. **The Breath** - This sounds almost too simple to be useful, but it's one of the most powerful tools you have for emotional regulation. When you feel a strong emotion rising, before you speak or act, take three slow, deep breaths. This isn't about suppressing the emotion. It's about creating a gap between stimulus and response. Viktor Frankl, who survived the Nazi concentration camps, wrote: "Between stimulus and response there is a space.

   In that space is our power to choose our response. In our response lies our growth and our freedom." These three breaths give you that space. They activate your parasympathetic nervous system, which helps calm your body's stress response. They give your prefrontal cortex, the thinking part of your brain, a chance to come back online so you're not just reacting from your emotional centre.

3. **Perspective** - Ask yourself Marcus Aurelius's question: "What does my emotional reaction accomplish?" Will getting angry at this team member improve their performance? Will showing anxiety to those around you increase their confidence in you? Will demonstrating frustration with this horse make them trust you more?

   Usually, the answer is no. That doesn't mean you ignore the underlying issue. If a team member's behaviour is problematic, address it. But do so from a place of clarity and decision, rather than reactivity.

4. **Practice** - You don't develop this skill by reading about it or thinking about it. You develop it by doing it. Repeat it over and over, in progressively more challenging situations.

Start small. Practice maintaining composure when someone cuts you off in traffic. When your coffee order is wrong. When a minor disappointment occurs. Build the muscle of emotional regulation in low-stakes situations so it's available when you really need it.

Working with horses accelerates this development because horses provide immediate, honest feedback. You can't fool a horse about your emotional state. If you're pretending to be calm while actually anxious, they'll show you. If you're claiming to be confident while actually nervous, they'll mirror that uncertainty back to you.

This makes the arena a perfect training ground for developing Emotionless Communication. Every interaction with a horse is an opportunity to practice awareness, breathing, perspective-taking, and regulated response.

The Power of Neutral

There's a concept in horsemanship called "neutral." It's the state you return to between every cue, every request, every interaction. You ask the horse to move forward. They respond. You immediately return to neutral. You ask them to stop. They stop. You return to neutral.

Neutral isn't about being passive or disengaged. It's about being present but not pressing. Available but not demanding. Ready but not tense.

This same concept applies to Emotionless Communication. Between every interaction, every conversation, every response, you return to neutral. You don't carry the frustration from the last meeting into the next one. You don't let yesterday's failure colour today's opportunity. You don't allow someone else's anger to determine your emotional state.

This is what both Marcus Aurelius and Jesus demonstrated so powerfully. Marcus could meet with his betraying general in the morning, make wise decisions about his trial, and then turn his attention to other matters without carrying the emotional residue of betrayal into every subsequent interaction. Jesus could be rejected by the religious leaders in one moment and still show them compassion in the next.

They had mastered the art of returning to neutral.

In practical terms, this might mean taking a moment between meetings to reset. Taking a walk around the block before you come home to your family so you're not bringing work stress into your living room. Pausing before you respond to that inflammatory email.

These moments of return to neutral are not wasted time. They're essential maintenance of your ability to communicate clearly, decide wisely, and lead effectively.

When Emotion is Appropriate

Having spent this entire chapter talking about emotional regulation and composure, I need to be clear about something: there are absolutely times when showing emotion is not only appropriate but necessary.

When someone you care about is suffering, they don't need your calm analysis. They need your compassion, which might include tears. When your team accomplishes something extraordinary, celebrating with genuine joy strengthens the bonds between you. When someone violates your values or boundaries, appropriate anger can be both healthy and clarifying.

Jesus wept at Lazarus's tomb. He overturned tables in righteous anger at the temple. He showed frustration with his disciples when they missed the point of his teachings. These weren't failures of emotional control. They were appropriate expressions of genuine feeling.

The key is consciousness and choice. Jesus wept with Mary and Martha because the moment called for grief to be shared. But when he stood before Pilate, the moment called for composed clarity, so that's what he brought.

Emotionless Communication doesn't mean never showing emotion. It means your emotions don't control your communication. It means you choose when and how to express what you're feeling based on what the situation requires, not just what you're experiencing in the moment.

With horses, there are times when a sharp correction is appropriate. Not delivered with anger, but with the clear, firm energy that communicates: this behaviour is not acceptable. There are other times when gentle, quiet reassurance is what's needed. The skilled horseman knows the difference and can move fluidly between them.

The same is true in all your relationships. Sometimes people need your strength. Sometimes they need your softness. Sometimes they need your celebration. Sometimes they need your commiseration. The leader who can only bring one emotional state to every situation is as limited as the one who brings a different emotional state every five minutes.

True mastery is being able to feel everything while choosing what to express and when.

How This Seed Grows

When you plant the seed of Emotionless Communication and tend it faithfully, something remarkable begins to happen. The seed doesn't stay a seed. It grows.

At first, you might notice small changes. You catch yourself before reacting. You take that breath. You pause before responding to that email. These are the first tender shoots breaking through the soil.

With continued practice, something deeper develops. Your words begin to match your actions more consistently. Your body language aligns with your intentions. You find yourself able to shift between states, focus and rest, assertiveness and softness, deliberately rather than being tossed about by every emotional current.

This is the growth stage, what I call Balanced Coordination. It's when Emotionless Communication matures into something more integrated, more embodied. Your mind, body, and emotions begin to move in harmony. The horse reads this as trustworthiness. People experience it as authentic presence.

And if you continue the practice, if you keep tending this growing plant with awareness and intention, it will eventually need pruning. Not everything that grows is worth keeping. Some patterns must be released. Some habits must be let go. This refinement, this careful pruning, leads to what comes next: Centred Transcendence.

But that's a lesson for another chapter. For now, focus on planting this seed well. Master the foundation of clear, emotionless communication. Learn to recognize your emotional state. Practice the three breath reset. Ask yourself what your emotional reaction accomplishes. Return to neutral between interactions.

This is the planting. This is where the journey begins. And like all good farmers know, the quality of your harvest depends on the care you take now, in these early stages, when the work is simple but the discipline is everything.

The Journey Continues

Marcus Aurelius spent his entire life practicing what he wrote about in his Meditations. Even at the end, dying from illness in a military camp along the Danube, he maintained his philosophical composure. His last words to his advisors were simply, "Go to the rising sun, for I am already setting."

Not dramatic. Not emotional. Just clear, present, accepting of what was.

Jesus's final words from the cross included, "Father, forgive them, for they know not what they do." Even in his agony, he maintained his purpose, his clarity, his compassion. His pain, His emotions didn't override his mission.

These weren't machines immune to feeling. They were deeply feeling people who had learned to master their responses. They had discovered that true freedom doesn't come from controlling external circumstances, but from choosing how we respond to them.

Every day in the arena, horses teach me lessons. And every day, I practice. Not to become emotionless, but to become more conscious. Not to stop feeling, but to stop being controlled by my feelings. Not to suppress my humanity, but to elevate it and how I communicate to the world around me.

This is the path of Emotionless Communication. It's not easy. It requires daily practice, constant awareness, and the humility to keep learning even when you fail. But the rewards are profound.

You will become the kind of person others trust in a crisis because they know you won't add to the chaos. You become the kind of leader people follow not out of fear or obligation, but because they know you can see clearly even when everyone else is panicking. You become the kind of person that horses choose to be with because they feel safe in your presence.

And perhaps most importantly, you will become free. Free from being controlled by circumstances you can't change. Free from being jerked around by every emotional current that flows through your day. Free to choose your response based on wisdom rather than reactivity.

As Marcus wrote, "You have power over your mind — not outside events. Realize this, and you will find strength." Horses can show you this truth, it's now your turn to learn it.

"The nearer a man comes to a calm mind, the closer he is to strength."

- Marcus Aurelius

CHAPTER 5

POWERFUL GENTILITY

"The greatest conqueror is he who overcomes the enemy without a blow."

- Chinese Proverb

The morning mist hung over the River Thames like a shroud as Prince Rupert of the Rhine rode slowly through the deserted streets of Windsor. It was October 1642, and England had descended into civil war. Behind him, his cavalry regiment waited in disciplined silence. Ahead, somewhere in that grey dawn, lay the army of Parliament.

At twenty-three years old, Rupert was already a veteran of the Thirty Years' War in Europe. Scarred by imprisonment and hardened by combat, his reputation preceded him. 'Prince Robber' his enemies called him, speaking of his fierce cavalry charges that shattered infantry formations like glass. Stories circulated of his dark moods, his quick temper, his willingness to hang deserters without ceremony.

But those who rode with him knew a different man. They knew the prince who spent hours training raw recruits with patience that surprised even his officers. The commander who refused to order a charge he wouldn't lead himself. The horseman who could gentle a terrified mount with nothing more than voice and presence.

As the sun began to burn through the mist, Rupert dismounted and approached a young trooper whose horse was acting up, ears pinned, muscles tense. The boy was yanking on the reins, his frustration building, his fear evident. The other cavalrymen watched, waiting to see if the prince's famous temper would flare at this breach of discipline just before battle.

Instead, Rupert spoke quietly to the trooper, took the reins, and stood beside the horse. Not pulling. Not forcing. Just standing there, his hand on the animal's neck, breathing slowly, waiting. The horse's ear swiveled toward him. The rigid muscles began to soften. Within minutes, the gelding was calm, responding to the lightest touch.

"Don't break my horse before the battle," Rupert said to the young trooper, his German accent still thick despite years in England. "You make a partner. This animal will carry you into hell today. The least you can do is treat him like he's worth something."

He remounted and, with a nod to his Sergeant-Major, turned to face his regiment. "Today we fight for King and country. But remember this. We are cavalry. Our power doesn't come from brutality. It comes from partnership. Partnership between you and your horse. The partnership between you and the man beside you. Your horse will give you everything if you give him trust. Now, to your places."

Hours later, when Rupert led the charge at Edgehill, his cavalry didn't just attack. They flowed across the battlefield like a living thing, each rider moving with their mount as one unit. The Parliamentarian cavalry broke and fled, not because they faced superior numbers or weapons, but because they faced something they couldn't match. They faced a force that had learned to harness power through partnership rather than dominance.

That was Rupert's secret, though he would never have called it that. In a world that valued brute force, he understood something more subtle. He knew that true power doesn't announce itself through violence. It reveals itself through the quiet confidence that comes from having nothing to prove.

The Paradox of Power

There's a paradox at the heart of exceptional horsemanship, and it extends far beyond the arena into every area of leadership and relationship. True influence comes not from force, but from calm, grounded presence. Not from domination, but from invitation. Not from breaking, but from building.

When you approach a nervous horse with steadiness, patience, and emotional clarity, the animal reads that energy long before it reads any physical cue. Horses in the wild are experts at sensing intention, and they retain this capacity in today's world of structure and intensity. A gentle, confident touch communicates safety, consistency, and leadership far more effectively than any amount of force ever could.

So, what is power? Power is that explosive quality that, on one hand, can send the unsuspecting handler flying when they're trying to ease a horse's pain from an injury. The horse, uncertain of your intention, only wants the pain to stop, or just to get back to its mates. It can be destructive and dangerous to anything that stands in its way, or anyone that tries to stop it.

On the other hand, power can be the roping horse that dives out of the box, in two strides is at full speed, then in perfect unison with the rider, slides to a stop as he dismounts to throw and tie the calf. Power is the thing that gets things done, whether that be using brute force to destroy, or finesse and grace to achieve a goal.

To be useful, to be productive, power needs to be tempered, controlled. Finessed with a gentleness that only comes from understanding. This is powerful gentility. It's confidence without aggression. Ability without fragility. Clarity without rigidity. It's the quality that creates the conditions for others, whether horses or humans, to achieve, collaborate, and commit.

But here's what most people miss: powerful gentility isn't just a technique or a strategy. **It's an act of service.** When you approach a frightened horse with gentleness, you're serving their need for safety before your need for accomplishment. When you wait patiently for trust to develop rather than forcing compliance, you're serving the relationship before your timeline. When you guide with invitation rather than demand, you're serving the partnership before your ego.

Prince Rupert understood this instinctively. History remembers him as a fierce cavalry commander, and he was. But those who served under him knew that his fierceness came not from rage but from absolute certainty. He could be gentle with a frightened horse and ruthless with an enemy in the same instant. He understood that different situations require different expressions of the same underlying quality: purposeful strength in service of something greater than himself.

Most people misunderstand power. They see it as something you demonstrate through dominance, through the ability to make others bend to your will. But that's not power. That's just force wearing power's clothing. Powerful gentility is something else entirely. It's the capacity to influence without coercion, to guide without dominating, to be strong without being harsh. It's power deliberately placed in service of others' growth and wellbeing.

This is the seed we're planting: the recognition that strength and gentleness aren't opposites to be balanced, but partners to be integrated in service of something greater than ourselves.

The Cavalry Commander and the Carpenter

Sixteen centuries before Prince Rupert led cavalry charges across English battlefields, another leader demonstrated the same principle in a radically different context. Jesus of Nazareth, a carpenter's son who commanded no armies and held no political office, somehow managed to transform the lives of everyone he encountered through nothing more than presence and purpose.

On the surface, Rupert and Jesus seem to have nothing in common. One was a prince and warrior, raised in royal courts and battlefield camps. The other was a tradesman who walked dusty roads with fishermen and tax collectors. One fought with sword and cavalry charge. The other taught with parables and quiet demonstrations of compassion.

But look closer, and you'll see the same quality expressed through different circumstances. Both men understood that true authority doesn't require constant demonstration. Both knew how to be simultaneously gentle and uncompromising. Both recognized that real strength reveals itself not through aggression but through the confidence that comes from knowing exactly who you are and what you stand for.

And both understood that their power existed to serve others, not themselves.

Consider Jesus's interactions with children. The Gospel accounts tell us that his disciples tried to keep children away, viewing them as distractions from important work. Jesus rebuked his own followers and invited the children to come to him. "Let the little children come to me," he said. "Don't hinder them." He took them in his arms and blessed them.

This wasn't weakness. This was a man so secure in his purpose that he could be gentle without losing any of his authority. But more than that, it was service. Jesus was serving the children's need to be seen, valued, blessed, even though it disrupted his schedule, frustrated his disciples, and offered him no strategic advantage.

The same man who tenderly blessed children also confronted religious authorities who oppressed the poor. The same voice that spoke comfort to the broken spoke judgment to the self-righteous. The same hands that touched lepers with compassion drove merchants from the temple with a whip.

Jesus demonstrated what Rupert would later show on the battlefield: that gentleness and strength aren't opposites. They're expressions of the same quality viewed from different angles. You can't have one without the other, not if you want to provide true service. Gentleness without power is just weakness pretending to be virtue. Power without gentleness is just domination.

When Jesus stood before Pontius Pilate, falsely accused and facing execution, he demonstrated powerful gentility in its purest form. He didn't defend himself aggressively. He didn't plead or beg. He didn't threaten or posture. He simply stood there, calm and centred, answering some questions and remaining silent for others.

His composure was so unnerving that Pilate, the man with all the visible power, became increasingly agitated while Jesus, the man apparently powerless, remained at peace.

"Don't you realize I have power either to free you or to crucify you?" Pilate demanded.

Jesus's response cut through Pilate's bluster: "You would have no power over me if it were not given to you from above."

This is powerful gentility in service of truth. Jesus wasn't denying Pilate's authority to execute him. He was putting that authority in its proper context. Pilate had power, yes, but it was derivative, temporary, and ultimately subject to a higher purpose. Jesus could afford to be gentle because he knew that Pilate's threats, while real, were not ultimate. His gentleness served the moment's need for clarity and dignity, even in the face of injustice.

Prince Rupert demonstrated the same quality in a different arena. Stories from the English Civil War describe how he could be merciless in battle but surprisingly compassionate toward prisoners and civilians. He hanged deserters without hesitation because he understood that discipline maintained his soldiers' effectiveness and ultimately saved more lives than it cost.

But he also paid for the funerals of enemy soldiers out of his own pocket and ensured that civilians in occupied territories were protected from his troops. His gentleness served the dignity of the dead and the safety of the innocent.

This wasn't inconsistency. It was the same principle expressed in different contexts. Be hard when hardness serves the greater purpose. Be gentle when gentleness serves it. Never confuse the two. Never use force when influence will suffice. Never hold back force when the situation genuinely requires it. And always, always, let service be your guide.

Why This Seed Must Be Planted

Before we go further, we need to understand what happens when this seed is never planted, when service operates without the integration of strength and gentleness.

When you have strength without gentleness, service becomes domination.

You "serve" by controlling. The horse complies from fear, not trust. Your leadership creates short-term results but long-term resentment. You tell yourself you're helping, but really you're just imposing your will. Your service is about your agenda, not their growth.

In the arena, this looks like the trainer who breaks horses through intimidation. The horse learns to obey, but never learns to trust. They perform out of fear of consequence, not from willing partnership. The moment the pressure is removed, so is the compliance.

In leadership, this looks like the manager who micromanages every detail, who uses their position to force compliance, who confuses obedience with engagement. People do what they're told, but they don't bring their best ideas, their creativity, their commitment. They serve your demands, but you never truly serve their development.

When you have gentleness without power, service becomes enabling.

You "serve" by removing all difficulty. The horse never develops capability because you never ask them to stretch. Your leadership creates dependent people who can't function without you. You rescue rather than strengthen. Your service is about your need to be needed, not their need to grow.

In the arena, this looks like the rider who never asks for anything challenging, who makes excuses for the horse's resistance, who interprets every difficulty as trauma. The horse never learns they're capable of more because you never show them. Your gentleness isn't serving their growth, it's protecting them from it.

In leadership, this looks like the manager who won't have difficult conversations, who lowers standards to avoid conflict, who protects team members from the challenges that would develop them. You think you're being kind, but you're actually being cruel, denying people the growth that comes from appropriately challenging work.

When you have neither strength nor gentleness, service becomes abandonment.

You don't actually serve at all. The horse is confused and unsafe. People feel unsupported and directionless. There's no leadership, no growth, no partnership.

Powerful Gentility is the seed that prevents all three failures. It's the recognition that true service requires both strength and softness, simultaneously. That your power exists to support others' growth, and your gentleness makes that power safe to receive. This is why planting this seed matters. Without it, every attempt at service will either dominate, enable, or abandon those you're trying to serve.

Recognizing the Need to Plant This Seed

Before you can plant this seed, you need to recognize whether it's already growing in you, or whether its absence is causing the problems you're experiencing.

Ask yourself these questions:

With horses:

- Do they comply from fear or from trust?
- Can you be firm without being harsh?
- Can you be gentle without being weak?
- Do they relax in your presence or tense up?
- When they resist, is your first impulse to increase force or to understand why?

In leadership:

- Do people bring you problems or hide them?
- Can you give difficult feedback without damaging relationships?
- Can you show compassion without lowering standards?

- Do your team members become more capable over time, or more dependent?
- When someone disagrees with you, can you be curious without being defensive?

In relationships:

- Do you dominate or do you invite?
- Do you rescue or do you support?
- Can you hold boundaries while remaining kind?
- Can you be vulnerable while remaining strong?
- Do people feel safe with you, or do they feel controlled by you?

If you find yourself consistently choosing either force or passivity, if you can't access both strength and gentleness simultaneously, then this seed needs to be planted in you.

Learning From the Dusty Road

Sometimes the seed gets planted not through success, but through spectacular failure. Not through doing it right, but through doing it so wrong that you're forced to recognize there must be a better way.

FLUBBA, FLUbba, Flubba…BANG! The sound of a horse float tyre disintegrating. Then slamming into the side of the float, and finally disappearing into the distance on the roadside, is as unique as it is disappointing. I just wanted to scream. I had been driving for the last 5 hours, along the dusty road between Diamontina Lakes Station and Winton, in western Queensland.

I had been working down on Diamontina Lakes, breaking in a bunch of horses there. Horses that ranged from a 14 hand high, two-year-old brumby, that obviously knew kung fu, and could cow kick my foot out of the stirrup without an ounce of effort; to a seven-year-old recently gelded thoroughbred, who I guessed was between 16 and 17 hands, with the remaining 6 horses ranging somewhere between these two extremes.

With one white eye, the big gelding would stare down at me, as if he was measuring how many pieces he could break me into in 5 long, slow minutes. This was a challenging time, during which I learnt a lot about starting horses of different types and temperaments. It was great experience, and each of the horses ended up working well for me. On the risk to reward spectrum however, I wasn't sure if it was where I saw my future going, and I was taking a break to think about my life choices.

Ironman, being reasonably mature, reliable and capable, had come with me to help with the breaking process. And he was as keen to get home as I was. We still had at least another 2 hours or so to go before I got back home to Longreach. But at least we would soon be back on the bitumen I thought, and the day's heat was quickly dissipating from the road as evening drew nearer. Hopefully that would mean no more blowouts.

But it looked like I wouldn't be home before dark now. That meant I'd have to travel over the jump-up, the home of about a billion kangaroos, the last 25 kilometres before Longreach, in the dark. With crappy lights. And the float pushing me if I did see them and try to stop. Damn it.

I pulled off the road, and quickly tried to wind the window of the old Toyota tray-back up, as a triple road train went roaring past in a cloud of bulldust. I got it about halfway up before the choking cloud turned everything dark brown. It didn't really matter, the passenger side window was down anyway.

It had been a hot day, with the heat of the engine blasting its way through the firewall into the cabin, so I had set the air conditioner on full… Both windows down. There was no way I could stop the car, and reach over, wind the passenger window up, at the same time as I wound the driver's side up, before the truck went past. The cabin filled with dust. Damn it.

I walked back to the float, reaching through the side opening to give Ironman a rub on his neck as I went around to inspect the damage. He was not happy. On the float for five hours already, on that rough, dusty track we called a road. The noise of the tyre exploding and coming apart, ringing in his ears. And that road train blowing past, spewing dust everywhere. He was not happy, at all! Damn it.

I knew if I took him off the float, it was highly unlikely that he would choose to go back on without a fight. But if I didn't take him off the float and another road train came past, he would probably jump around enough to cause the float to fall off the jack. If this happened when I had the wheel off, I would never be able to get the spare on with the tools I had. Well, not before dark anyway.

I wanted to get him off, to give him a break from being confined inside the float in any case. I untied him, opened the back door. Ironman was always a horse that liked to do everything full-bore, and when I unhooked the rump chain, he came out a hundred-miles an hour. He wasn't overly upset, but glad to get off, for sure. I gave him a drink from the drum I carried, tied him to the fence and set about changing the wheel.

In the remains of the long hot day, with a covering of dust, I undid the wheel nuts, feeling the long dry stems of the Mitchell Grass poking me in the ears and eyes as I worked. Flies magically appeared to "help" get the job done, adding to my frustration. As I was putting the remains of the wheel into the back of the Landcruiser, another road train went thundering past loaded, headed to a sale somewhere I guessed.

As the dust cleared again, I looked toward the western horizon, guessing I had about an hour of daylight left. Ironman was raised as a poddy, fed on a bottle after his mother died, so he was quieter than most horses, and more used to the bizarre ways of humans, so he wasn't unduly fazed by the events of the day, and I knew that he might argue a little, but he would soon get back on the float. We would be in Winton before dark.

The thing about poddies is that, because they have to get old soon to survive, they learn to make decisions quickly and are often unwilling to let go of those decisions easily, regardless of the consequences. As I led him back to the float, I began to sense an unwillingness on his part to get back on the float. It soon became obvious that he had decided this was not a thing that he would be doing today.

For the next hour, I pulled him, I pushed him, I tempted him with food, I threatened him with violence. At one point he was nearly on, he had nearly given in and another road train came past. I used a breaching rope behind him to force him forward, which did little but burn the hair off his rump.

This was strength without gentleness. Pure force. And it wasn't working.

Back then I didn't know what else to do. Gentleness wasn't a major part of my toolkit yet. I only had more force, or giving up entirely. Strength or weakness. Domination or surrender. I didn't know there was a third option.

Finally he relented, and I closed the door on the float just as the last hint of sunlight disappeared from the sky. I had kind of won, I told myself. But neither of us felt like winners.

I still had a three hour drive in front of me, and I was exhausted. On the long slow drive home, the thought that I could have done that better; that I should have been better prepared, and that I had to know why I had so much difficulty getting him back on the float, kept me awake.

And just like that the seed was planted.

Not planted because I succeeded, planted because I failed. Planted in the recognition that there had to be a better way. That strength alone wasn't enough. That force, even when it eventually produces compliance, destroys something essential in the process.

I had no concept of Powerful Gentility that day on the dusty road. I didn't have access to both strength and softness simultaneously. I only had force, and when that didn't work, I only had more force.

But that failure planted a seed. The seed of a question: What if there's a way to be strong without being harsh? What if gentleness isn't the opposite of strength, but its necessary partner?

This journey started in the early 1990's, when I was nearly thirty, and it took me many years to understand where I went wrong, what I could have done better. It was a difficult situation, there is no doubt. But eventually I saw how I could have served both Ironman, and myself better.

That seed would grow over the coming years into Determined Understanding, the patient, persistent pursuit of truth that would eventually teach me how to load any horse in any situation. We'll explore that growth in Chapter 8. And years later still, some of what I learned would need to be carefully dismantled and rebuilt through Creative Destruction, which we'll examine in Chapter 11.

But it all began here, on a dusty road in western Queensland, with a tired horse, an exhausted handler, and the recognition that force alone would never be enough. That true service requires something more, the integration of strength with gentleness.

That's the seed. Once planted, it changes everything about how you approach horses, people, and leadership. Not immediately. Not dramatically. But steadily, surely, growing into something you couldn't have imagined when you first planted it.

The Nature of Service

Before we discuss how this seed begins to take root, we need to understand what service actually means in the context of powerful gentility. Because service has been so misunderstood, so corrupted by false humility and performative self-sacrifice, that many people recoil from the word entirely.

True service isn't about diminishing yourself. It's not about becoming a doormat or suppressing your needs or pretending you don't matter.

That's not service, that's self-abandonment dressed up in virtuous language.

Service, properly understood, is the deliberate use of your strength on behalf of another's growth. It's choosing to place your power, your knowledge, your presence in support of someone else's development. Not because they deserve it. Not because you'll get something in return. But because you've decided that your capabilities exist, at least in part, to create conditions where others can flourish.

In the arena, this looks like patience. When a horse is confused or frightened, service means staying calm while they work through it, even when you're frustrated. It means breaking down a complex request into manageable pieces, even when they 'should' already understand. It means celebrating small victories, even when progress feels painfully slow. Your expertise serves their learning. Your strength serves their confidence.

But service isn't always soft. Sometimes service requires you to do difficult things, to insist on a boundary, to maintain a standard, to say no when yes would be easier. The difference between service and dominance is always the same: who benefits? Service asks, 'What does this being need?' Domination asks, 'What do I want?'

In leadership, service means creating environments where your team can succeed, even when that requires you to set aside your preferences. It means having difficult conversations because growth demands honesty, not because you enjoy confrontation. It means sometimes taking the blame publicly while giving credit privately. It means using your position not to accumulate power but to distribute it.

This is why powerful gentility matters so profoundly. Without gentleness, your service becomes harsh and controlling. Without power, your service becomes ineffective and empty. But when you can be both strong and gentle, when you can guide without dominating and support without coddling, you create something remarkable: you create conditions where transformation becomes possible.

Service is the soil in which all other virtues grow. Courage serves a purpose beyond self-interest. Communication serves understanding rather than manipulation. Ambition serves collective benefit rather than personal glory. And when powerful gentility serves something greater than itself, it plants seeds that will grow into the wisdom we'll explore in the chapters ahead.

As This Seed Takes Root in the Arena

When you plant the seed of Powerful Gentility and begin to tend it faithfully, you'll start to notice changes in your work with horses. These aren't dramatic transformations, seeds don't become trees overnight. But they're real, and they mark the beginning of genuine growth.

1. **You begin to notice the difference between dominance and direction.** You start to see that firmness isn't the same as harshness. You can insist on respect without intimidating. You can maintain boundaries without creating fear. The horse feels the difference immediately, they respond to your clarity, but they don't shut down emotionally. This is the seed beginning to sprout.

2. **You become aware of when you're acting from ego versus acting from purpose.** You catch yourself pushing because you're frustrated, not because the horse needs more pressure. You notice when you're trying to prove something rather than teach something. This awareness is the seed sending down roots, creating the foundation for real growth.

3. **You develop comfort with stillness.** You begin to understand that horses learn in the quiet moments, the pauses between actions. You can stand with a horse without demanding anything, just being present. This stillness serves their need to process, to think, to integrate. The constant noise that used to characterize your training starts to give way to purposeful silence.

4. **You start to feel the horse's response differently.** You become more attuned to whether they're complying from fear or from trust. You notice the difference between submission and partnership. When the horse tries, even if they don't succeed, you recognize that effort deserves acknowledgment. This sensitivity is the seed reaching toward light.

5. **You learn to modulate your energy.** With a hot, reactive horse, you instinctively bring calm, grounded energy. With a shut-down horse, you naturally offer patient invitation. You're not thinking about it consciously yet, it's just starting to happen. The seed is growing.

These early signs don't mean you've mastered Powerful Gentility. They mean the seed has taken root and begun to grow. There will still be days when you revert to force or collapse into passivity. That's normal. Seeds don't grow in straight lines. But each time you notice yourself choosing, strength-with-gentleness over strength-without-gentleness, you're watering the seed.

As This Seed Takes Root Outside the Arena

The same principles that begin to transform your horsemanship also start to reshape how you lead people, though the changes are often subtle at first.

In professional settings, you begin to notice:

You catch yourself before responding defensively to criticism. Just catching it, not necessarily changing your response yet, but noticing the impulse. This awareness is the seed germinating.

You start to recognize when you're about to micromanage, and sometimes, you step back instead. You create space for others to solve problems, even when you could solve them faster. This restraint is the seed developing roots.

You find yourself more curious about resistance instead of immediately frustrated by it. When someone pushes back, you wonder why before assuming they're being difficult. This curiosity is the seed reaching upward.

In difficult conversations, you begin to feel:

The difference between clarity and cruelty. You can deliver hard truths without weaponizing them. Your body language starts to support your message rather than contradict it. You're learning to be firm and kind simultaneously.

In relationships, you begin to experience:

Moments when you hold a boundary without anger. Times when you offer support without rescuing. Instances where you're vulnerable without being weak. These moments are still inconsistent, the seed is young, but they're real.

This is what early growth looks like. Not mastery. Not consistency. Just the first tender shoots of something that could become strong if you continue to tend it.

Tending the Newly Planted Seed

Now that you've recognized the need for this seed and perhaps experienced the failure that created space for planting it, how do you tend it so it can grow?

- **Start with your body.** You can't embody **powerful gentility** if your body is chronically tense or collapsed. Your body tells the truth about your internal state, and horses read that truth instantly. Practice releasing unnecessary tension while maintaining purposeful strength.

Stand with your spine aligned but your shoulders relaxed. Breathe deeply but don't force it. Feel grounded but not rigid. This physical practice prepares the soil for the seed to grow.

- **Practice stillness.** In a culture that values constant action, the ability to simply be present without doing anything is revolutionary. Stand with a horse and do nothing. Sit in a meeting and listen without needing to respond immediately. Be in a difficult moment without rushing to fix it.

  Learn to be comfortable with space, with pause, with the silence where real understanding develops. This stillness serves others by giving them room to think, to feel, to find their own answers. It's watering the seed.

- **Examine your first impulses.** When someone, human or horse, doesn't do what you want, what's your immediate reaction? If it's to increase pressure, to force compliance, to prove you're in charge, that's important information.

  You're seeing where force has replaced gentleness. If it's to back down completely, to make excuses, to avoid any conflict, that's equally important. You're seeing where weakness has replaced strength.

  The seed of Powerful Gentility grows when you catch these impulses and choose differently. Not perfectly. Not every time. But more often. You take a breath. You get curious about the resistance. You consider whether your request was clear, your timing appropriate, your approach serving the relationship.

- **Get comfortable with not knowing.** Powerful gentility doesn't require you to have all the answers immediately. It requires you to be present with the questions. When you're working with a horse and something isn't working, you don't always need to know what to do differently right away.

  Sometimes you just need to acknowledge that your current approach isn't serving the partnership and be willing to try something else. This humility, this willingness to not know, is itself a form of service. It serves truth over the illusion of expertise. It's giving the seed room to grow.

- **Ask the essential question repeatedly:**

> "What does this moment need from me?"
> And **See** the answer.
> Not: What do I need from this moment?
> Not: What would make me look good?
> Not: What's the fastest way to get compliance?
>
> But what does service require of me right now?
> And **See** the answer.
>
> Sometimes the answer is strength. Sometimes it's gentleness.
> But **See** the answer.
>
> Often, as the seed grows, the answer is both.
> But **See** the answer.

When I say, "**See** the answer", I don't mean that if you look it will magically appear. Rather I mean if you look, you will see where to find the answer. Many people have said, "Seeing is believing", meaning they will believe it when they see it, but in this instance that will get you nowhere.

Instead "Believing is Seeing", is the most important aspect. The most important way to look at it. The farmer plants the seed believing it will grow. If you look for the answer, you will see where to find it. It might take days, months or years to find the solution, but if you believe you will find it, you are seeing the answer. This is the seed that is planted.

The Weight of Gentleness

Here's what most people miss about powerful gentility, and what you'll discover as this seed begins to grow: true gentleness is harder than force.

Force is easy. Anyone can dominate someone weaker than themselves. Anyone can impose their will through threat or coercion. That doesn't require strength. It just requires willingness to use power without conscience.

But to be gentle? To be patient when you're frustrated? To stay calm when someone is testing every boundary? To give others space to find their own way when you could just tell them what to do? That requires immense strength. The kind of strength that most people never develop because they mistake aggression for power.

And here's the deeper truth: gentleness is harder because it's service. When you're forceful, you're serving your own needs, your need for control, for compliance, for immediate results. But when you're gentle, you're serving the other's needs, their need for dignity, for agency, for growth at their own pace. Service is always harder than selfishness.

Prince Rupert understood this. Leading a cavalry charge is terrifying, yes, but it's also straightforward. Point your horse at the enemy. Hang on. Hope you survive. But standing beside a frightened horse, waiting as long as it takes for trust to develop? That's a different kind of courage. The kind that doesn't get celebrated in ballads or remembered in history books. The kind that shapes character rather than reputation. The kind that serves the relationship more than the resume.

Jesus understood this too. He had the power, according to his followers' beliefs, to call down angels and escape his execution. To prove his divinity through overwhelming force. To make his enemies pay for what they were doing to him. Instead, he chose gentleness. "Father, forgive them, for they don't know what they're doing." That's not weakness. That's strength of a kind that most people can't even comprehend. Strength deliberately placed in service of reconciliation, even at the cost of his own life.

As the seed of Powerful Gentility grows in you, you'll feel this weight. The weight of choosing patience over expedience. The weight of serving others' growth over your own convenience. The weight of being strong enough to be gentle.

This weight is the sign the seed is growing. Don't resist it. Tend it.

The Seed and Its Future Growth

This chapter has focused on planting the seed of Powerful Gentility, recognizing the need for it, understanding what it is, beginning to cultivate it. But a planted seed is just the beginning of a much longer journey.

As you continue to practice this integration of strength and gentleness in service of others, the seed will grow. That growth is the subject of Chapter 8: Determined Understanding. There, you'll learn how the gentle touch must deepen into persistent pursuit of truth. How you can't serve what you don't understand. How understanding requires patience, attention, and the willingness to be wrong about your initial assessments.

That's where my journey with Ironman led. The seed planted on that dusty road grew over many years into the ability to load any horse in almost any situation. Not through force. Not through passivity. But through the integration of strength and gentleness in service of the horse's actual needs, which I had to learn to understand truly.

And eventually, that understanding itself will need refinement. Chapter 11 explores Creative Destruction, the wisdom to recognize when patterns must be released to make room for new growth. Sometimes what you've built must be carefully dismantled and rebuilt. Sometimes the gentlest thing you can do is help someone let go of what's no longer serving them.

But none of that future growth is possible without first planting this seed. Without recognizing that strength and gentleness aren't opposites to be balanced, but partners to be integrated. Without choosing to place your power in service of others' growth.

Prince Rupert's cavalry was devastating not because of superior numbers or equipment, but because of something more fundamental. His troopers had learned to be powerful and gentle simultaneously. Gentle with their mounts. Powerful in battle. This integration made them more effective than forces that relied on brutality alone. And it all began with a young prince who understood that his strength existed to serve his men, his king, and his cause.

Jesus's influence lasted not because he dominated people, but because he invited them. Gentle in his treatment of the broken. Powerful in his confrontation of injustice. This integration made him more transformative than any king or emperor of his era. And it all flowed from his understanding that his power existed to serve humanity's redemption.

My own journey began not with success, but with failure. With a tired horse on a dusty road and the recognition that force alone would never be enough. That seed, planted in frustration and exhaustion, has grown over decades into something I couldn't have imagined then.

Your journey will be different. Your seed-planting moment might look nothing like mine. But the principle is the same: at some point, you have to recognize that true service requires the integration of strength and gentleness. You have to plant that seed deliberately, understanding that what seems impossibly paradoxical today will become natural tomorrow.

Not because it's easy. Because you've tended it faithfully.

The Invitation

The seed of Powerful Gentility is available to anyone willing to plant it. Anyone willing to recognize that strength without gentleness is domination, that gentleness without strength is enabling, and that true service requires both.

The question isn't whether you'll plant this seed perfectly. You won't. I didn't. The question is whether you'll plant it at all. Whether you'll recognize when force has replaced partnership, when harshness has replaced clarity, when your need to control has replaced your commitment to serve.

And then whether you'll choose differently. Not every time. Not immediately. But more often. Whether you'll water this seed with practice, protect it with awareness, and give it room to grow.

The horse doesn't follow your strength. They follow the integration of your strength and gentleness in service of the partnership. The team doesn't follow your power. They follow your use of that power to create conditions where they can flourish. The child doesn't follow your control. They follow your demonstration that strength and kindness can coexist.

This is what powerful gentility offers: a way of being in the world that doesn't require you to choose between strength and kindness, between decisiveness and compassion, between power and love. It suggests that maybe those apparent opposites aren't opposites at all. Maybe they're different aspects of the same quality, the quality of showing up fully present, fully human, fully alive, and fully in service.

The seed has been planted, in Rupert's gentle hand on a frightened horse's neck, in Jesus's quiet composure before Pilate, in my frustration on a dusty road when I realized force alone would never be enough.

Now it's your turn to plant it. To recognize where you've relied on strength without gentleness or gentleness without strength. To see where service has become domination or enabling or abandonment. To choose the integration instead.

The seed is small. The growth will be gradual. But tend it well, and it will transform everything about how you serve.

"In true partnership, power is shared, not hoarded. Gentleness is offered, not withheld. And strength reveals itself not through dominance, but through the confidence to invite rather than demand."

— The Horseman's Way

PART III

GROWING THE PLANT

CHAPTER 6

COMPASSIONATE AMBITION

"You intended to harm me, but God intended it for good to accomplish what is now being done, the saving of many lives."

- Joseph, Genesis 50:20

The cramped riding hall at West Point was thick with dust and tension. It was June 1843, graduation day for the senior class, and the air inside felt heavy despite the cool morning outside. The academy horses were notoriously difficult, half-broken cavalry mounts that made every riding session a test of will. Most cadets dreaded their time in this hall.

But twenty-one-year-old Ulysses Grant was different.

He stood at the far end of the hall, one hand resting on the neck of a large chestnut stallion named York. The horse had a reputation. Not a single cadet could ride him, most couldn't even get close without York exploding into violence. The riding master, Sergeant Henry Hershberger, had all but given up on the animal. One more incident and York would be condemned, removed from the academy string, his fate uncertain.

Grant had asked to work with York three months earlier. Not because he wanted to prove something to his classmates, though they certainly noticed. Not because he enjoyed the challenge, though he did. But because he saw something in the big chestnut that others missed. Beneath the explosion and panic, beneath the reputation for violence, Grant recognized fear. And fear, he understood, could be transformed through patient, persistent care.

The assembled crowd, cadets, officers, dignitaries, families, watched as Hershberger prepared the final demonstration of the day. He had saved the best for last. Or perhaps the most dramatic. He strode to the jumping bar and raised it. Higher. Then higher still. Until it stood above the height of an average man's head. Six feet, perhaps more.

A murmur rippled through the crowd. That wasn't just high. That was dangerous. A horse clearing that height with a rider would need perfect timing, absolute courage, and complete trust in the person on his back.

Hershberger turned to face the mounted cadets. "Cadet Grant."

Grant touched York's neck once more, then gathered the reins. The big chestnut's ear swivelled toward him. They'd done this jump a hundred times in practice. Not this high, never this high. But Grant had methodically, patiently, built York's confidence over three months. Each session ending on a good note. Each success celebrated. Each failure met with patience rather than punishment.

He moved York to the far end of the hall. Silence fell over the assembly. Grant could feel York's tension, the slight tremble in the powerful muscles beneath him. The horse was afraid. Of course he was afraid. But he trusted Grant more than he feared the jump.

Grant took a breath. Let it out slowly. He felt York's breathing synchronize with his own. Then, with the subtlest shift of weight, he asked.

York exploded forward. Not in panic this time, but in purpose. His hooves thundered across the packed dirt. Grant gauged the pace, felt the rhythm, knew the exact moment when York would need to gather himself, compress that power into the coiled spring that would launch them skyward.

York's muscles bunched. The take-off was perfect. For a moment that seemed to stretch impossibly long, horse and rider hung suspended in dusty air, clearing the bar with room to spare. They landed smoothly, cantered a few more strides, then came to a calm halt.

Sergeant Hershberger's voice rang out: "Very well done, sir."

The assembly erupted in applause. Grant had just set a high-jump record that would stand at West Point for twenty-five years. But as he dismounted and stroked York's neck, accepting the horse's soft nicker of pride, he wasn't thinking about records. He was thinking about what had made this possible.

Not force. Not dominance. Not breaking York's spirit to impose his will. But something else entirely. Something he'd understood instinctively since he was five years old, standing on the back of a trotting horse while other children still struggled with simple riding.

Power was meaningless without care. Ambition achieved nothing if it trampled those who helped you reach it. The height of that jump mattered less than the partnership that made it possible.

Twenty-two years later, in a modest house in rural Virginia, Grant would demonstrate the same principle on a scale that would shape a nation's healing.

The Growing Season

Compassionate Ambition is the second stage in the Courage and Vision pillar of the Faithful Enthusiasm framework. It's the growing season that follows the planting of Fearless Guidance.

Remember the progression: Fearless Guidance plants the seed, the willingness to step into uncertainty first, demonstrating that courage is possible. That planted seed was Alexander throwing his spear into Persian soil. Joshua commanding priests to step into flooded waters. You approaching the frightened horse with calm certainty.

But a seed that's planted doesn't immediately produce fruit. It requires a growing season. Time when the fragile shoot pushes through soil toward sunlight. Months when roots dig deep and stems stretch skyward. A period when the vision that inspired the initial leap of courage must mature into sustained drive.

This is where many leaders fail. They have the courage to begin. They can inspire people to take that first step. But they lack the capacity to maintain momentum without becoming harsh. They don't understand how to push forward while still honouring the wellbeing of those who follow them.

Fearless Guidance says, "Follow me into the unknown, I'll go first." Compassionate Ambition says, "We're going to keep moving forward, and I won't sacrifice you to get there."

When Grant worked with York, he wasn't content with one successful ride. He had the ambition to transform the horse completely, to prepare him for that record-breaking jump. But that ambition was tempered by compassion, by understanding what York could handle in each session, by celebrating progress, by never pushing so hard that fear replaced trust.

This is Compassionate Ambition in its essence: healthy drive rooted in empathy. Ambition aligned with values, not ego. Drive that acknowledges its impact on others. The ability to foster growth without activating shame or pressure. Energy that expands rather than contracts.

The Weight of Victory

April 9, 1865. Appomattox Court House, Virginia.

General Robert E. Lee rode toward Wilmer McLean's house wearing a spotless dress uniform, his ceremonial sword at his side. He'd spent the morning preparing for this moment, not for battle, but for surrender. After four years of war, after Petersburg had fallen and Richmond burned, after his army had been reduced to 25,000 starving men surrounded by 125,000 Union troops, there was nothing left but this.

The dignity of an honourable end.

Grant arrived thirty minutes after Lee, riding in from where his troops were positioned to prevent any Confederate escape. He dismounted wearing what he called a "soldier's blouse", a private's shirt with lieutenant general's stars hastily sewn on the shoulders. His boots and pants were spattered with mud. He'd been riding hard, suffering from a blinding headache until he received Lee's note that morning agreeing to meet. The headache had vanished instantly, replaced by the weight of what this moment represented.

They met in McLean's parlour. Lee in his tall, caned armchair, impeccable in grey. Grant in his swivel chair with its padded leather back, looking more like a working soldier than the architect of Union victory. Grant's staff crowded into the room, watching history unfold.

The two men had fought together in the Mexican-American War, nearly twenty years earlier. Before the nation tore itself apart. They spoke of those days, of shared battles and shared friends, giving Lee a few more minutes before the inevitable. Softening what could have been a humiliating experience. Making space for dignity.

Finally, Lee brought the conversation to its purpose. "I suppose, General Grant, that the object of our present meeting is fully understood. I asked to see you to ascertain upon what terms you would receive the surrender of my army."

Grant could have crushed Lee in that moment. The Confederacy had waged war against the United States. Lee's own army had threatened Washington, had won battles at Manassas and Fredericksburg, had killed Union soldiers by the tens of thousands. Many in the North wanted Lee and his officers prosecuted for treason. Wanted Confederate soldiers imprisoned or executed. Wanted the South punished for every drop of blood spilled.

Grant's ambition had driven him through four years of war. He'd fought at Fort Donelson and Shiloh, through the Vicksburg Campaign and Chattanooga, across the Wilderness and Cold Harbor and Petersburg. He'd earned his reputation through relentless pursuit, refusing to let Confederate armies rest or regroup. "Unconditional Surrender" Grant, they called him, for his response at Fort Donelson: "No terms except unconditional and immediate surrender can be accepted."

But at Appomattox, facing the defeated commander of the Army of Northern Virginia, Grant demonstrated something more complex than simple ambition. He outlined terms that shocked everyone present with their generosity.

Officers could keep their sidearms, horses, and personal baggage. All soldiers would be paroled, allowed to return home without being prosecuted or imprisoned. They wouldn't even have to turn in their horses and mules. "Let every man of the Confederate army who claims to own a horse or mule take the animal home with him to work his little farm," Grant said simply.

Lee read the terms carefully. When he reached the part about officers keeping their horses, Grant later recalled, Lee "remarked, with some feeling, I thought, that this would have a happy effect upon his army."

Grant went further. Lee mentioned that his men were starving, they'd had no rations for days. Grant immediately ordered 25,000 rations sent to Confederate soldiers. Most came from Confederate supply trains that Union cavalry had captured the day before, but Grant made sure they reached the hungry men.

As Lee prepared to leave the McLean house, Union troops began cheering in celebration of victory. Grant immediately ordered them to stop. "The war is over," he told his men. "The Rebels are our countrymen again."

This was Compassionate Ambition fully realized. Grant had pursued victory with relentless drive. His strategic brilliance and tactical persistence had won the war. But at the moment of triumph, he tempered that ambition with profound compassion. That crushing the Confederate soldiers would make reunification harder, not easier. That the nation needed healing more than it needed vengeance.

His ambition was to end the war. His compassion determined how that ending would unfold.

Two Men Separated by Millennia, United by Principle

Nearly four thousand years before Grant and Lee met in that modest Virginia parlor, another man faced a moment that tested whether power would be used for revenge or redemption.

Joseph stood in his audience chamber in Egypt, second only to Pharaoh in authority. Before him knelt a group of men from Canaan, desperate and frightened, begging to purchase grain during a famine that had devastated the entire region.

He recognized them immediately. His brothers. The men who had sold him into slavery when he was seventeen years old. Who had stripped him of the multi-colored coat his father gave him. Who had thrown him in a pit and debated killing him before deciding slavery was more profitable. Who had gone home and told their father that Joseph had been killed by wild animals, letting Jacob grieve for a son who was still alive.

Twenty years had passed. Joseph had been a slave in Potiphar's house. Had been falsely accused and thrown in prison. Had spent years forgotten in an Egyptian dungeon until his ability to interpret dreams brought him before Pharaoh. Had risen from prisoner to prime minister in a single day when he correctly interpreted Pharaoh's dreams and proposed a plan to prepare for the coming famine.

Now he was Lord of all Egypt. Governor of the storehouses. The man every nation sent representatives to when their own crops failed. And his brothers stood before him, not recognizing the well-dressed Egyptian official as the boy they'd betrayed.

Joseph could have destroyed them. One word from him and they'd be imprisoned, executed, or enslaved themselves. No one would question it. They were foreigners in a time of famine, desperate men with no power, no protection, no recourse.

Instead, Joseph tested them. He wanted to know if they'd changed in the years since they'd sold him. Accused them of being spies. Kept Simeon imprisoned while the others returned home. Demanded they bring Benjamin, his youngest brother, back with them. Planted his silver cup in Benjamin's sack and threatened to enslave the boy.

He watched as Judah, the brother who had proposed selling Joseph in the first place, stepped forward and offered to take Benjamin's place. Watched as men who had once been willing to destroy one brother now risked everything to protect another.

Joseph broke. He couldn't maintain the pretence any longer. He sent all the Egyptian attendants out of the room, what he had to say was for his brothers alone. Then he wept so loudly that people outside the chamber heard him.

"I am Joseph," he said in Hebrew, the language of their childhood. "Is my father still alive?"

His brothers were terrified. They stood frozen, unable to speak. They knew what they'd done. They knew what they deserved.

Joseph moved closer to them. "I am your brother Joseph, whom you sold into Egypt. And now, do not be distressed and do not be angry with yourselves for selling me here, because it was to save lives that God sent me ahead of you."

Think about what he was saying. He had every right to be angry. Every justification for revenge. But instead, he reframed their betrayal within a larger purpose. God had sent him to Egypt ahead of them. His suffering had positioned him to save not just his family but entire nations during this famine.

"God sent me ahead of you to preserve for you a remnant on earth and to save your lives by a great deliverance. So then, it was not you who sent me here, but God. He made me father to Pharaoh, lord of his entire household and ruler of all Egypt."

This is what Compassionate Ambition looks like when fully mature. Joseph had risen through slavery, false accusation, and imprisonment to become one of the most powerful men in the world. His ambition had driven him to interpret dreams, propose solutions, administer Egypt's grain storage, and ultimately manage the economic survival of multiple nations.

But that ambition was inseparable from his compassion. When he had the power to punish those who had wronged him, he chose instead to save them.

When he could have used his position for revenge, he used it for reconciliation. When his brothers expected judgment, he gave them grace.

He sent them back to Canaan with Egyptian carts loaded with provisions. He gave them new clothes and silver. He sent twenty donkeys carrying Egyptian goods for their father. He told them to bring Jacob and the entire extended family to Egypt, where he would provide for them during the remaining five years of famine.

When Jacob died seventeen years later, Joseph's brothers became afraid again. They thought Joseph had only shown them kindness while their father lived. Now that Jacob was gone, surely Joseph would take his revenge.

They came to Joseph and begged for forgiveness, saying Jacob had requested before his death that Joseph forgive them.

Joseph wept when he heard this. That they still didn't understand. That they still expected punishment.

"Don't be afraid," he told them. "Am I in the place of God? You intended to harm me, but God intended it for good to accomplish what is now being done, the saving of many lives. So then, don't be afraid. I will provide for you and your children."

The Pattern That Connects

Look at the pattern that emerges when we place Grant and Joseph side by side:

Both men possessed extraordinary ability. Grant was perhaps the finest horseman of his generation at West Point. James Longstreet, his classmate who would become a Confederate general, said Grant was "noted as the most proficient in the Academy" in horsemanship, that rider and horse held together "like the fabled centaur." Joseph had the God-given ability to interpret dreams and the administrative genius to prepare an entire nation for famine.

They demonstrated relentless ambition in pursuing their goals. Grant campaigned through the Western Theatre and then Virginia with single-minded determination. He didn't stop after victories, he pressed forward, giving Confederate armies no time to recover. Joseph rose from slavery to second-in-command of Egypt. He didn't just survive his circumstances, he excelled in every position he held, from Potiphar's house to Pharaoh's palace.

Each of the men understood that ambition without compassion destroys what it achieves. Grant could have humiliated Lee at Appomattox. Could have paraded Confederate soldiers through Northern cities in chains. Could have prosecuted Southern officers for treason.

Instead, he offered terms so generous that they laid the foundation for national reconciliation. Lee himself remarked that Grant's terms would "have a happy effect" on the Confederate army, and on the Southern population trying to rebuild their lives.

Joseph could have imprisoned or executed his brothers. Could have seized their property and enslaved their families. Could have used his power to extract revenge for twenty years of suffering. Instead, he chose to see his suffering as preparation for a larger purpose, saving lives during the famine. He used his position not to punish but to preserve.

Both men recognized that their power existed to serve something beyond themselves. Grant's ambition was never personal glory, it was preserving the Union. At Appomattox, when he had achieved that goal, he immediately shifted from conquering to healing. His ambition had been for the nation, not himself, so he could afford to be generous with the defeated.

Joseph explicitly stated that his elevation to power was God's doing, not his brothers' cruelty or his own cleverness. "God sent me ahead of you," he told them. His ambition had always been to serve God's purposes, so he could afford to forgive those who had tried to destroy him.

This is the heart of Compassionate Ambition. It's not ambition diluted by compassion, as if caring for others weakens your drive. It's not compassion limited by ambition, as if achieving goals requires you to sacrifice people. It's a complete integration where ambition and compassion strengthen each other.

The peaceful surrender that Grant achieved at Appomattox was elevated by the compassion that he showed there. He won not just a military victory but the possibility of peace. A peace that would eventually rebuild the nation. Joseph's forgiveness of his brothers didn't weaken his position, it fulfilled his purpose. He saved lives not just during the famine but across generations.

When ambition serves a purpose larger than ego, compassion becomes possible. When power is held as a trust rather than a possession, mercy becomes natural.

When Ambition Forgets Compassion

I need to tell you about Silver.

Silver is one of the most skilled cutting horses I've ever ridden. Quick, athletic, intelligent. When he's prepared properly, he can read a cow's movement before I can, anticipating its next move with precision that makes my job almost unnecessary. We'd won the open the month before. He was in top form. I was proud of what we'd built together.

There was a small show coming up. Nothing important, but good for building confidence. Good for my business profile. Good for proving that the previous win wasn't a fluke.

But it had rained. For days leading up to the show, rain turned each of the practice areas into a muddy mess. Silver didn't get worked much. He needed that work, not so much for training his physical skills, but for strengthening the mental bond between us. The riding that builds trust. The time together that reminds him he can depend on me.

In hindsight, I should have scratched him from the show. My ego got in the way. He'd won the month before. I thought it would be good for business if he did well again. I convinced myself that he wouldn't need much prep because he's so naturally talented.

The warmup areas were almost unusable. Silver has always been cautious about unusual surfaces, shadows in the arena, tractor tracks in the dirt, anything that looked different made him wary. The muddy puddles in the warmup made it difficult to get his mind right. I should have scratched him then. But I persevered. Got him to a place where I thought he could handle the show.

Then I tied him to the side of the gooseneck trailer while I helped other competitors for a couple of hours. I thought I'd have time to warm him up again before our run. I was wrong about that too.

When I returned to the trailer, Silver was a mess. Not physically, he looked fine. But I could see in his eyes that he'd lost it mentally. Looking around, I noticed one of the trailer's side lights was broken. The bar that holds the tailgate up was lying on the ground. While I'd been away helping others, this faithful friend who had given me his all whenever I had asked for it. That could show with the best of them when he's properly prepared, had been left to face his demons alone.

Being alone scares him. Then something, anything can startle him. Then he gets more scared. Like a self-defeating cycle. This is how the sidelight got shattered. How the tailgate bar had been broken off. I don't know exactly what happened. But I know Silver had panicked. And I hadn't been there.

I tried to show him anyway. My ambition to succeed, to maintain the winning streak, to prove my training methods work, that ambition overrode my compassion for what he needed. He wasn't there mentally. He couldn't perform. I'd broken something between us that had taken years to build. … Trust.

Looking back, I realize what I did. I sacrificed the relationship for a momentary goal. I prioritized my business reputation over his wellbeing. I let ambition, selfish, ego-driven ambition, override the compassion that should have made me recognize he wasn't ready.

Many will read this and say I'm wrong. They'll say he should be able to handle being tied up by himself. That I need to make him tougher, more resilient. That coddling him makes him weak. This is the old way. The "tough" way. The "right" way. They say. But when you've broken the trust someone had in you, when you realize you weren't there when they needed you, you'd give anything to get it back.

This is what happens when ambition loses compassion. I had the vision, success at the show. I had the courage, I wasn't afraid to compete. But I'd forgotten the growing season, the patient cultivation that Compassionate Ambition requires. I'd skipped from Fearless Guidance straight to trying to harvest fruit from a plant I hadn't properly tended.

Silver needed more than training. He needed partnership. He needed to know I'd be there when things got difficult. He needed the kind of care that Grant showed York, the understanding that exceptional performance comes from trust, not from forcing someone to overcome their fear alone.

It will be a long road back with Silver, if we make it at all. Not because the physical skills aren't there. But because I demonstrated that my ambition mattered more than his welfare. And horses, like people, remember when you fail them.

This is the danger of ambition without compassion. You can achieve your immediate goal and lose everything that matters. You can win the show and break the partnership. You can conquer the territory and poison the ground you're trying to build on.

The Growing Season Requires Time

When Grant began working with York at West Point, he didn't set a record in the first week. He spent three months building trust, establishing partnership, proving to York that success was possible without panic. Every session had to end on a positive note, even if they didn't accomplish much. Every attempt was met with patience rather than punishment. Every small success was celebrated. The growing season can't be rushed.

When Joseph was sold into slavery at seventeen, he didn't become prime minister the next day. He served faithfully in Potiphar's house for years. Then spent more years in prison after being falsely accused. The growing season for his eventual elevation involved patience through circumstances he couldn't control, maintaining integrity when it would have been easier to become bitter, choosing to serve excellently even when he wasn't being rewarded.

The ambition was always there. Joseph could interpret dreams, he told his brothers about his dreams of their sheaves bowing to his when they were children. He knew he was meant for something. But that ambition had to mature through the growing season. Had to be refined by suffering. Had to learn compassion through experiencing the absence of it.

When Grant finally met Lee at Appomattox, his compassion wasn't spontaneous generosity. It was the fruit of a growing season that began in his childhood. His father Jesse Grant had confidence in young Ulysses's ability with horses and gave him tasks that were considered difficult for a youth. By age five, Ulysses was performing stunts bareback. At age ten, he tamed an unbroken colt after others failed.

He learned early that force wasn't the path to partnership. That patience produced better results than domination. Those lessons with horses shaped how he led men, how he dealt with enemies, how he understood power.

The growing season for both Grant and Joseph involved setbacks. Grant resigned from the army in 1854, struggled with alcohol, failed at farming and business before the Civil War gave him another chance. Joseph spent years as a slave and prisoner before his opportunity came. Neither man's ambition had a smooth path from vision to fulfillment.

But that's precisely what the growing season requires. Time to develop resilience. Experience with failure. Practice maintaining your vision when circumstances suggest you should give up. The roots have to go deep before the plant can reach high.

If I'd been intent on developing this with Silver, I would have scratched him from the show. I would have recognized that we weren't in harvest season yet, we were still in the growing season. More time was needed to strengthen our partnership after the rain had limited our preparation. My ambition to compete immediately was trying to harvest fruit before the plant had matured.

This is what Compassionate Ambition teaches: discernment about timing. Knowing when to push forward and when to wait. Understanding that rushing the growing season produces shallow roots and weak fruit. Having the humility to recognize when more time is needed, even when your ego wants immediate results. Let's look at what we can do on a daily basis to work toward that.

Resilience through Ambition

You must learn to push forward while maintaining care for those who follow you. To drive toward goals while honouring the humanity of those who serve beside you, those who help you reach those goals. To maintain ambitious vision while staying grounded in compassionate reality. And you need to consciously put yourself on top of the list of those you care for. After all, you are your number one supporter.

Back in 2012, I was on deployment in Afghanistan, working as an Engineering Surveyor in the Australian Army. I had originally joined the Army Reserve, six years earlier, while I was studying at university. I had started a practise of running every second day, and weight training, or swimming, the alternate days, in order to keep my weight down.

When I joined the full-time army, I was no longer responsible for my personal fitness. It was a requirement to do Physical Training (PT) every morning, and most of us loved it. It was a great way of building resilience through disciplined effort, challenging ourselves and each other in an atmosphere of friendly rivalry.

In his 2024 book, "Military Mindset: Lessons from the Battlefield", Ant Middleton says, "The great thing about discipline is that after a while, once you achieve consistency of discipline, it turns into motivation." Ant talks about how having the discipline to get fit, builds his motivation to want to stay fit, for the physical, mental and psychological benefits.

I found that having the ambition to compete in the Cairns Ironman drove my desire to build my fitness, getting me out of the door even on those days when the last thing I wanted to do was run. Being based in the middle of Afghanistan was not conducive to improving my swimming though, but I had a set of rubber bands attached to my bunk that let me practise this a little at least.

We had a good gym set up at the Tarin Kot base, where I could practise my cycling, and a track around the airfield where we could run. These factors were great for my motivation, and I would run that track every other day, trying to push my fitness to that next level. Early one morning, I was about halfway through my first lap, and I nodded at three guys jogging toward me as I was fiddling with the heart rate monitor on my watch.

After they passed, I thought to myself, "Hang on a second, that was Ben Robert-Smith!" These guys were the elite of our defence force. Ben had just received the Victoria Cross for Gallantry the year before, but here he was, just like me, doing the 1% things that make a difference in your life.

6 years later (2018), James Clear published "Atomic Habits", in which he stresses the importance of the cumulative effect of doing the small things every day. The 1% rule's focus is on compounding improvements, eliminating the pressure to achieve immediate perfection.

Clear says that if you improve by 1% every day, by the end of a year, you'll be nearly 37 times better at that skill. Conversely, neglecting small actions can lead to gradual decline, making it harder to achieve your goals. It all comes back to the old African proverb that asks, "How do you eat an Elephant?" Ambition leads to discipline, and disciplined daily actions lead to resilience.

What It Looks Like in the Arena

When you bring Compassionate Ambition into your work with horses, several things become clear:

1. **You learn to distinguish between the horse's capacity and your agenda**. I can want Silver to perform brilliantly at a show. That's my ambition. But what matters more is whether Silver is prepared mentally and emotionally to handle that pressure. Compassionate Ambition asks the horse, "What do you need right now?" before it asks, "What do I need right now?" This doesn't mean you never challenge the horse.

   Grant challenged York with increasingly difficult jumps. But each challenge was matched with support. Each new difficulty came only after the previous one had been mastered. The ambition pushed forward; the compassion ensured the foundation was solid.

2. **You develop the ability to celebrate small victories while maintaining vision for larger goals.** Grant didn't expect York to clear six feet in their first session. He celebrated the smaller jumps.

Acknowledged every instance when York chose trust over fear. Built confidence incrementally rather than demanding immediate perfection.

This requires patience that most people lack. We want dramatic transformation now. We want the horse to understand completely after one explanation. We want visible progress every single session. Compassionate Ambition accepts that growth is often invisible in the moment but becomes apparent over time.

3. **You learn to end sessions before you've pushed too far.** The temptation is always to get one more repetition, try one more time, push just a little further. But that "one more time" can undo the trust you've been building. Compassionate Ambition knows when enough is enough, not because you lack drive, but because you're thinking longer term than this single session.

4. **You become sensitive to the horse's mental and emotional state, not just their physical performance.** Silver's body was fine. He could have performed physically. But his mind wasn't ready. He'd been left alone when something frightened him, and he needed reassurance before being asked to perform. Compassionate Ambition reads beyond the surface.

   It asks not just "Can they do this?" but "Should they do this right now?" It recognizes that forcing performance when the foundation is shaky doesn't prove capability, it erodes trust.

5. **You develop the wisdom to sacrifice short-term goals for long-term relationships.** Scratching Silver from that show would have cost me the entry fee. Would have meant no chance to build on the previous win. Would have looked like giving up. But keeping the relationship intact would have been worth far more.

   A horse who trusts you completely is more valuable than any single show result. Compassionate Ambition understands this math. It counts the cost of success and sometimes decides the price is too high.

What It Looks Like Outside the Arena

The same principles that govern Compassionate Ambition with horses apply to leading people, though the stakes are often much higher.

In professional settings, Compassionate Ambition means:

1. **Setting ambitious goals while remaining attentive to your team's capacity.** Like Grant preparing York for that record jump, you push toward excellence. But you're constantly assessing whether people have what they need to succeed. Not just skills and resources, but psychological safety, support during difficulty, recovery time between intense efforts.

   Leaders without compassion push their teams until people break. They hit their targets but lose their best people. They win the quarter but destroy morale. They achieve their objectives and create organizational wreckage in the process. Leaders with ambition tempered by compassion push just as hard, but they do it while maintaining awareness of impact.

   They notice when someone is struggling. They adjust timelines when necessary. They celebrate progress even when final results aren't yet achieved. They understand that burning people out to hit a deadline destroys the capacity to hit future deadlines.

2. **Creating environments where people can fail safely while still maintaining high standards.** Joseph tested his brothers, he needed to know if they'd changed. But the testing had a purpose beyond his own satisfaction. He was determining whether they were capable of being part of the solution to the famine. Once he confirmed they'd changed, he immediately moved to restoration and support.

   Compassionate Ambition doesn't lower standards. It creates conditions where people can reach for high standards without fear that failure will be met with punishment. Mistakes become learning opportunities. Setbacks become chances to adjust approach. The ambitious goal remains clear, but the path toward it allows for human reality.

3. **Recognizing when to push and when to provide support**. Grant gave his troops rest between campaigns when possible. He ensured they had supplies and reinforcements. He pushed them hard when he needed to, but he didn't break them unnecessarily. At Appomattox, when the war was won, he immediately shifted from conqueror to reconciler.

   The leader with Compassionate Ambition can shift fluidly between pushing and supporting. Sometimes people need challenge. Sometimes they need rest. Sometimes they need you to demand their best. Sometimes they need you to give them permission to step back and recover. Wisdom lies in knowing which is needed when.

4. **Being willing to sacrifice personal glory for collective wellbeing**. Grant could have been the vengeful victor at Appomattox. History would have understood. Many Northerners wanted it. His reputation would have been secure as the man who crushed the Confederacy completely. Instead, he chose terms that served the nation's need for healing over his own potential for glorification.

   He let Lee keep his dignity. He fed Confederate soldiers. He sent them home with their horses for spring ploughing. He made reunion possible. Compassionate Ambition understands that leadership isn't about the leader. It's about what gets built, what gets achieved, what gets preserved for those who come after. Sometimes that requires setting aside ego.

   Sometimes it requires letting others receive credit. Sometimes it requires doing the harder thing, showing mercy, when the easier thing would be showing power.

5. **Maintaining vision while adapting tactics.** Joseph never lost sight of his purpose, saving lives during the famine. But how he achieved that purpose changed dramatically over twenty years. As a slave, he served faithfully. In prison, he interpreted dreams. As prime minister, he administered Egypt's resources. The vision remained constant; the tactics adapted to circumstances.

   Leaders with Compassionate Ambition are fierce about their ultimate purpose but flexible about methods.

   They don't confuse the goal with the path. They're willing to adjust, pivot, or completely change approach if the original plan isn't serving the greater purpose. The ambition provides direction; the compassion ensures the journey doesn't destroy what you're trying to build.

The Integration: When Ambition and Compassion Become One

Here's what took me years to understand: Compassionate Ambition isn't two separate qualities balanced against each other. It's not ambition pulling one direction while compassion pulls the other, while you try to find equilibrium.

It's one integrated quality where ambition and compassion amplify each other.

Grant's compassion at Appomattox didn't limit his ambition, it fulfilled it. His ambition was always to preserve the Union. Crushing Lee would have preserved the geographical Union but destroyed the possibility of true reunion. Showing mercy made reunification possible. The compassion served the ambition.

Joseph's forgiveness of his brothers didn't compromise his position. It completed his purpose. God had sent him to Egypt to save lives. Punishing his brothers would have saved his ego but violated his purpose. Reconciling with them and providing for their family saved many lives. The compassion fulfilled the ambition.

When I work with a horse properly, my ambition to develop their skills and my compassion for their wellbeing aren't competing interests. They're the same interest viewed from different angles. I want the horse to reach their full potential because I care about them. I care about them by helping them reach their potential. The ambition and compassion reinforce each other.

This integration only happens when your ambition is aligned with values, not ego. When what you're driving toward serves something beyond yourself. When your goals include the wellbeing of those who help you reach them.

Grant's ambition wasn't personal glory, it was preservation of the nation. So his compassion toward Lee served that ambition. Joseph's ambition wasn't revenge or power, it was fulfilling God's purpose. So his compassion toward his brothers served that ambition.

If Grant's ambition had been personal glorification, compassion would have contradicted it. If Joseph's ambition had been proving his superiority over his brothers, forgiveness would have undermined it. The integration is only possible when ambition is rightly ordered.

The Pruning That Must Come

But even Compassionate Ambition isn't the final stage. It's the growing season, not the harvest. And growing seasons eventually require pruning.

There will come a time, we'll explore it in the next chapter on Peaceful Directedness, when even ambition tempered by compassion must be refined further. When the drive to achieve must be mellowed into calm, clear guidance. When the push forward must become peaceful presence.

Grant demonstrated this at Appomattox, but he'd been developing it for years. The ambitious general who drove through the Western Theatre and Virginia with relentless determination became, in that moment of victory, the peaceful leader who could set aside triumph for reconciliation.

Joseph demonstrated it when his brothers feared revenge after Jacob's death. The powerful prime minister who could have crushed them became the peaceful brother who wept and reassured them of his continued care.

These moments of transcendence, moving from Compassionate Ambition to Peaceful Directedness, don't happen automatically. They require another stage of growth, another level of refinement, another pruning of what no longer serves.

But that's the subject of the next chapter. For now, focus on this: the seed of Fearless Guidance must grow into Compassionate Ambition before it can mature into anything more refined.

Grant didn't jump from graduation day at West Point to the surrender at Appomattox. Twenty-two years of war and peace, success and failure, military triumph and personal struggle stood between that record-breaking jump and those generous surrender terms. The growing season took time.

Joseph didn't jump from the pit his brothers threw him in to the throne room where he saved them. Twenty years of slavery and imprisonment, of faithfulness unrewarded and dreams deferred, stood between betrayal and reconciliation. The growing season required patience.

You won't jump from your first courageous step into uncertainty to mature leadership that integrates ambition and compassion. The growing season demands time, attention, and persistent cultivation.

But if you tend it properly, if you maintain your ambitious vision while developing genuine care for those you lead, if you push forward without sacrificing people to progress, if you achieve your goals while preserving the relationships that made achievement possible, then Compassionate Ambition will mature in you.

Then, you'll discover what Grant and Joseph learned. That your achievements aren't measured by what you accomplish but by what you preserve while accomplishing it. That the greatest victories aren't over enemies but over the temptation to let ambition override compassion. That the most lasting legacy isn't what you built but how you treated the people who helped you build it.

The Lesson From the Arena

Every time I walk out to work with a horse now, I carry Silver's lesson with me. Before I make any decision about what we'll do that day, I ask myself: Is this serving the partnership, or just my agenda? Am I pushing because they're ready to grow, or because my ego needs validation?

Sometimes the ambitious thing to do is work hard. Sometimes it's to not work at all. Sometimes it's to compete. Sometimes it's to scratch from the show and take more time to prepare. The ambition stays constant, building the best partnership possible. But compassion determines how that ambition gets expressed in this particular moment with this particular horse.

Grant knew this with York. Three months of patient work led to one record-breaking jump. The ambition was always there, preparing York for that demonstration. But compassion determined the pace, the approach, the daily decisions about when to push and when to rest.

Joseph knew this with his brothers. His ambition was always to save lives during the famine. But his compassion determined how he used his power when those specific lives, his brothers' lives, were in his hands. He could have saved the region while destroying his family. Instead, he saved both.

The horse doesn't care about your ambitions. They care about whether you can be trusted. Whether you see them as a partner or a tool. Whether your drive to achieve will sacrifice their wellbeing or honour it. Whether your strength will be used to dominate them or to lift them higher than they could reach alone.

Leadership is the same. People don't follow your ambitions. They follow you. And they only follow you consistently if they trust that your ambition includes their wellbeing. That your drive to succeed won't require them to be sacrificed. That your vision of achievement has room for their humanity.

Grant gave Confederate soldiers rations and horses. Joseph gave his brothers provisions and land. Both men achieved their ambitious goals not despite their compassion but through it. The compassion made the ambition sustainable.

This is what the growing season teaches: that true achievement requires you to care about more than the achievement itself. That lasting success must include the wellbeing of those who make success possible. That the height you reach matters less than who's still standing beside you when you get there.

Plant the seed with Fearless Guidance. Tend the growing season with Compassionate Ambition. And trust that when the time comes for pruning and harvest, you'll have built something worth preserving.

The horse will tell you if you're getting it right. Not through perfect performance, but through willing partnership. Through trust that grows deeper with each session. Through the willingness to try difficult things because they know you won't sacrifice them to your ambition.

Grant knew he'd gotten it right with York when that big chestnut gathered himself and launched skyward over a bar set higher than anyone thought possible. Not because Grant forced him, but because York trusted him.

Joseph knew he'd gotten it right when his brothers finally understood that he'd forgiven them completely. Not just said the words, but lived the reality day after day, year after year, until they could believe it.

You'll know you're getting it right when the horse you're working with stops seeing you as a source of pressure and starts seeing you as a partner. When the person you're leading stops waiting for you to sacrifice them and starts trusting you to support them. When your ambition and your compassion become indistinguishable because they're serving the same purpose.

That's the harvest of Compassionate Ambition. Not just achievement, but achievement that preserves partnership. Not just success, but success that honours those who made it possible. Not just reaching your goals but reaching them with your relationships intact.

The growing season takes time. Tend it with patience. Water it with care. Protect it from the shortcuts that promise faster results at the cost of deeper relationships. And trust that what grows from this season will be worth the wait.

York cleared that record-breaking jump. Joseph saved two nations. Grant preserved a union. And you, if you tend this growing season properly, will build something equally remarkable in your own arena.

Not because you had the courage to begin. That was Fearless Guidance. And not yet because you've refined everything down to its peaceful essence. That will be Peaceful Directedness. But because you learned to maintain ambitious drive while honouring the wellbeing of those who accompany you on the journey.

That's Compassionate Ambition. That's the growing season. That's what transforms a planted seed into a plant that will eventually bear fruit. Tend it well.

"The terms of surrender, however, would be a simple gentlemen's agreement."

- National Museum of American History, describing Appomattox

CHAPTER 7

BALANCED COORDINATION

"The horse is a mirror to your soul, and sometimes you might not like what you see in the mirror."

- Buck Brannaman

The Silver Medal

The morning of July 29, 1952, dawned cool and overcast in Helsinki. Lis Hartel woke in her hotel room and immediately began the ritual she'd performed every morning for the past eight years. Before her feet touched the floor, before she attempted to walk on legs that no longer fully obeyed her, she closed her eyes and breathed.

Three slow breaths. Feeling her centre. Aligning her intention with what her body could actually do.

She was thirty-one years old. A mother of two. Paralysed from the knees down since 1944, when polio had struck her down in the eighth month of her pregnancy. And today, she would compete in the Olympic Games against the finest dressage riders in the world.

The doctors had told her she would never ride again. That was eight years ago. Today, she would prove them wrong in front of the world.

But first, she had to get dressed. Then walk to breakfast. Then make it through the morning without her legs giving out completely. The Olympic dressage test would come later, the easy part, ironically, because once she was on Jubilee's back, the paralysis didn't matter as much. On the ground, she was disabled. On her horse, she was complete.

Her husband Einar helped her down the stairs of their lodging. She moved carefully, deliberately, each step requiring concentration. Her right leg was worse than her left. She'd learned to distribute her weight, to use her hip flexors and core muscles to compensate for what her lower legs couldn't provide. She'd learned to make intention and execution meet somewhere in the middle, bridging the gap her body had created.

This was Balanced Coordination at its most fundamental level, not the graceful synchronization of a healthy body, but the painstaking construction of harmony from broken pieces.

At the Olympic stadium, the stands were beginning to fill. Dressage was still relatively unknown to most spectators, but something about this Danish woman's story had captured attention. The newspapers had written about her: "The Polio Victim Who Rides," "Paralysed Mother Defies Doctors," "Danish Rider Overcomes Impossible Odds."

She hated those headlines. They made her sound like a curiosity, a medical miracle, when what she'd actually done was work. Eight years of relentless, grinding, unglamorous work. Three hours of physical therapy every morning. Two hours with Jubilee every afternoon. Learning to feel through her seat and thighs what she could no longer feel through her calves. Learning to communicate with her mind and heart what she couldn't communicate with her heels.

Every ride was an exercise in coordination, not just between her and Jubilee, but within herself. Her mind knew what the movement should look like. Her emotions felt the connection with her horse. But her body had to find new pathways, new ways to translate intention into action when the old pathways were severed.

When Jubilee was led into the warm-up arena, Lis felt the familiar tightness in her chest. Not fear, she'd stopped being afraid years ago. Just the awareness of what was about to be demanded of her. She approached her horse carefully, placed her hands on his neck, breathed with him. Felt his steadiness flow into her.

Two grooms helped her mount. This part was always humiliating, needing help to do what any child could do alone. But she'd learned to accept it. Pride was a luxury she couldn't afford. Once she was in the saddle, she took a moment to settle. To let her spine align with her seat bones. To feel her seat bones align with Jubilee's back. To bring her scattered pieces into harmony.

Then she gathered the reins, and the transformation happened.

On Jubilee's back, Lis Hartel was not paralysed. She was not disabled. She was not broken. She was a rider, and he was her partner, and together they were capable of something approaching perfection.

The test began. Collected walk. Extended trot. Half-pass. Flying changes. Movements that required split-second timing, absolute precision, seamless communication between rider and horse. Movements that most able-bodied riders struggled to execute cleanly. Movements that Lis Hartel, who couldn't walk without assistance, performed with such fluidity that watchers had to remind themselves she was paralysed.

Because what they were seeing wasn't physical strength overcoming disability. It was something more profound: the complete alignment of mind, emotion, and body, however limited that body might be, in service of a shared purpose. This was coordination achieved not through perfection, but through integration. Not through having all the pieces, but through making all the pieces you did have work together flawlessly.

When the final salute came and Lis rode out of the arena, she knew. Not that she'd won, she could never predict judges' scores, but that she'd done what she came to do. She'd shown that Balanced Coordination isn't about having a perfect instrument. It's about bringing every part of the instrument you have into perfect harmony.

The scores were announced hours later. Silver medal. Second place in the world. Behind only Sweden's Henri Saint Cyr, and ahead of riders from nations with centuries of dressage tradition.

But the moment that would define her Olympic experience came during the medal ceremony. When her name was called for silver, she needed help climbing the podium steps. Her legs, exhausted from the day's effort, were barely holding her weight.

Henri Saint Cyr, the gold medalist standing on the highest step, did something unprecedented. He stepped down from his podium, walked to Lis, and helped her up the steps to the silver medal platform. Then he lifted her, gently, so she could stand steady while they raised the flags and played the national anthems.

A Swedish man helping a Danish woman. A gold medalist honouring a silver medalist. A moment that transcended competition because both riders recognized what they'd witnessed: not disability overcome, but coordination achieved at a level so profound that physical limitation became irrelevant.

Years later, Henri would say, "I was not helping a competitor. I was honouring an achievement far greater than my own."

The Growing Season

In the framework of The Horseman's Way, Balanced Coordination represents the growing season of the Communication Pillar. It's what emerges when the seed of Emotionless Communication, planted in the Chapter 4 (Emotionless Communication), begins to mature into something more integrated, more embodied, more complete.

Remember the progression:

- **Emotionless Communication** planted the seed, learning to communicate without emotional distortion, to remove the static that prevents clear transmission. You learned to recognize your emotional state, to breathe and centre before speaking, to deliver messages that arrive uncoloured by reactivity.

- **Balanced Coordination** is the growing season, when that clear communication matures into embodied congruence. Your words align with your actions. Your body language matches your intentions. Mind, body, and emotion move together in synchronization. You become trustworthy because there's no gap between what you say and what you are.

- **Centred Transcendence** will lead to the harvest, the pruned and refined state where this coordination becomes so consistent that your awareness can expand beyond yourself, where your presence remains stable regardless of external circumstances. But we're not there yet. Right now, we're in the growing season. And growing seasons require patience, persistent care, and acceptance that development happens incrementally, not instantly.

Think about what growing season means for a farmer. The seed has been planted. You can't dig it up every day to check if it's sprouting. You can't force it to grow faster by pulling on the shoot. You can only provide consistent conditions, water, sunlight, protection from pests, and trust the process of development.

Balanced Coordination requires the same patience. You've learned to communicate without emotional distortion (the planted seed). Now you must practice, day after day, bringing your body language into alignment with your words. Training your physical responses to match your intentions. Building the muscle memory of congruence until it becomes automatic.

Lis Hartel's eight years between paralysis and Olympic silver represent this growing season perfectly. She couldn't rush it. She couldn't skip steps. She had to show up every day, through pain, through frustration, through setbacks, and do the work of building coordination from broken pieces.

The Exile's Daily Practice

Twenty-five hundred years before Lis Hartel mounted Jubilee in Helsinki, another person was learning about Balanced Coordination through sustained practice in hostile territory.

Daniel was probably fourteen or fifteen years old when Nebuchadnezzar's army conquered Jerusalem in 605 BCE. Old enough to remember his home, his family's standing, his life before exile. Young enough to be reshaped by the Babylonian Empire's re-education program for promising captives.

The Babylonians had a system. They took the brightest young men from conquered nations, particularly from royal and noble families, and trained them to serve the empire. Three years of intensive education in Babylonian language, literature, and culture. The goal was to create a class of administrators who understood their conquered homeland, but whose loyalty belonged to Babylon.

Daniel and his friends Hananiah, Mishael, and Azariah (renamed Belteshazzar, Shadrach, Meshach, and Abednego by their captors) were selected for this program. It should have been an honour. Instead, it was a crisis of identity.

Everything about the program was designed to erase their Jewish identity and remake them as Babylonians. New names. New language. New gods. Even new food, they were assigned daily portions from the king's table, rich foods that would have been impressive under normal circumstances but were unacceptable under Jewish dietary law.

This is where most people focus on Daniel's story, the dramatic moments. Refusing the king's food. Interpreting Nebuchadnezzar's dream. Surviving the lion's den. These are the crisis points, the climactic scenes that demonstrate courage and faith.

But Balanced Coordination isn't built in crisis moments. It's built in the daily, undramatic practice of aligning your actions with your beliefs when no one's watching. When there's no drama, no audience, no immediate consequence. Just the steady, persistent work of making your external behaviour match your internal conviction.

The real story of Daniel is what happened between the dramatic moments. Seventy years of daily practice. Seventy years of maintaining the coordination between his Jewish identity and his Babylonian responsibilities. Seventy years of serving pagan kings faithfully while remaining faithful to his God.

Every morning, Daniel opened his windows toward Jerusalem and prayed. Three times a day. It's mentioned casually in Scripture, almost as an aside, but think about what this represents. Not occasional prayer. Not prayer when he felt like it or when things got difficult. Three times every day, without fail, for seventy years.

This wasn't dramatic. It was disciplined. It was the daily alignment of his physical body (kneeling, facing Jerusalem), his mind (focusing on prayer), and his spirit (maintaining connection to God). Day after day. Year after year. Decade after decade.

This is Balanced Coordination as a way of life.

The dietary restrictions were the same. Every day, Daniel had to choose foods that maintained his Jewish identity without insulting his Babylonian hosts. Every meal required him to coordinate his beliefs with his behaviour in a hostile environment. Not once. Not occasionally. Every single day for seventy years.

And the work itself, serving as a high official in multiple pagan administrations, required a different kind of coordination. He had to be competent enough to justify his position, which meant learning Babylonian systems thoroughly. But he also had to maintain enough distance from Babylonian practices to preserve his Jewish identity. He had to be simultaneously insider and outsider, fully present but never fully assimilated.

The book of Daniel tells us he was exceptionally skilled at this balance. He rose to become one of the top three administrators in the entire Persian Empire under Darius. Not because he compromised his convictions, but because his integrity made him trustworthy. His external competence matched his internal character. His professional behaviour aligned perfectly with his spiritual beliefs.

This is what made him dangerous to his rivals. They knew they couldn't attack him for incompetence or corruption, his coordination was too complete. So they attacked the source of that coordination itself: his prayer practice. They convinced King Darius to pass a law forbidding prayer to anyone but the king for thirty days, knowing Daniel would violate it.

And Daniel did. Not dramatically, not defiantly, but exactly as he'd always done. Windows open. Facing Jerusalem. Three times a day. The coordination between belief and practice was so deeply established that even the threat of death couldn't disrupt it.

That's seventy years of growing season producing a harvest of unshakeable coordination.

When Daniel was thrown into the lion's den and survived, it wasn't a miracle that saved him. Well, it was, but the miracle happened because of the coordination he'd built over a lifetime. His trust in God wasn't theoretical. It was embodied. His faith wasn't abstract. It was practiced daily until it became as automatic as breathing.

The same pattern appears throughout his life. When he interpreted Nebuchadnezzar's dream, he didn't just understand the symbols intellectually. He aligned his spiritual insight with practical wisdom, his knowledge of God with his understanding of Babylonian culture. When he read the writing on the wall at Belshazzar's feast, he integrated prophetic vision with historical analysis.

This is what Balanced Coordination produces: the ability to bring all parts of yourself, mind, body, emotion, spirit, into unified action. Not occasionally, but consistently. Not just in crisis, but in daily life.

Two Kinds of Paralysis

On the surface, Lis Hartel and Daniel seem to have little in common. She was a Danish dressage rider in the twentieth century. He was a Jewish exile in ancient Babylon. She fought physical paralysis. He navigated cultural exile.

But both faced the same fundamental challenge:

How do you maintain coordination when circumstances try to fracture you?

Lis' paralysis was physical. Polio had severed the connection between her brain and her lower legs. The neural pathways that should have carried signals from intention to execution were damaged. To ride again, she had to build new pathways, learning to communicate through her seat and thighs what she could no longer communicate through her calves and heels. Learning to feel through different parts of her body. Learning to make her limited physical capacity coordinate with her unlimited mental and emotional capacity.

Daniel's paralysis was cultural. Exile had severed him from everything that had defined his identity, his homeland, his temple, his community, his way of life. He was surrounded by a culture that wanted to reshape him, to fracture the coordination between his beliefs and his behaviour. To maintain his identity, he had to build new pathways, learning to serve Babylonian kings faithfully while remaining faithful to his God. Learning to function in a hostile environment. Learning to make his external circumstances coordinate with his internal convictions.

Both discovered the same truth:

Balanced Coordination isn't about having perfect circumstances or a perfect body. It's about aligning every part of yourself toward your purpose, regardless of limitation.

For Lis, this meant three hours of physical therapy every morning. Painful, unglamorous work that most people never saw. Stretching paralysed muscles that would never fully function. Building strength in the muscles that still worked. Training her core and seat to compensate for what her legs couldn't do. This was her growing season, daily practice building coordination from broken pieces.

For Daniel, this meant three times daily prayer. Consistent, disciplined practice that integrated his physical body (kneeling, facing Jerusalem), his mind (focusing prayer), and his spirit (maintaining connection to God). This was his growing season, daily practice maintaining coordination in hostile territory.

Both understood something essential:

Coordination is built in the mundane moments, not the dramatic ones.

By the time Lis entered the Olympic arena, she'd spent eight years practicing the coordination that would make those eight minutes possible. By the time Daniel entered the lion's den, he'd spent seventy years practicing the coordination that would sustain him through that night.

The dramatic moments revealed the coordination that had been built during thousands of undramatic ones.

What Makes This Different from the Planting Stage?

In Chapter 4 (Emotionless Communication), we talked about removing emotional distortion from communication. About learning to recognize your emotional state, breathe through it, and respond from clarity rather than reactivity. That's the planted seed, the foundational practice.

Balanced Coordination is what grows from that seed when you practice it consistently over time. The difference is embodiment.

Emotionless Communication is primarily cognitive. You catch yourself before you react. You pause. You choose your response. There's still a gap between stimulus and response, and you're actively managing that gap.

Balanced Coordination is embodied. Your body language naturally aligns with your words because you've practiced long enough that congruence becomes automatic. You don't have to think about matching your tone to your message, they align naturally. You don't have to monitor whether your facial expression contradicts your words, they coordinate without conscious effort.

This is what Balanced Coordination looks like in reality. Your communication isn't just emotionally clean, it's physically congruent. Your body isn't contradicting your words. Your facial expressions aren't undermining your message. Your energy isn't broadcasting anxiety while your voice claims calm. Everything aligns.

Lis demonstrated this perfectly. On the ground, she was obviously disabled. Her walk was laboured, her balance uncertain. But once on Jubilee, the coordination was so complete that judges had to remind themselves she was paralysed. Her limited physical capacity coordinated so perfectly with her mental focus and emotional connection to her horse that the disability became almost invisible.

Daniel demonstrated the same principle in a different domain. He served pagan kings faithfully, learning their language and culture, rising to the highest levels of their government. To observers, he appeared fully integrated into Babylonian society. But his daily prayer practice revealed the coordination beneath the surface, his external competence was perfectly aligned with his internal conviction. There was no gap between who he appeared to be and who he actually was.

This is the growing season's gift:

The gap between intention and execution narrows until they become nearly indistinguishable.

The Daily Practice of Growing Coordination

So how do you move from planted seed to growing plant? How do you develop the kind of embodied coordination that Lis and Daniel demonstrated? The answer is both simple and demanding: consistent daily practice of aligning body, mind, and emotion.

For Lis Hartel:

The details of her daily routine reveal the unglamorous reality of growing season work:

- **Morning (6:00 AM - 9:00 AM):** Physical therapy. Every day, without exception, even when it hurt, especially when it hurt. Stretching paralysed muscles. Building core strength. Training her hip flexors to compensate for her calves. This wasn't glamorous. It was painful, slow, often discouraging. Many days she couldn't see any progress. But she showed up anyway.

- **Midday:** Rest. Not because she was lazy, but because building coordination requires recovery time. The growing season includes periods of apparent dormancy where integration happens beneath the surface.

- **Afternoon (2:00 PM - 4:00 PM):** Riding with Jubilee. Not just mounting and riding around. Focused practice of specific movements. Working on half-passes until her seat and thighs could communicate what her legs couldn't. Practicing flying changes until the timing became automatic. Learning to feel through different parts of her body what most riders felt through their calves.

- **Evening:** Mental rehearsal. Visualizing the movements. Feeling them in her mind. Building the neural pathways that would support physical coordination. Athletes call this "mental practice," but it's actually coordination training, aligning your mental image with your physical capacity and your emotional intention.

This was eight years of growing season. Not eight years of constant progress. Eight years of showing up daily, even when progress was invisible. Eight years of trusting that the seed planted (her decision to ride again) was developing roots and shoots beneath the surface.

For Daniel:

The specifics of his practice were different but the principle was identical:

- **Morning, Noon, and Evening:** Prayer. Three times daily, windows open toward Jerusalem, aligning his body (kneeling, facing home), his mind (focusing on prayer), and his spirit (maintaining his relationship with God). This wasn't occasional devotion. It was disciplined coordination practice.

- **Daily Work:** Serving in Babylonian and Persian administrations with excellence. Not compromise, competence. His professional behaviour had to align with his personal character. He couldn't be sloppy at work and then claim his faith was strong. The coordination had to extend through every domain of his life.

- **Dietary Practice:** Every meal was a coordination exercise. Maintaining Jewish dietary restrictions in a pagan court without insulting his hosts or drawing negative attention to himself. Finding the balance between conviction and context. This required both principle and wisdom, holding firm to what mattered while being flexible about what didn't.

- **Study and Interpretation:** Daniel didn't just maintain his Jewish identity passively. He studied. He grew. He developed the ability to integrate Babylonian knowledge with Jewish wisdom, to read both cultures fluently while belonging fully to neither. This cognitive coordination supported his behavioural coordination.

This was seventy years of growing season. Most of it routine. Most of it invisible. Most of it undramatic. But by the time crisis came, whether interpreting dreams or facing lions, the coordination was so deeply established that it held under pressure.

The Horse Teaches Coordination

As I stepped into the yard, I watched how the four young mares reacted. It was not a big yard, about 30 metres square, with a small shed in the centre that provide shelter from the sun, the wind, and the rain. This was where our stallion, Harry, spent most of his days. A good place for him to stay out of mischief, but it was big enough that, if a horse wanted to play hard to catch, they could make a good game of it.

The mares were all rising two-year-olds that had just been purchased from a sale. The plan was to start them all under saddle, along with the two that we had bred that were the same age, and after 12 months sell some of them as working horses. The ones that would be kept would become competition horses, and would eventually become broodmares, if they proved themselves.

Out of the four in the yard on this day, two were the Alpha females, which was unusual in itself. But they had not been together long enough to see who the true Alpha would be. Of the other two, one was the epitome of Phoebe from Friends, a true blonde in a chestnut body. The life of the party. Someone who never takes things too seriously, and always sees everyone as her friend, whether they thought it or not.

The other was Smarty, and if she was a teenage girl, I'm sure you would always find her in the library. The little geeky girl, with the heavy glasses. She would be there, not because she was that keen about learning, although she was pretty smart, but because she was the shy girl. The one who didn't want to be seen and would be hiding out in there.

The two Alpha mares, one of which was Sunny, who you met in Chapter 4 (Emotionless Communication), and Missy, a beautiful tall Bay filly, both came up to me, vying for my attention, and Smarty followed them over. I gave the two bigger mares a neck rub, and went to do the same to Smarty. She stood there until I got to within a metre, and then she ran away. Over to where Roxy was watching the butterflies dance.

My first thought was that I can't afford to let this situation get any worse. I caught the Alpha mares, and Roxy, taking them out of the yard. Smarty was not a fan of being suddenly being left alone. Of being the centre of attention. For the next half hour, we went around, and around that yard. She knew that the other side of the shed provided the best place for her to hide, and so when I walked on one side, she would move around the other.

This game continued for some time, but eventually she decided that I wasn't going to give up, and that, even though she didn't really trust me, perhaps it might be a slightly better fate to allow herself to be caught, than to keep endlessly going around this yard. The seed was planted.

A couple of months later I started breaking in the mares. This is a process where I introduce a young horse to the saddle and bridle, and over the period of the next month or so, build a partnership with that horse. The partnership I form is based upon trust. A trust that allows me to hand that horse over to a competent rider, confident that the horse will go wherever they want the horse to go and do whatever they want the horse to do.

Unlike the ways of old, which were often based around "breaking the horse's spirit", the process that I use is more like "breaking in" a pair of new boots. And like breaking in new boots, I don't try to do too much in one day, because this just causes blisters. Instead, I do a little each day, letting the horse get used to the new experiences, and to ask me what it is I am trying to get them to do. Quitting in that good place, if I can, and pushing them through the bad stuff when I've got to.

Smarty gradually grew more, and more, confident in me with each new day. I could sense though, that a lot of her uncertainty wasn't based upon how she felt about me, but instead it was almost like she lacked confidence in herself. At the culmination of the breaking in process, I like to ride each horse with the owner watching to show their good points, and if there are any areas that need further work.

When it came time to ride Smarty, to show her off, I started in the arena where I train the cutting horses. This is deep sand designed to lessen the impact when the young horses exert themselves working cattle, and as I changed Smarty onto the offside lead, she tripped and fell. We both rolled headfirst into the sand. While neither of us were hurt, I could tell that her confidence was badly shaken. To me it felt like she said to herself, "I knew you would mess this up, your hopeless. You'll never be as good as the others."

As sad as this made me feel, it also made me smile. Not because we ate sand that day, but because the reality was that she was the most capable of the six horses I broke in that time. Where the others would push on through a task, relying on bravado to get them through, she would think her way through it, asking how much I wanted and when. Where the others had natural ability in varying quantities, she had natural caution that made her question every move. And she had a surprising amount of natural talent hiding away as well.

When the others went back to the sale the following year, Smarty stayed on, continuing her training each day. Each day we exposed a little more of her hidden talent. Developing the skillset that she would need when she went to compete at the futurity. Building the trust in herself, in me, and in us as a team, so that when we walked into that arena, we could confidently communicate with each other.

The training went on for the next two years. There were good days and there were hard days. Days when I wondered if she would get it, days when she got it almost before I could ask. Days when she clearly wondered what all this was in aid of, why she should care enough to make the effort I asked for. But it was the days when we communicated like we were hard wired together, when I thought and she responded, that I knew that all of the effort, all of the training would be worth it.

Over time our coordination developed, and her ability did too. Over time my ability to guide her, to ask her the right way, the best way for her to understand, grew also. Over time her trust in me developed, when she saw me coming, she would look forward to me scratching her head. We had developed Balanced Coordination, and the world was our oyster.

Smarty's two-year journey from the shy filly hiding behind the shed to a confident partner mirrors exactly what Lis spent eight years building, and what Daniel maintained for seventy. The specifics were different, Smarty didn't face paralysis or exile, but the principle was identical: **Balanced Coordination develops through daily practice, not dramatic breakthroughs.** Every session where I aligned my body language with my intentions, where I coordinated my patience with clear expectations, where I synchronized what I asked with what she could give, we were both practicing coordination.

The coordination wasn't built in the moments when everything clicked perfectly. It was built in the hundreds of moments when something was slightly off, and we both adjusted until we found alignment again. This is what the growing season looks like in practice. Not constant progress, but persistent practice. Not immediate mastery, but incremental integration. Smarty taught me that you can't rush coordination any more than you can rush a plant's growth by pulling on the shoot.

You can only show up daily, provide consistent conditions, and trust that beneath the surface, roots are deepening and strength is building. When we finally competed together, what they wouldn't see were the years of morning sessions where we learned each other's language, where my body learned to speak what my mind intended, where her trust in me became embodied rather than theoretical.

That's how Balanced Coordination is built, not in the spotlight of performance, but in the ordinary repetition of practice. And once built, it changes everything about how you work with horses, and how those lessons translate into every other domain of your life.

What It Looks Like in the Arena

When you bring Balanced Coordination into your work with horses, several things become evident:

1. **Your body language begins to match your intentions without conscious effort.** You think "forward" and your seat, legs, and hands automatically coordinate to communicate that intention clearly. You don't have to remember to relax, soften your shoulders, breathe deeply, these behaviours become automatic because you've practiced coordination long enough that it's embodied.

   This is what separated Lis from other paralysed riders who have returned to horses. Many ride very well, often facing greater disabilities than Lis. But to her credit, Lis achieved world-class coordination because she'd trained her body, mind, and emotions to work together so seamlessly that her disability became nearly irrelevant. The horse didn't feel confusion or contradiction from her cues. Jubilee felt clear, coordinated communication.

2. **You develop the ability to notice when you're out of coordination before the horse tells you.** You feel the tension creeping into your shoulders. You recognize that your breathing has become shallow. You notice that your jaw is clenched. These physical markers reveal your internal state, and you can address them before they distort your communication with the horse.

   This requires the self-awareness planted in Emotionless Communication, but now it's physical as well as emotional. You're not just monitoring your feelings, you're monitoring your embodiment. Are your hands tense? Is your seat following the horse's movement or fighting it? Is your weight evenly distributed or are you collapsing to one side?

3. **You learn to shift between different states deliberately rather than reactively.** You can move from calm observation to active correction smoothly. You can be soft and yielding in one moment, then firm and clear in the next, without losing your centre. The horse experiences this

as reliability, you're responsive to what they need without being reactive to what they do.

The master horseman moves fluidly between assertiveness and softness, focus and release, work and rest. These aren't contradictions, they're coordinated responses to changing circumstances. But this fluidity only comes after years of practice aligning your intentions with your physical expression.

4. **You become trustworthy to the horse in a deeper way.** When your words, actions, and internal state all align, the horse can relax their vigilance. They don't have to constantly monitor you for incongruence. They can trust that what you're communicating externally matches what you're experiencing internally. Think about working with a person whose body language contradicts their words.

   They say "I'm not angry" through clenched teeth. They claim "I'm listening" while scrolling their phone. They promise "I care about your development" while their impatience radiates off them. You can't relax around these people because you know you can't trust them. Horses feel the same way. When your coordination is consistent, they can trust you. When there are gaps between your layers of communication, they remain guarded.

5. **You discover that less becomes more.** As your coordination improves, your cues become subtler. You don't need big gestures, or loud aids because your feather-light touches are felt clearly. The advanced dressage rider makes movements that look effortless because every part of their communication is aligned, a slight shift of weight, a minimal adjustment of rein tension, a thought toward the next movement, and the horse responds.

   This is what spectators saw watching Lis at the Olympics. Her aids were nearly invisible. She couldn't use strong leg aids because she was paralysed. So she'd developed such profound coordination between her seat, her weight distribution, her mental focus, and her emotional connection with Jubilee that visible aids became unnecessary. The coordination itself was the communication.

What It Looks Like Outside the Arena

The same principles that create Balanced Coordination with horses apply to every area of leadership and relationship.

In professional settings:

Your team learns to trust you because there's no gap between what you say and what you do. When you commit to a decision, your subsequent actions align with that commitment. When you express concern about workload, your behaviour demonstrates that concern through adjusted timelines or additional resources. When you claim transparency is important, your communication patterns actually embody transparency.

This trustworthiness isn't built in dramatic moments. It's built through daily alignment. Hundreds of small moments where your words and actions coordinate. Thousands of interactions where your stated values and actual behaviour match.

I've worked with executives who's teams don't trust them. Usually, the problem isn't dramatic betrayal, it's chronic misalignment. They say they value work-life balance while sending emails at midnight. They claim feedback is welcome while becoming defensive when it's offered. They advocate for collaboration while making unilateral decisions. The words and the behaviour are out of coordination.

Daniel's rise through multiple Babylonian and Persian administrations demonstrates the opposite pattern. He was trusted with increasing responsibility precisely because his behaviour consistently aligned with his character. When he said he'd handle something, he handled it. When he gave advice, it was sound. When he claimed loyalty to the king, his actions demonstrated that loyalty (even while maintaining his ultimate loyalty to God). This coordination made him invaluable.

In difficult conversations:

Balanced Coordination means your body language supports rather than undermines your message. If you're having a hard conversation about performance, your posture is open rather than closed, your tone is firm but not harsh, your facial expression shows concern rather than judgment. Every part of you communicates the same message: "This conversation is necessary, and I'm approaching it with respect for you and commitment to improvement."

Without this coordination, the conversation fails regardless of your words. You might say all the right things, but if your body is broadcasting anxiety, impatience, or disdain, the other person responds to what you are, not what you're saying.

In family relationships:

Your children (and partners) develop trust when your stated values align with your lived behaviour. Can you tell children that honesty is important while lying to them about Santa Claus without creating confusion? Wait, maybe that's too controversial. Let me try again.

You can't tell teenagers to manage their screen time while you're constantly on your phone. You can't claim family dinners matter while scheduling meetings through dinner time. You can't say you value their emotions while dismissing their feelings as overreaction.

Lis Hartel's children learned about perseverance not from lectures about never giving up, but from watching their mother spend eight years coordinating every part of herself toward a goal that seemed impossible. Her words about persistence aligned with her lived reality of daily practice. That coordination taught more powerfully than any speech could.

In community leadership:

People follow leaders whose private character aligns with their public persona. When there's coordination between who you are behind closed doors and who you present publicly, trust develops naturally. When there's misalignment, when you're inspirational on stage but petty in private meetings, when you're generous publicly but stingy with your time, when you advocate for values you don't personally live, people sense the incongruence even if they can't name it.

The Physical Markers of Coordination

One of the most practical aspects of Balanced Coordination is learning to read your own body's signals. Your body tells you when you're coordinated and when you're not, if you learn to listen.

Tension patterns reveal misalignment:

Notice where you hold tension. Clenched jaw often indicates suppressed frustration or anger. Raised shoulders typically signal anxiety or stress. Tight lower back can indicate control issues or fear of letting go. Shallow breathing almost always accompanies emotional dysregulation.

These aren't just physical discomforts, they're information. They tell you that your body isn't aligned with what you're trying to project or accomplish. Lis had to become exquisitely sensitive to her body's signals because she couldn't afford to ignore them. Tension in her upper body would transmit down the reins to Jubilee. Imbalance in her seat would confuse him. She learned to scan her body constantly, releasing tension before it disrupted their coordination.

Daniel would have developed similar awareness through his prayer practice. Kneeling three times daily makes you aware of your body, how you're holding yourself, where you're tight, how your breath flows. This physical awareness supported his ability to maintain coordination in high-pressure political situations.

Breath is the bridge between mind and body:

Your breathing pattern reveals your internal state more reliably than almost anything else. Rapid, shallow breathing indicates stress. Held breath suggests tension or fear. Deep, slow breathing reflects calm or deliberate regulation. Long exhales activate your parasympathetic nervous system, creating physical calm that supports emotional composure.

Learning to regulate your breath is fundamental to Balanced Coordination. When Lis mounted Jubilee, one of the first things she did was breathe, consciously, deliberately, aligning her nervous system before asking her body to coordinate complex movements. When Daniel prayed three times daily, the physical act of kneeling and speaking prayers naturally regulated his breathing, creating the physiological foundation for mental and spiritual coordination.

Posture reflects intention:

Stand up right now. Slump your shoulders, let your head hang forward, collapse your chest. Notice how that feels. Now straighten your spine, lift your chest, roll your shoulders back. Feel the difference?

Posture isn't just about looking confident; it's about creating the physical structure that supports confident action. When your posture is aligned, your breathing improves, your mental clarity sharpens, and your emotional state stabilizes. This isn't mystical, it's biomechanical. Your physical structure supports or undermines everything else.

Horsemen know this intuitively. You can't ride effectively while slouching. Your seat needs structure to follow the horse's movement and communicate clearly. Similarly, you can't lead effectively while physically collapsed. Your body needs structure to support the coordination you're trying to achieve.

The Practice: Building Coordination Daily

So how do you develop Balanced Coordination? The same way Lis spent eight years preparing for eight minutes in the Olympic arena. The same way Daniel spent seventy years maintaining his identity in exile. Through daily, consistent practice that gradually aligns body, mind, and emotion.

Morning Coordination Practice (10-15 minutes):

Before you do anything else, before checking email, before coffee, before the day's demands hit you, spend a few minutes establishing coordination. Choose a physical practice that develops body awareness, yoga, Qi Gong, tai chi, dance, martial arts, or simply deliberate movement. The specific practice matters less than the intention behind it: you're training your ability to coordinate mind and body deliberately.

1. **Body scan:** Notice where you're holding tension. Don't judge it, just notice. Jaw? Shoulders? Lower back? Breath?

2. **Breath regulation:** Five minutes of deliberate breathing. Inhale for four counts, hold for four, exhale for six. The longer exhale activates your parasympathetic nervous system, creating physiological calm.

3. **Posture alignment:** Sitting or standing, align your spine. Feel your head balanced over your shoulders, your shoulders over your hips. Notice how this physical alignment affects your mental state.

4. **Intention setting:** What coordination do you want to practice today? Maybe it's keeping your body language open during a difficult conversation. Maybe it's maintaining calm breathing during a stressful presentation. Choose one specific aspect of coordination to focus on.

This isn't meditation, though meditation helps. This is coordination training. You're practicing the alignment of body, mind, and emotion before the day demands it from you.

Throughout the Day: The Coordination Check. Every few hours, pause for sixty seconds and ask yourself:

- What's my body doing right now?
- What's my emotional state?
- Do they match what I'm trying to accomplish?
- What needs to adjust?

This is what Daniel's three daily prayer times provided, regular checkpoints to realign body, mind, and spirit. You need regular moments of conscious realignment throughout the day.

Evening Integration Practice (10 minutes):

Before bed, review the day:

- When was I most coordinated today? What supported that?
- When did I lose coordination? What triggered it?
- What physical patterns did I notice? (Tension, breathing, posture)
- What do I want to practice tomorrow?

Lis would have done something similar after every training session with Jubilee. Not beating herself up for what didn't work, but noting what created coordination and what disrupted it. This reflection is how practice becomes progress.

When Coordination Breaks Down

Here's what no one tells you about the growing season: plants don't grow steadily upward. They grow in spurts. They plateau. Sometimes they look like they're dying when they're actually developing deeper roots. Progress isn't linear.

Lis didn't spend eight years in steady improvement. Some weeks she made progress. Some weeks she regressed. Some months she wondered if she'd ever ride at the level she once had. The growing season included frustration, setbacks, plateaus where nothing seemed to change despite daily practice.

This is normal. This is expected. This is part of the growing season.

When you notice coordination breaking down:

1. **Acknowledge it without judgment.** "I'm out of alignment right now." Not "I'm failing" or "I'll never get this." Just observation.

2. **Return to basics.** Breath. Posture. Present moment. You're not trying to fix everything, you're just reestablishing the foundation.

3. **Identify the source of misalignment.** Usually, it's one of three things:
   - Physical fatigue (your body is too tired to maintain coordination)
   - Emotional overwhelm (your feelings are too intense to regulate)
   - Mental distraction (your attention is scattered)

4. **Address the source directly.** If you're physically exhausted, you need rest, not more practice. If you're emotionally overwhelmed, you need to process those feelings, not suppress them. If you're mentally scattered, you need to simplify and focus, not add more complexity.

5. **Rebuild gradually.** Lis couldn't jump straight back to advanced dressage movements after a setback. She'd return to basics, walk, basic trot transitions, simple patterns. Rebuilding coordination from the foundation up. Daniel couldn't maintain perfect coordination every moment, but when he noticed misalignment, his daily prayer practice brought him back to centre.

The Integration Forward

Balanced Coordination is the growing season of the Communication Pillar, but it's not the final stage. When you practice coordination consistently over years, aligning body, mind, and emotion in daily life, something deeper becomes possible.

The coordination that requires conscious effort becomes automatic. The alignment you have to work to maintain becomes your natural state. The gap between intention and execution narrows until they're nearly simultaneous. This is when Balanced Coordination matures into Centred Transcendence, the subject of the next chapter.

Centred Transcendence isn't about being more coordinated. It's about being so deeply coordinated that your awareness can expand beyond yourself. When you're not constantly monitoring and managing your own internal alignment, your attention becomes available for something more: the ability to remain centred regardless of external circumstances, to maintain inner stillness even during activity, to access a state of grounded presence that others can rely on absolutely.

But you can't skip to transcendence. You earn it through the growing season of coordination. Through years of daily practice aligning your pieces. Through thousands of moments choosing congruence over convenience.

Lis Hartel earned her Olympic silver through eight years of coordination practice. Daniel earned his unshakeable faith through seventy years of daily alignment. Neither could have accessed what they demonstrated in their dramatic moments without the undramatic accumulation of coordinated practice that preceded them.

The same is true for you. The centred presence you'll develop in Chapter 10 (Centred Transcendence) will grow from the coordinated practice you establish now, in Chapter 7. The growing season is preparing you for the harvest.

But first, you have to tend the plant.

The Daily Choice

Every morning, Lis Hartel faced a choice: spend three hours in painful physical therapy or accept that she'd never ride again. The choice wasn't dramatic. It was quiet, daily, unglamorous. But it was the choice that made everything else possible.

Every morning, afternoon, and evening, Daniel faced a choice: pray toward Jerusalem or assimilate more fully into Babylonian culture. The choice wasn't life-or-death (except when it was). Most days, it was just the quiet decision to maintain coordination between his beliefs and his behaviour.

You face the same choice every day. Multiple times each day. Will you take the sixty seconds to notice when you're out of alignment and correct it? Will you practice the morning coordination routine even when you're tired? Will you monitor whether your body language matches your words during that difficult conversation?

These choices don't feel significant in the moment. They're not dramatic. No one's watching. No one will know if you skip a day, or a week, or a month.

But these daily, undramatic choices are what build coordination. They're the growing season. And the harvest, the moments when your coordination holds under pressure, when your alignment creates breakthrough, when your embodied practice produces extraordinary results, comes only after the growing season has been faithfully tended.

Lis Hartel spent eight years in the growing season so she could experience eight minutes of harvest in Helsinki. Daniel spent seventy years in the growing season so his faith could hold through the lions' den. The ratio isn't encouraging from an efficiency standpoint. But it's honest about what coordination requires.

Most of your life will be growing season. Daily practice. Incremental progress. Setbacks and plateaus. This is normal. This is the process. This is how coordination is built.

The dramatic moments, the Olympic arena, the lions' den, the high-stakes presentation, the crisis that tests everything you are, these are brief. They reveal the coordination you've built during all the undramatic moments that preceded them.

So tend your growing season. Show up daily. Practice alignment between body, mind, and emotion. Notice when you drift out of coordination and gently guide yourself back. Trust that beneath the surface, roots are deepening, strength is building, integration is happening.

The horse doesn't follow your intentions. They follow your coordination. The team doesn't trust your words. They trust the alignment between your words and your being. The child doesn't learn from your lectures. They learn from watching your life coordinate with your values.

Balanced Coordination isn't glamorous. But it's real. And it works. And it's worth the daily practice required to develop it.

Lis Hartel proved it on Jubilee's back in Helsinki. Daniel proved it through seven decades in Babylon. And every day in arenas, boardrooms, and living rooms around the world, people prove it again: when you align every part of yourself toward your purpose, remarkable things become possible.

Not because you're extraordinary. But because coordination itself is extraordinary. And it's available to anyone willing to tend their growing season with patient, persistent care.

"The horse will teach you, if you'll listen."

- Ray Hunt

CHAPTER 8

DETERMINED UNDERSTANDING

"The measure of intelligence is the ability to change."

\- Albert Einstein

The pre-dawn darkness hung heavy over Quinn's Post on the morning of May 12, 1915. Brigadier General Harry Chauvel moved quietly through the maze of trenches, checking on his men as he had done every morning since arriving at Gallipoli. The position was a death trap. Open to Turkish observation on two sides, these four advanced posts at the top of Monash Valley formed the linchpin of the entire ANZAC defense. Lose Quinn's Post, and the whole line would collapse.

Chauvel paused at a firing step where a young trooper from Queensland kept watch. The boy couldn't have been more than nineteen, his face gaunt from weeks of constant vigilance, hands trembling slightly as they gripped his rifle. But his eyes were sharp, focused on the Turkish trenches barely twenty meters away.

"How long have you been up here, son?" Chauvel asked quietly.

"Since midnight, sir. They've been moving around over there. Can hear them digging."

Chauvel nodded, scanning the enemy positions himself. He could hear it too.

The scrape of shovels against rock. Voices carrying across the narrow gap between the lines. The Turks were planning something. They always were. Every day brought a new assault, a new attempt to drive the Australians back into the sea.

"Get yourself some rest when your relief comes," Chauvel said. "You've done well."

The trooper glanced at him, surprised that a general would take time to speak to a private soldier. But that was how Chauvel led. He knew every commander along this line. He knew which posts had the best fields of fire, which trenches flooded when it rained, where the snipers had the clearest shots. He knew because he walked these trenches every single day, often multiple times. Not to inspect. To understand.

As he moved on, he found Major Hugh Quinn organizing his company's defenses. Quinn was one of his best officers, strong, brave, quick-thinking. The kind of man who led from the front, who his soldiers would follow anywhere.

"Morning, Harry," Quinn greeted him. Officers and men alike had taken to calling him by his first name, a familiarity he permitted because it built trust. "They're up to something. I can feel it."

"I know. Keep the men alert, but make sure they rest in shifts. We need them sharp when it comes."

This was the balancing act Chauvel performed every day. Maintaining vigilance without exhausting his men. Holding positions that seemed impossible to defend. Making decisions that could save lives or waste them, and never quite knowing which until after the fact.

Over the following weeks, Chauvel established patterns that saved countless lives. He reorganized the defence, appointing permanent commanders for each post rather than rotating them through unfamiliar positions. He formed special sniper groups who gradually suppressed the Turkish marksmen, making it safe for mule trains to move up Monash Valley. When the inevitable assaults came, as they did on May 19th when the Turks launched a massive attack along the entire line, his preparations held.

But it was what happened after these battles that revealed something deeper about Chauvel's leadership. Following the massive Turkish assault of May 19th, where thousands of Ottoman soldiers were killed in futile charges against prepared positions, Chauvel spent days walking the battlefield. Not celebrating the victory. Not congratulating himself on his defensive arrangements. Walking among the Turkish dead, many of them boys barely old enough to shave, understanding the terrible cost of this war on both sides.

When one of his officers asked why he was spending so much time studying the enemy casualties, Chauvel replied simply: "Because I need to understand them. What drove them forward? What made them so brave? What failures in their leadership put them in this position? If I'm going to fight them effectively, I have to know more than how to kill them. I have to understand them."

Later, when Chauvel commanded the Desert Mounted Corps across Sinai and Palestine, this pattern continued. After the Battle of Romani, where his forces achieved the first decisive British victory of the war, he visited each brigade personally to congratulate them. Not a perfunctory inspection, but genuine conversations about what had worked, what had been difficult, what they needed next time. He didn't assume that victory meant he'd understood everything. He treated success as an opportunity to deepen his knowledge.

When battles didn't go as planned, as at the Second Battle of the Jordan where he was forced to withdraw despite initial success, Chauvel studied those failures even more carefully. He filed detailed reports analysing what had gone wrong. Not to excuse himself or blame others, but to understand. What had he missed in his assessment? Where had his assumptions proven false? What could he learn that would help him avoid similar failures in the future?

Perhaps most telling was his approach to the famous charge at Beersheba. Facing a desperate situation where his mounted troops would perish without water, Chauvel authorized what many considered a suicidal cavalry charge against entrenched Turkish positions. But he didn't order it blindly. He spent hours studying the ground, understanding the Turkish defensive positions, calculating the risks. He talked with his brigade commanders, listening to their assessments, weighing their concerns. And when he finally gave the order, it was because he understood, as clearly as any human could, exactly what he was asking his men to do and why it might succeed.

It did succeed. The 4th Light Horse Brigade's charge at Beersheba became one of history's great cavalry actions. But Chauvel didn't celebrate it as proof of his tactical brilliance. He spent the following days understanding why it had worked, what factors had aligned to make success possible, so he would know when such tactics might work again and, more importantly, when they wouldn't.

This was what made Chauvel extraordinary. Not his tactical skill, though that was considerable. Not his personal courage, though he had plenty of that. What set him apart was his relentless determination to understand. To see clearly. To resist the human temptation to settle for comfortable explanations or convenient assumptions. To stay curious even when certainty would have been easier.

From Gentility to Understanding

Determined Understanding is what grows when Powerful Gentility matures. In Chapter Five, we explored how true strength expresses itself through deliberate softness, how the most effective leadership often comes not from force but from calm, grounded presence. We learned to approach with patience, to guide with invitation rather than demand, to create environments where others can thrive.

That was the planted seed. Powerful Gentility is where service begins. But a seed planted must grow. And growth requires something more than initial gentleness. It requires the determination to understand truly, deeply, persistently. Even when understanding is uncomfortable. Even when easier answers present themselves. Even when the truth you discover contradicts your initial assumptions.

This is the growing season of the Service pillar. Gentleness without understanding can become enabling. Patience without insight can become passivity. Support without comprehension can become ineffective. The gentle touch that planted the seed must mature into something more robust: the persevering clarity that stays with complexity until real understanding emerges.

Chauvel demonstrated this progression throughout his military career. His gentility with his men, his concern for their welfare, his servant leadership approach, all of these were expressions of Powerful Gentility. But what made him truly exceptional was how that gentleness deepened into determined pursuit of understanding. He didn't just care about his men. He worked relentlessly to understand them, understand the enemy, understand the terrain, understand the situation. And that understanding informed every decision he made.

In working with horses, we see this same pattern. The gentle approach gets you started. The horse learns you're safe, learns you won't hurt them, begins to trust. That's Powerful Gentility at work. But if you stop there, you limit what's possible. To develop a real partnership, to help the horse reach their potential, to address problems that arise, you need more than gentleness. You need determined understanding.

What does that look like in the arena? It means when a horse resists, you don't immediately assume they're being stubborn. You pause. You observe. You wonder. Is this pain? Fear? Confusion? Justified resistance to poor communication from you? Each of these requires a completely different response, and only understanding will tell you which.

It means staying curious long enough to see patterns. The horse that pins their ears might be protective of their space. Or they might be responding to discomfort in their back. Or they might have learned that pinning ears makes people leave them alone, a strategy that once kept them safe. Same behaviour, completely different meanings, requiring completely different approaches. Determined Understanding means you don't settle for the first explanation that occurs to you.

It means being willing to question your own assumptions. Maybe the horse isn't "disrespectful." Maybe you're asking for something they don't physically understand yet. Maybe your timing is off. Maybe your body language is sending mixed signals. Determined Understanding requires the humility to look first at yourself, to wonder if the problem might be in your perception rather than in the horse.

And it means persisting through frustration. Understanding doesn't always come quickly. Sometimes you have to try multiple approaches, observe carefully, consult with others, revisit your assumptions again and again before clarity emerges. This is where determination comes in. The commitment to keep seeking understanding even when it would be easier to give up, to settle for a superficial explanation, to blame the horse and move on.

The Man Who Demanded Truth

Centuries before Chauvel walked the trenches at Gallipoli, another man demonstrated this same quality of Determined Understanding in a radically different context. His name was Job, and his story has echoed through millennia precisely because of how he pursued understanding in the face of inexplicable suffering.

Job was, by all accounts, a good man. Scripture describes him as "blameless and upright," someone who feared God and turned away from evil. He had wealth, family, position, respect. Everything a person of his time could want. And then, in a series of catastrophic events, he lost it all. His children died. His wealth vanished. His health failed. He found himself sitting in the dust, scraping his sores with broken pottery, wondering what had happened to his life.

His friends came to comfort him. And they did what friends often do in such situations: they tried to make sense of his suffering. They offered explanations. Theories. Theological frameworks that would make Job's disasters understandable, manageable, fixable. "You must have sinned," they said. "This is divine punishment. Confess your secret transgressions and God will restore you."

It was a tidy explanation. A clear cause-and-effect relationship. Suffering equals punishment. Punishment means sin. Therefore, Job must have sinned. Simple. Clean. Wrong.

And Job knew it was wrong. This is what makes his story so remarkable. He could have accepted his friends' explanation. It would have been easier. It would have given him something concrete to do, some path toward restoration. Confess. Repent. Fix the problem. Move forward.

But Job refused. He refused because he clearly understood his own integrity. He knew he hadn't committed the kind of sins his friends were suggesting. He knew the simple cause-and-effect framework they were offering didn't match the reality of his situation. And he was determined to hold onto that understanding, even when everyone around him was telling him to let it go.

"Though he slay me, yet will I trust in him," Job declared. "Even so, I will defend my own ways before Him." This wasn't arrogance. This was clarity. Job understood something true about himself and about God, and he refused to pretend otherwise just because the truth was uncomfortable.

For thirty-seven chapters, Job held this position. His friends kept offering their explanations. Job kept rejecting them. Not because he had all the answers, he didn't. But because he clearly understood that their answers were wrong. He would rather live with the discomfort of not knowing than accept a false understanding just to ease his pain.

This is Determined Understanding in its purest form. The willingness to stay with complexity. The courage to reject easy answers. The clarity to distinguish between what you genuinely understand and what you're being pressured to accept. The determination to keep pursuing truth even when truth is elusive and the cost of that pursuit is isolation from those who think they're helping you.

Like Chauvel studying the battlefield, trying to understand the enemy even after victory, Job insisted on understanding his situation truly rather than accepting comfortable falsehoods. Like Chauvel questioning his own assumptions after setbacks, Job examined his own life with brutal honesty, maintaining his clarity about his integrity while remaining open to whatever truth God might reveal.

And in the end, God confirmed that Job had spoken what was right, while his friends had not. Job's determined pursuit of understanding, his refusal to settle for false clarity, his willingness to live with uncomfortable questions rather than comfortable lies, all of this was vindicated. When God finally spoke, Job didn't receive a neat explanation for the cosmic reasons behind his suffering. Instead, he achieved something deeper: a personal encounter with divine wisdom that transcended all prior human understanding.

"My ears had heard of you," Job confessed, "but now my eyes have seen you." This is the harvest of Determined Understanding. Not always the specific answers you sought, but a depth of comprehension that wouldn't have been possible without the persistent pursuit of truth.

Both Chauvel and Job show us that Determined Understanding isn't about knowing everything. It's about persistently holding onto core truths while remaining honestly uncertain about what you don't yet comprehend. It's about distinguishing between genuine insight and convenient explanation. It's about staying curious long enough for real understanding to emerge, even when that takes longer and costs more than you expected.

What Letty Taught Me

I learned a lot about Determined Understanding from a mare we call Letty. She came to us a number of years ago, after being passed in at auction. I rode her a bit after we got her home, cut some cows on her also. She could handle herself, but I felt that the process of making up for all of the training time that she had missed out on was not worth the effort, in comparison to breeding some foals out of her.

She was due to foal in October, so we brought her home to keep an eye on her, and give her a bit of extra feed in the lead up to the birth. One day, not long after we brought her back, I took her some feed and noticed that she had some unusual swelling around the lymph nodes at the top of her neck. My immediate thought was, "Is it Strangles, or some other infectious disease?"

A quick query to Dr Google confirmed to me that it wasn't Strangles, but most likely just a little pregnancy-related fluid. When I checked her the next morning, the swelling seemed to have eased, so I was happy with my diagnosis. But something kept nagging at me. Was I understanding this correctly? Or was I accepting the first explanation that made me feel better?

We kept monitoring her, feeding her each evening, checking her condition. About a week after the initial swelling was noticed, I went to check her earlier than usual. She still seemed bright and alert as I approached, but I noticed her jowls were quite swollen. As I got closer, I could see some discharge high up, under her jaw.

Wanting a closer look, I took her up to the wash-bay. As I sprayed the wound, large pieces of skin fell away. When I had removed the dead tissue, an ugly wound about the size of a large tomato was visible. My easy explanation, my comfortable diagnosis, my assumption that everything was fine, all of it fell away like that dead tissue. I had failed to understand what was really happening.

We called the vet. After inspecting the wound and taking some x-rays, the vet said that she believed the cause of the injury was a rotten tooth that would have to come out. But, she said that the best option would be to leave it in there, given how close she was to foaling, rather than put her through additional trauma. That it would be better to attempt to control the infection, and deal with the tooth issue about six weeks after the birth.

So it began. Every day we would cut the bandage off, spray the wound with water to remove whatever discharge was there, and replace the bandage again. Morning and night she would receive oral antibiotics in her feed to control the infection. The wound reduced in size from about four inches across to a little over an inch across within a week.

But here's what struck me most. Through all of this, through the pain that must have been excruciating, through the daily treatment that must have been frightening and uncomfortable, Letty never lost sight of what mattered most to her: the foal growing inside her.

Despite her pain, she never stopped eating. She never lost condition. She never started a fight about the treatment she was getting. And this is significant, because when she is not pregnant, when she doesn't have a foal at foot, she can be the most obnoxious, belligerent animal to deal with. Normally to drench her is a major mission, but during this period she willingly accepted numerous pastes and potions in her mouth.

While we were treating her, she would have one eye on the foal after it was born. If it wandered off, she would call it back to her. Looking back through the course of this whole episode, I can see how her sole focus was the foal, even before it was born. She clearly understood what mattered, and she controlled herself to ensure all of her goals were met.

The foal was a month old before the tooth flared up again. I suspect that what had happened was that the wound had finally closed over, trapping the infection inside her head. Her pain was extreme. The swelling was so severe that the hair fell out along the bottom of her jaws. That first day of the new flare up, the temperature of skin around her face, and particularly the top of her head, around her brain, was like she was on fire. The pain must have been intolerable.

But despite the pain, despite all of the inconvenience she faced, she never lost sight of her foal. This is what Letty taught me about Determined Understanding: it's not about controlling the situation to make the outcome suit your goals. It's about controlling yourself to ensure all of your goals are met. For her, it was all about whatever was best for her baby.

But Letty's lesson went deeper than I first understood. She wasn't just being gentle, she was serving a purpose greater than her own comfort. Every moment of compliance, every acceptance of painful treatment, every instance of patience with our clumsy care, all of it was service. Service to her foal's wellbeing. Service to the life growing inside her and then depending on her.

She demonstrated something I'm still learning, that Determined Understanding requires you to subordinate your immediate desires to a larger purpose. Not in a way that destroys you, Letty never stopped eating, never gave in to her pain. But she showed me, by the way she handled it, a different way forward. A way by which I could transform my own relationship with discomfort.

When you're serving something you love, pain becomes bearable. Inconvenience becomes acceptable. Patience becomes possible.

Powerful Gentility plants the seed. Determined Understanding is the growth that follows. The understanding that your strength exists not just for your benefit, but for the benefit of those who depend on you. That your capacity to endure, to remain steady, to stay gentle under pressure, all of it can be placed in service of something larger than yourself.

Three Teachers, One Lesson

Chauvel, Job, and Letty seem to have nothing in common. A military commander in the trenches of Gallipoli. An ancient patriarch suffering unexplainable loss. A pregnant mare fighting infection. Three different contexts, three different challenges, three different outcomes.

But they all demonstrate the same essential quality: Determined Understanding in the service of something greater than themselves.

155

Chauvel served his men. His relentless pursuit of understanding, studying battlefields, walking trenches, questioning assumptions, all of it was in service of keeping his soldiers alive and using them effectively. He didn't seek understanding for its own sake or to prove his own intelligence. He sought it because lives depended on the quality of his comprehension.

Job served truth. His refusal to accept false explanations, his determination to maintain clarity about his own integrity, his willingness to live with uncomfortable uncertainty, all of it was in service of preserving genuine understanding over comfortable fiction. He didn't pursue truth to win arguments or prove his friends wrong. He pursued it because truth mattered more than comfort.

Letty served her foal. Her willingness to endure pain, accept treatment, control her typically difficult behaviour, all of it was in service of her baby's welfare. She didn't become compliant because we'd finally trained her properly. She became compliant because she clearly understood what mattered most and was determined to serve that purpose.

This is what Determined Understanding looks like in practice: clarity about what you're serving, combined with the determination to pursue genuine comprehension even when it's difficult, uncomfortable, or costly. It's not understanding for understanding's sake. It's understanding in service of something that matters.

What This Looks Like in the Arena

When working with horses, this is how we see the same pattern play out. The gentle approach gets you started, the horse learns you're safe to be around, learns you won't hurt them, begins to trust. That's Powerful Gentility at work. But if you stop there, you limit what's possible. To develop a real partnership, to help the horse reach their potential, to address problems that arise, you need more than gentleness. You need determined understanding.

What does that look like practically?

When Resistance Appears

A horse refuses to load in a trailer for instance. Your first instinct might be to assume they're being stubborn or difficult. And try to push them through it, try to force them on. But Determined Understanding means you pause. You observe. You wonder.

Is this fear? Can they see out? Some trailers seem designed more like claustrophobic torture chambers than the relaxing cruise liner we imagine them to be. Is the problem past trauma? Did this horse have a bad experience in a trailer before? Or is the problem physical discomfort? Does the floor feel slippery, the ramp too steep, the space too tight for them to balance comfortably? Is the roof too low?

Or is it about you? Are you broadcasting anxiety about the loading process? Are you rushing because of some human timeline? Is your body language unclear, or overly aggressive? Have you thought about what you're asking? Have you looked at the float through the eyes of the horse? Have you made loading such a big deal that the horse now associates it with tension?

Each of these possibilities requires a different approach. If you start with the first thing that pops into your head and insist on making that work, if settle on the first explanation for the problem that occurs to you, you'll likely apply exactly the wrong solution. Determined Understanding means staying curious long enough to discover what's actually happening.

Recognizing Patterns

A horse that pins their ears every time you approach from the left side. Once might be coincidence. Twice might be chance. But consistent behaviour across multiple sessions? That's communication. What are they saying? Is it a threat, an attempt at domination. Or are they feeling threatened? Look for the signs that they show as you are working with them.

This is a fundamental part of how I work with horses, and most of the top horsemen that I have trained under speak about the importance of this. I guess it is one of those things that becomes so ingrained in your understanding, your consideration of how the horse works and what he does that I haven't spoken of it before this.

It might be that they feel the need to protect their space on that particular side. Horses, like people, are left-handed or right-handed. On one side, their dominant side, they will be open accepting. This is the side that if they feel threatened, they will be able to more easily defend themselves. This is the side that they prefer to kick, strike or bite from when threatened.

The other side, their weaker side, they will try to protect. They will be less likely to open this side to you when lunging. They might find it difficult to pick up the correct lead on this side. This may be the side on which they are more easily triggered to start bucking when feeling tight.

Their propensity to use any of these defence mechanisms, increases with the level of threat that they feel from whatever is attacking them, tempered by the level of acceptance or submission they feel towards the intruder in their space.

Alternatively, they may have discomfort in their left shoulder or ribcage. Maybe a previous owner or handler would normally approach them from that side to do something unpleasant, to give injections, or maybe was rough handling them. Same behaviour, completely different meanings, requiring different approaches.

Determined Understanding means you don't settle for the first explanation. You track patterns. You pay attention across sessions. You note what makes the behaviour better or worse. You consult with others who might see what you're missing. You let understanding emerge from accumulated observation rather than jumping to conclusions from isolated incidents.

Questioning Your Own Assumptions

A young horse struggles with a simple manoeuvre you've taught dozens of others successfully. The easy explanation: this horse is slow to learn, resistant, maybe not very bright.

But Determined Understanding requires humility. Before concluding the horse has a problem, check yourself. Is your timing off today? Are you asking for something their body isn't ready to do yet? Is your body language sending mixed signals? Are you assuming they understand something that actually needs to be broken down into smaller steps?

The biggest obstacle to understanding is often our own certainty. We think we already know what's happening, so we stop looking for evidence that might contradict our assumptions. Determined Understanding means looking at yourself first, wondering if the problem might be in your perception rather than in the horse.

Persisting Through Frustration

Understanding doesn't always come quickly. Sometimes you have to try multiple approaches, all of which fail, before clarity emerges. The horse that won't pick up the right lead. The mare that kicks at other horses in the arena. The gelding that won't stand for mounting. Each problem has a cause, but finding it requires patience.

This is where determination comes in. The commitment to keep seeking understanding even when it would be easier to label the horse as "difficult," to accept a surface-level explanation, to give up and move on. It's the discipline to revisit your assumptions again and again, to consult with vets or trainers who might see what you're missing, to stay curious about what this horse is trying to tell you.

Letty helped me to see this. It would have been easy to treat her as a commodity, as just a broodmare, to leave her out in the paddock to foal. But determination to care led to trying to truly understand what was happening, even after the initial improvement, even when the problem seemed solved, that determination meant dealing with the deeper issue that needed addressing.

If I'd stopped pursuing understanding after the wound began to heal, the tooth infection would have killed her, and her baby.

What This Looks Like Outside the Arena

The principles of Determined Understanding extend far beyond horsemanship into every area of leadership and relationship.

In Leadership

A team member's performance declines. The surface explanation: they've become lazy or unmotivated. But Determined Understanding means you dig deeper before acting on that assumption.

Are they dealing with personal struggles you don't know about? Have you been unclear about expectations? Did something change in the team dynamic that's affecting their work? Are they actually performing poorly, or have your standards shifted without you communicating that clearly?

Like Chauvel walking the trenches to understand his men's actual conditions rather than relying on reports, effective leaders pursue understanding before jumping to solutions. They stay curious about the real causes of problems. They question their own assumptions before questioning their people's commitment.

In Parenting

Your teenager becomes withdrawn, spending more time alone in their room. The easy explanation: typical teenage rebellion, pulling away from parents, nothing to worry about.

But Determined Understanding means you stay curious. Is this normal development or something more concerning? Are they dealing with social struggles at school? Mental health challenges they don't know how to articulate? Pressure from activities or academics that's overwhelming them?

You don't immediately assume the worst, but you also don't dismiss what you're seeing just because it makes you uncomfortable. You observe patterns. You create safe opportunities for conversation. You question whether your own behaviour might be contributing to their withdrawal. You persist in trying to understand even when they're not making it easy.

In Business

A product launch fails to meet projections. The immediate response might be to blame marketing, the sales team, or market conditions. But Determined Understanding means examining the failure thoroughly before making changes.

Was the product itself flawed? Was the market research accurate but the execution poor? Did timing play a role? Were internal communication problems creating disconnects between teams? Was the failure really a failure, or did expectations need adjusting?

Like Chauvel studying his failures at the Second Battle of the Jordan, not to excuse himself but to genuinely understand what went wrong, business leaders who practice Determined Understanding investigate problems deeply. They look for root causes, not convenient scapegoats. They're willing to discover that their own decisions contributed to the problem.

In Relationships

Your partner becomes distant or irritable. The quick assumption: they're upset with you, or maybe just in a bad mood. But Determined Understanding means staying curious rather than reactive.

What's actually happening? Are they stressed about work? Dealing with family issues they haven't fully shared? Processing something difficult that has nothing to do with you? Or yes, maybe they are upset with you, but about what specifically, and why?

Instead of defending yourself or withdrawing in response, you maintain curiosity. You ask questions. You listen for understanding rather than to defend your position. You question whether you're interpreting their behaviour accurately or projecting your own insecurities onto the situation.

Like Job refusing to accept his friends' false explanations even though accepting them would have been easier, you commit to understanding what's true rather than what's comfortable. Even when that truth reveals something difficult about yourself or the relationship.

Cultivating Determined Understanding

Cultivating, preparing soil, tending growth, is exactly what we must do with Determined Understanding. How do you move from Powerful Gentility's planted seed to mature growth? Communication Pathologist and Neuroscientist, Dr. Caroline Leaf's 'thought tree' concept offers a helpful framework that shows how to develop this quality.

In her 2021 book, "Cleaning Up Your Mental Mess", Dr Leaf explains the natural progression of mental growth, detailing how it is possible to move from Powerful Gentility's planted seed to Determined Understanding's mature growth.

Picturing the thought tree creates an image of a thought. The branches and the leaves represent our conscious thinking and our memories, the tree trunk represents our subconscious, and the roots of the tree represent our nonconsciousness. The nonconscious level is working 24/7, whether we are awake or asleep, it is still working away all the time, trying to help us make sense of our world.

Just like an actual tree, the thought tree comes from a seed, a single thought. Although it is not the common understanding, this same concept fits what Jesus was speaking about when he said, "'The kingdom of heaven is like a mustard seed, which a man took and planted in his field. Although it is the smallest of all seeds, yet when it grows, it is larger than the garden plants and becomes a tree, so that the birds of the air come and nest in its branches."

Like that mustard seed, the thought forms roots, sprouts out of the ground, grows and changes over time. Once a thought is planted, every conversation you have, what you hear, or read; each thing encourages the roots to grow and shoots to develop. And the more that you think about something, the more that little thought plant develops.

If we don't think about it the little tree will die, and conversely when we give it our full attention, that little tree can grow into a giant of the forest. A nagging worry, continually watered by our thinking, can become a big tree which can dominate and influence our behaviour. This is how thoughts good or bad develop.

Remember to Resist the First Explanation

Our conscious minds crave closure. When something happens that questions our understanding, at the conscious level we want to solve it quickly and move on. But the first explanation that occurs to you is rarely the complete picture. Train yourself to pause. "That might be true," you can think. "But what else might be happening here? What am I not seeing? What assumptions am I making?"

Remember the trailer loading example, they might have learned that refusing to load gets them out of work. Or they might associate the trailer with some traumatic past experience. The trailer might look like a trap, or smell a like they don't know what. Or they might be picking up on your anxiety about loading them. Each explanation suggests a different approach. If you settle on the first explanation that occurs to you, you could land on the wrong solution.

Keep Looking for Patterns Over Time

Single incidents can mislead you. A single memory could be completely out of context. But patterns over time can reveal the truth. They can give us that "Aha" moment. Chauvel didn't make strategic decisions based on one battle. He studied multiple engagements, looking for what consistently worked and what consistently failed. Job didn't base his understanding of God on one experience of suffering. He drew on a lifetime of relationship and knowledge.

With horses, this means paying attention across sessions. The horse that may rear or throw its head back might just be having a bad day. The horse that consistently pins their ears or reacts negatively in the same situation is telling you something important. Keep note of their actions and reactions throughout every interaction that you have with them. Track patterns. Let understanding emerge from accumulated observation rather than jumping to conclusions from isolated incidents.

Always Question Your Own Assumptions

The biggest obstacle to our understanding is often our own certainty. We think we already know what's happening, so we stop looking for evidence that might contradict our assumptions. Determined Understanding requires the humility to question yourself first.

Is the horse really being disrespectful? Or are you asking for something they don't understand? Is your employee really unmotivated? Or have you failed to provide clear direction? Is your partner really being difficult? Or are you projecting your own stress onto them?

This doesn't mean you're always wrong. Sometimes the horse is being disrespectful, the employee is unmotivated, the partner is being difficult. But you have to check your own contribution to the problem before you can understand the situation clearly.

Don't Let Frustration Kill your Curiosity

Understanding doesn't always come quickly. Sometimes you have to try multiple approaches, all of which fail, before clarity emerges. This is where determination comes in. The commitment to keep seeking understanding even when it would be easier to give up, to label the horse as "difficult," to blame the person as "impossible," to accept surface-level explanations rather than digging deeper.

If I'd stopped pursuing understanding after the wound began to heal, the tooth infection probably would have killed her. It is important not to let frustration kill your curiosity. To paraphrase Dr Leaf, if you're stuck (if your curiosity wanes) remember these things to get curious:

- There is nothing new in life, keep looking for the answer.
- Keep experimenting – explore, test, analyse and pivot if it doesn't work.
- Keep learning, listening and asking.
- Be open to suggestions.
- Don't think that you have to be the best to try something.
- Ask difficult questions.

(Leaf 2021, 228-229)

Know What You're Serving and Why

Determined Understanding requires a purpose larger than your curiosity. Chauvel pursued understanding to serve his men. Job pursued truth to serve his integrity and his relationship with God. Letty endured treatment to serve her foal. What are you serving?

Dr Leaf uses a pathway to process challenging problems called the Neurocycle of Brain-Building, and we can use this same pathway to determinedly transform our understanding from an intellectual exercise into a meaningful practice.

1. *Gather.* Gather as much information as you can about the subject. But process it in bite sized chunks. You might use books, YouTube, podcasts, or notes at clinics. Read or listen for a minute or two then go to 2.

2. *Reflect.* Ask yourself how you could the apply the information to the situation or problem before you. Reread or listen to the information again. Discuss with, or explain to, yourself what it means.

3. *Write.* Write down the key points of what you've learnt, and develop your plan for dealing with the situation or problem in a meaningful way moving forward.

4. *Recheck.* Take the time to actively review the plan. Recheck what you have written. Does it make sense, and did you get the true sense of what the original information was saying?

5. *Active Reach.* Teach what you've learnt. It might be to a horse, your dog, a group of colleagues. Put the plan into action train the team. Be the leader.

(Leaf 2021, 229-233)

When your working with horses, you're not trying to understand the horse just to prove you're a good trainer. You're trying to understand them so you can serve their wellbeing and development. You're not trying to understand your team just to manage them better. You're trying to understand them so you can help them to thrive, or perhaps just to survive.

Dr. Leaf herself demonstrated this process under the most difficult circumstances imaginable. She recounts a story in her book when her son was attacked while studying in Rome. He was speaking to her on the phone the night of the attack, talking to her in Washington, DC, when the phone went dead. Every parent's worst nightmare!

But as she explains in her book, falling into the trap created by her fears would have been worse than useless. It would have been counterproductive to follow that path. But through strength of will, she was able to proactively serve her son, her family and ultimately her own well-being, by working through the 5 steps of the Neurocycle.

It sounds almost superhuman, but she was able to master self-management that night, and when I think about it, how empowering it would be to be able to apply these skills to any traumatic experience we faced inside, or outside the arena.

The process that she used to master her self-management was as follows:

> She began by using breathing to prepare herself, to calm her mind. In this instance, she specifically used box breathing. In for 4 counts, hold for 4 counts, out for 4 counts, and hold for 4 counts. She repeated this 4 times to gain control over her mind.
>
> Then she moved onto the 5 steps program:
>
> 1. *Gather.* She gathered awareness of her racing thoughts.
>
> 2. *Reflect.* She reflected on how she was losing control and starting to let negative emotions dictate what she was doing.
>
> 3. *Write.* She wrote down the negative thoughts that were causing her to freeze up.
>
> 4. *Recheck.* She reconceptualised the toxic thoughts she had about this situation that was totally out of her control. Changing, "Is he dead", into "He will live and not die", and repeating this statement over and over as she calmed her breathing.
>
> 5. *Active Reach.* She actively did what she could. Calling her husband, and a friend with global connections to begin the search for her son.

Her son was ultimately found in a hospital emergency ward in Rome, and eventually recovered from the attack.

(Leaf 2021, 237-240)

This scenario begs the question, the next time you were faced with a traumatic event could you use a similar course of action. Or better yet, will you use the 5-step formula to discover how to grow Determined Understanding with your horse. Or perhaps your partner, your children or your business associates.

When you're clear about who or what you're serving, the determination to understand becomes easier. Discomfort is bearable when you know it's in service of something that matters. Frustration is manageable when you're pursuing understanding for a purpose beyond yourself.

The Growing Season

Powerful Gentility was the seed. That gentle, grounded approach that creates safety and invites trust. That strength deliberately moderated to serve others' growth. That was where we began, and it was necessary.

But seeds must grow. And growth requires more than the qualities that enabled planting. Determined Understanding is the growing season. The time when gentleness deepens into committed pursuit of truth. When patience evolves into persevering clarity. When service becomes not just an attitude but a practice sustained through difficulty.

This is harder than planting. Planting can be done in a moment of insight, a decision to approach differently, a commitment to be gentle. Growing takes time. It requires daily attention. It demands that you show up consistently even when you don't feel like it, that you keep pursuing understanding even when clarity is elusive, that you maintain your service even when no one is watching or appreciating your effort.

But this is where real transformation happens. Not in the moment you decide to be gentle, but in the months and years of determined effort to understand truly. Not in the initial commitment to serve, but in the sustained practice of subordinating your immediate comfort to larger purposes.

Chauvel's greatness wasn't revealed in a single battle or decision. It was built through years of daily practice, walking trenches, studying battlefields, questioning assumptions, staying curious about what he didn't yet understand. Job's integrity wasn't demonstrated in one moment of faith.

It was sustained through months of suffering, persistent rejection of false explanations, determined maintenance of clarity even when everyone told him to let it go. Letty's service to her foal wasn't a one-time choice. It was practiced every day, every treatment, every moment she controlled her typical difficult behaviour in service of her baby.

And eventually, after sufficient time in this growing season, the plant will be ready for pruning. Determined Understanding will mature into something even more refined: the wisdom to know what must be released, what must be deconstructed, what must be allowed to die so that new growth can emerge. That's Creative Destruction, the harvest that comes after the growing season. But we're not there yet.

For now, focus on the growth. Gentle strength is maturing into determined understanding. Patience is deepening into persevering clarity. Service is becoming more than an attitude; it's becoming a daily practice. The seed is growing. Tend it well.

"What will it be for you? What purpose is worthy of your strength? What relationship deserves your gentleness? What vision requires your service?"

- The Horseman's Way

PART IV

PRUNING THE TREE

CHAPTER 9

PEACEFUL DIRECTEDNESS

For what the horse does under compulsion... is done without understanding; and there is no beauty in it either, any more than one should whip and spur a dancer."

- Xenophon, On Horsemanship

The snow had stopped falling sometime during the night. Xenophon stood in the predawn darkness outside the makeshift stable his men had constructed from timber and stones scrounged from abandoned Armenian villages. His breath formed clouds in the bitter air. Behind him, stretched across the mountainside in ragged encampments, lay what remained of the Ten Thousand.

Nine months. Nine months since Cyrus had fallen at Cunaxa.

It had started so well. September morning, north of Babylon, at a place called Cunaxa. Cyrus the Younger had promised his Greek mercenaries wealth and glory if they'd help him overthrow his brother Artaxerxes and claim the Persian throne. And when the two armies finally met, the Greeks had done their part brilliantly. Their hoplite phalanx had charged the Persian left wing, shouting their war cry, pounding shields with spears to terrify the enemy horses. The Persians broke and fled before the Greeks even came within bowshot. Barely a single Greek casualty. A perfect victory.

Except it wasn't a victory at all.

While the Greeks were routing their opposition, the centre of the battle had collapsed. Cyrus, impatient and brave and perhaps too eager to prove himself, had personally led his cavalry of six hundred against his brother's position. He'd broken through the royal guard, wounded Artaxerxes in the chest with his own hand. For a moment, the throne had been within reach.

Then a javelin, thrown by a man whose name was Mithridates, caught Cyrus in the temple near his eye. He fell from his horse. In the chaos of combat, wounded and disoriented, he was struck again, this time in the leg. Falling, he dashed his wounded temple against a rock. The pretender to the Persian throne died in the dust of Babylon, and with him died every Greek soldier's reason for being there.

The Greeks didn't learn of Cyrus's death until after they'd finished celebrating their tactical victory. Only when they returned from pursuit did they discover the rest of Cyrus's forces had fled, their camp had been plundered, their employer was dead, and they were stranded eleven hundred miles from home, deep in the heart of the Persian Empire, surrounded by enemies. More than ten thousand Greek soldiers. No supplies. No money. No allies. And winter approaching.

Tissaphernes, the Persian satrap who had warned Artaxerxes of Cyrus's approach and commanded the troops that fled from the Greek charge, somehow still retained the king's favour. He was shrewd enough to see that attacking the Greeks frontally would be costly, even suicidal. These were veteran hoplites in disciplined formation. But he was also cunning enough to know he didn't need to defeat them in battle.

The Persians shadowed the Greeks as they began their retreat north. Sometimes visible on the ridgelines, sometimes just a felt presence that kept every man on edge. Tissaphernes arranged a truce. He promised to escort the Greeks safely to the Greek cities of Asia Minor if they'd promise not to pillage along the way. Many Greeks were suspicious, double-dealing and treachery were Tissaphernes' stock in trade, but the alternative was marching through hostile territory without provisions or guides.

Clearchus, the Spartan general who had emerged as de facto commander after Cyrus's death, wanted to end the mounting tension between the Greeks and their Persian "escorts." He proposed a face-to-face meeting with Tissaphernes to address grievances on both sides and solidify the truce. Most Greeks opposed this plan. The risks were obvious. But Clearchus was stubborn, confident in his ability to negotiate, perhaps too proud to believe a satrap would dare move against Greek generals.

He convinced four other generals to accompany him: Proxenus the Boeotian, Menon the Thessalian, Agias the Arcadian, and Socrates the Achaean. Twenty captains went with them. Two hundred soldiers followed, most of them just hungry men hoping for extra provisions rather than bodyguards prepared for treachery.

Tissaphernes welcomed them with smiles and warm words. The five generals were invited into his tent. The captains waited outside. Everything seemed cordial, diplomatic, exactly as Clearchus had expected…Then a blood-red flag rose above Tissaphernes' tent.

At that signal, Persian troops fell upon the captains and soldiers outside. Two hundred men, unarmed and unprepared, were cut down where they stood. Those who tried to run were hunted by cavalry and killed on the plain. Inside the tent, the five generals were seized before they could draw weapons.

Only one man escaped the massacre. A soldier named Nicharchus staggered back to the Greek camp hours later, his hands pressed against his own abdomen where a Persian sword had slashed him open. His intestines were visible through the wound, held in place by gore-soaked fingers. Before he collapsed, he told the horrified Greeks what had happened.

The five generals were dragged before King Artaxerxes. He wanted to witness their execution personally. Four were beheaded on the spot. Menon, who had an unsavory reputation and was suspected of conspiring with Tissaphernes, was reserved for special treatment. He was tortured for nearly a year before being finally killed.

Clearchus, the veteran Spartan who had fought for Cyrus and tried to negotiate in good faith, died far from home at the order of a king who considered him a mercenary and a traitor. Queen Mother Parysatis, who had loved Cyrus and grieved his death, tried to intervene to save Clearchus's life. She arranged for him to receive comforts in prison through her physician. But Queen Consort Statira's influence proved stronger, and her hatred of anyone associated with Cyrus's rebellion was absolute.

The night after Nicharchus brought news of the massacre, the remaining Greeks expected immediate attack. They rushed to arms, forming defensive positions. But the attack didn't come. Instead, Ariaeus, Cyrus's former second-in-command who had apparently conspired with Tissaphernes in the betrayal, rode to the Greek camp with three hundred Persian cavalry. He claimed that only Clearchus had been killed, for the crime of breaking his oath, and urged the Greeks to surrender their weapons.

The Greeks refused. But they also understood their situation with new clarity. They were leaderless, stranded in the heart of the Persian Empire, surrounded by forces that had just demonstrated they considered oaths worthless and truce flags an opportunity for murder. They were, as one officer put it, sheep without a shepherd, facing wolves that had already tasted blood.

That was when Xenophon, a thirty-year-old scholar from Athens who had joined the expedition as an observer out of curiosity about the wider world, stood up in the assembly. He wasn't a career soldier. He wasn't seeking command. But someone had to speak, and the words came.

"We have Zeus, who punishes perjurers and violators of hospitality," he reminded the demoralized troops. "We have defeated these Persians in battle before. And we still have each other. If we maintain discipline and unity, we can march out of here alive."

They elected new officers. They reformed their ranks. And they began the long march north toward the Black Sea and home, through territory where every valley held potential ambush, every mountain pass a possible dead end, every village a question of whether they'd find food or arrows.

Nine months ago, that decision had been made. Nine months of daily battles, of negotiating with hostile tribes, of watching men fall to arrows or exhaustion or the cold that froze toes and fingers and sometimes entire men in their sleep. Nine months of Xenophon learning what it meant to lead not through rank or title, but through the daily choice to remain calm when everything justified panic, to maintain direction when the path ahead was obscured by snow and uncertainty and death.

Still, somehow, they endured. Xenophon had not sought command. He was a scholar, a student of Socrates, not a career soldier. He'd joined as an observer, curious about the world beyond Athens. But when leadership fell into chaos and men looked for someone to speak, he'd found words. And when those words had given them hope, they'd chosen him to lead their retreat.

Leadership. He was still learning what that meant.

Inside the stable, his gelding shifted restlessly. The horse had carried Xenophon faithfully through ambushes and river crossings, up mountain passes where the snow came to their knees. Like all the cavalry mounts, he'd grown lean, his ribs visible despite the army's efforts to find fodder. But his spirit remained unbroken.

Xenophon entered the stable with slow, deliberate movements. No sudden gestures. No harsh commands. Just his presence, steady and calm.

The gelding's ear swivelled toward him. Xenophon approached, speaking quietly in that conversational tone he'd discovered worked better than shouting. "Good morning, old friend. I know you're hungry. I know you're tired. But we have work to do today. Just a few more mountain passes. Just a little further."

He placed his hand on the horse's neck, feeling the warmth beneath the winter coat. The gelding lowered his head slightly, a gesture Xenophon had learned to recognize. Not submission. Trust.

"I won't ask more than you can give," Xenophon murmured. "But I need you to give what you can. The men watch how we move together. They take courage from seeing you follow me willingly. They need to believe that following leadership through darkness leads somewhere worth reaching."

The horse stood quietly, processing. Xenophon didn't rush him. Didn't pull or force. Just waited, his hand on the warm neck, his breathing slow and even.

After a moment, the gelding took a step forward. Not because he was compelled. Because he'd chosen.

Xenophon smiled slightly. This was the lesson he was learning, day by day, horse by horse, soldier by soldier. True direction wasn't about domination. It was about creating conditions where others chose to follow because they trusted your judgment more than their fear.

Outside, officers were beginning to stir. Soon they'd need to brief the men, plan the day's march, make decisions that could mean life or death for thousands. But for this moment, Xenophon stood with his horse in peaceful companionship, both of them gathering strength for what lay ahead.

Years later, when he was an old man living on his estate at Scillus, Xenophon would write about horsemanship. He would counsel that a horse should never be approached in anger. That force creates only resistance and fear. That the most beautiful movements emerge when the horse performs them willingly, "of his own free will."

He would write from experience. Not just from his years of study, but from those desperate months leading the Ten Thousand through territory where every day demanded that men and horses find courage they didn't know they possessed. Nine months of finding creative solutions within the constraints of

Greek military discipline, forming improvised cavalry units when the situation demanded it, negotiating with hostile tribes when force would have been suicidal, adapting tactics to impossible terrain while maintaining the cohesion that kept his army from disintegrating.

Direction through darkness. Guidance through uncertainty. Leadership that whispered rather than shouted. This was what Xenophon had learned in the mountains of Armenia, what he'd teach in the pastures of Elis, and what would echo through twenty-three centuries of horsemanship philosophy.

This was Peaceful Directedness.

The Third Level

Peaceful Directedness is the third and final level in the Courage and Vision pillar of Incorporeal Competence. It represents the refinement of everything that's come before, when Fearless Guidance has matured into Compassionate Ambition, and that ambition has been distilled into something purer still: direction given calmly, movement initiated from stillness, clarity maintained without aggression.

This is action without urgency. Purpose without pressure. The ability to guide others toward a destination while allowing them to bring themselves to the journey willingly.

The progression is crucial to understand. Fearless Guidance plants the seed, stepping into uncertainty first, showing others it's possible to move through fear. That's the courage that begins everything.

Compassionate Ambition is the growing season, when that initial courage develops into sustained motivation, when you learn to push forward while honouring the wellbeing of those you're leading. That's drive matured by empathy.

And Peaceful Directedness, when combined with the refined states of the Communication and Service pillars, contributes to the ultimate harvest of Incorporeal Competence. When courage and compassion have been thoroughly integrated, and the excess has been pruned away, then your direction feels like partnership rather than command. This is leadership refined to its essential form. No wasted energy. No unnecessary force. Just clear, calm, consistent guidance that others trust enough to follow.

Think about the contrast between a novice instructor and a master guiding someone on how to complete a task. The novice becomes anxious, speaks rapidly, gestures frantically, overwhelms with too much information delivered with too much intensity. Their anxiety transfers to the learner, who becomes more confused rather than less.

The master, by contrast, speaks slowly. Makes eye contact. Gives one clear instruction at a time. Checks for understanding. Remains calm even if the person asks the same question twice. The learner relaxes, absorbs the information, feels confident about finding their way through the job.

Same destination. Same information. Completely different experience. The difference isn't knowledge, it's the peaceful directedness with which that knowledge is delivered.

This principle applies universally, but nowhere is it more evident than with horses. A horse can feel your heartbeat. They sense tension in your shoulders, uncertainty in your hands, aggression in your energy. You cannot fake peaceful directedness with a horse. You must embody it.

What Gets Pruned Away

Before we can fully embody Peaceful Directedness, we must understand what this third level requires us to release. Pruning isn't destruction, it's strategic removal of what prevents flourishing. Just as a gardener cuts away good branches to make room for great fruit, developing Peaceful Directedness means letting go of patterns that once served but now limit.

1. **Urgency without purpose must be pruned away.** Not all urgency, sometimes speed genuinely matters. But the manufactured panic that makes everything feel like a crisis, the anxiety that broadcasts itself to everyone around you, the desperate need to rush that actually slows progress by creating resistance, these must go.

    When you approach a frightened horse with frantic energy, they become more frightened. When you lead a team with constant urgency, they become numb to actual priorities. Peaceful Directedness requires you to distinguish between genuine urgency and your own impatience dressed as importance.

2. **Reactive intensity gets cut away through practice.** This is the pattern of meeting every challenge with heightened emotional response, every setback with dramatic reaction, every difficulty with

visible struggle. Reactive intensity feels powerful in the moment, it demonstrates that you care, that you're engaged, that you're fighting for what matters. But it's exhausting to maintain and unsustainable for those who follow you.

The horse learns to brace against your intensity rather than soften into partnership. Your team learns to manage your emotions rather than focus on the work. Pruning reactive intensity doesn't make you passive; it makes you steady.

3. **The need to control outcomes must be deliberately released.** This is perhaps the hardest pruning for most leaders. You want to ensure success. You want to prevent failure. So you grip tightly to every detail, every decision, every step of the process. But this stranglehold prevents the very growth you're trying to facilitate.

The horse who's micromanaged never develops confidence in their own judgment. The team member who's never trusted with meaningful autonomy never develops capability. Peaceful Directedness requires you to control what actually needs controlling, direction, standards, boundaries, while releasing your grip on how others navigate within those parameters.

4. **Impatience with process gets pruned through painful experience.** You want results now. You want to see progress immediately. You want confirmation that your guidance is working without having to wait through the awkward middle phase where nothing seems to be working.

This impatience shows up as frustration when the horse doesn't understand your cue by the third repetition. It manifests as disappointment when your team doesn't immediately implement your vision perfectly. It reveals itself in the constant temptation to abandon one approach before it's had time to work and try something else. But development happens on its own timeline, not yours.

Pruning impatience doesn't mean lowering standards, it means extending timeframes to match reality.

5. **Attachment to specific methods must be cut away.** You discovered what works, developed your approach, proved its effectiveness. Now that approach has become The Way Things Must Be Done. But Peaceful Directedness understands that different horses need different

approaches, different people respond to different communication styles, different situations require adapted tactics.

The master isn't attached to one method, they're committed to one principle (serving growth) while remaining flexible about application. This pruning feels like loss initially. It feels like abandoning what made you successful. But it's actually expansion into greater effectiveness.

6. **Ego-driven ambition gets refined away until only purpose-driven ambition remains.** Ambition is essential, it provides the energy to push through difficulty, the vision to see beyond current limitations, the drive to pursue excellence. But when ambition serves your ego rather than your purpose, it creates the kind of leadership that uses people as stepping stones and horses as proving grounds.

   Peaceful Directedness requires you to examine every ambitious impulse: Is this serving growth? Or is this serving my need to be seen as successful? The pruning of ego doesn't eliminate ambition, it purifies it.

7. **Fear-based pressure must be released.** This is the pattern of pushing harder when you're afraid, of applying more force when you're anxious about outcomes, of demanding more when you're worried about not being enough. Fear-based pressure communicates itself instantly.

   The horse feels your anxiety and mirrors it back. Your team senses your fear and either absorbs it or resents it. Peaceful Directedness requires you to feel your fear fully, acknowledge it, examine it, understand it, then choose to lead from vision rather than from that fear.

This pruning isn't a one-time event. It's an ongoing practice. Each time you catch yourself broadcasting urgency, you prune a little more. Each time you choose steady presence over reactive intensity, you refine further. Each time you release control of outcomes while maintaining clarity of direction, you develop more fully into Peaceful Directedness.

And what remains after the pruning? Clear, calm, consistent guidance. Direction that doesn't waver based on your internal state. Leadership that others can rely on precisely because it's been refined of everything that made it unstable. Presence that creates safety because the chaos has been cut away.

This is what Xenophon learned during those nine months leading the Ten Thousand. This is what David cultivated during years alone with his sheep. This is what every master horseman discovers: that true power emerges not from adding more force, but from pruning away everything that prevents peaceful, purposeful direction.

Two Shepherds, One Truth

A thousand years before Xenophon led the Ten Thousand through Armenia, another shepherd-warrior lived in the hills of Judea. David, youngest son of Jesse, spent his youth watching over his father's flocks. Like Xenophon, he would rise from those humble beginnings to lead thousands through danger. And like Xenophon, he would write about what he'd learned.

But where Xenophon wrote practical treatises on horsemanship and military command, David wrote poetry. Psalms that captured the emotional and spiritual dimensions of guidance, trust, and leadership. None more famous than the twenty-third.

"The LORD is my shepherd; I shall not want."

When David wrote those words, he wrote from lived experience. He knew what it meant to be a shepherd. The long hours of solitude in the hills. The constant vigilance required to spot threats. The patience needed to guide sheep to water and pasture without frightening them. The willingness to put himself between the flock and danger, David had killed both lion and bear to protect his sheep.

But more than technique, David understood the psychology of shepherding. Sheep are nervous creatures, prone to panic. They have questionable eyesight and worse judgment. Left to themselves, they'll wander into danger, eat poisonous plants, get trapped in ravines. They need guidance.

But not just any guidance. Sheep won't follow a shepherd they don't trust. You can't force a flock of sheep to move anywhere they don't want to go, try it and they'll scatter in every direction. The shepherd's authority comes not from power but from relationship. The sheep know his voice. They've learned through experience that following him leads to safety, food, water, rest.

"He makes me lie down in green pastures. He leads me beside still waters."

Notice the verbs. Makes. Leads. This is directive leadership. The shepherd doesn't ask permission or hold a committee meeting to decide where the flock will graze. He decides, based on his knowledge of the terrain, the season, the condition of the flock.

But notice also what he doesn't do. He doesn't drive. He doesn't force. He doesn't create panic. He leads to green pastures, not barren ground. Still waters, not turbulent rivers. His direction serves their needs, not his ego.

"He restores my soul. He leads me in paths of righteousness for his name's sake."

The shepherd's guidance isn't arbitrary. It has purpose. But that purpose encompasses both the shepherd's reputation and the sheep's wellbeing. A shepherd whose flock starves or scatters has failed, regardless of his intentions. The quality of his leadership is measured by the condition of those who follow him.

"Even though I walk through the valley of the shadow of death, I will fear no evil; for You are with me; Your rod and Your staff, they comfort me."

Here's the paradox at the heart of Peaceful Directedness. David isn't saying he never walks through dangerous valleys. He's saying he walks through them without fear because of the shepherd's presence. The rod and staff, instruments of guidance and protection, are a comfort precisely because they represent directed purpose.

The sheep in the dark valley can't see the path ahead. Can't know whether this route leads to safety or disaster. But it feels the shepherd's presence. Hears his voice. Knows from experience that this guidance, however uncomfortable the present moment, leads somewhere worth reaching.

This is Peaceful Directedness in its purest form. Direction that others trust enough to follow even when they can't see the destination. Guidance that comforts precisely because it's consistent, competent, and focused on their welfare alongside the larger purpose.

The Philosopher-General and the Shepherd-King

The parallels between Xenophon and David run deeper than their shared experience as shepherds who became leaders.

Both men led people through territories where death was a constant companion. Xenophon guided the Ten Thousand through mountains swarming with hostile tribes, pursued by Persian forces, starving in winter cold. David led Israel against Philistines, Moabites, Ammonites, Arameans, a lifetime of warfare defending and expanding his kingdom.

Both understood that their leadership was being watched. Xenophon knew the Ten Thousand took courage from seeing their commanders remain calm under pressure. David knew his soldiers fought more bravely when they saw their king lead from the front, but he also knew recklessness would inspire foolishness rather than courage.

Xenophon wrote, "The one best precept, the golden rule, in dealing with a horse is never to approach him angrily. Anger is so devoid of forethought that it will often drive a man to do things which in a calmer mood he will regret."

David wrote, "The LORD is my shepherd", casting himself in the role of sheep, acknowledging his need for guidance, modelling the trust he wanted his people to have in his own leadership.

Both men understood something essential: leadership isn't about the leader. It's about creating conditions where those who follow can flourish. The shepherd exists for the sheep, not the sheep for the shepherd. The cavalry officer exists for his troops and their horses, not the troops and horses for the officer.

This is Peaceful Directedness as service. Your vision, your courage, your ambition, all of it channelled into helping others reach destinations they couldn't reach alone.

But perhaps most striking is what both men understood about walking through dark valleys. Xenophon led the Ten Thousand through mountain passes where the cold killed as readily as arrows. Nights when men froze to death in their sleep. Days when they marched through snow up to their waists while hostile forces harassed them from the heights.

David wrote about valleys of death's shadow. Periods when enemies surrounded him. Times when even his own son turned against him. Moments when God seemed distant and disaster seemed certain.

Neither man promised their followers an easy path. Both were honest about the dangers ahead. But both provided what those who followed needed most: a steady presence that didn't waver regardless of circumstances. Direction that remained clear even when everything else was chaos. Peaceful guidance through valleys that weren't peaceful at all.

This is the culmination of the Courage and Vision pillar, the result of the pruning of Peaceful Directedness. Not fearlessness, both Xenophon and David experienced fear. Not false optimism, both were realists about threats and costs.

But the capacity to maintain clear, calm direction even in circumstances that would justify panic.

When everything in you wants to shout or force or demand, Peaceful Directedness whispers and waits and trusts that relationship will accomplish what urgency cannot.

The Horse Who Needed Certainty

Fatty was a character. Even as a colt he was fun to have around, fun to be around. Always getting into mischief. I remember the day that I got home from work to find him in the fork of a tree. It wasn't a big tree, and the fork was just high enough that he could reach the ground, if he stood on tiptoes, so he wasn't in any real danger.

The thing was though, this tree had countless little twigs rising up from the top of the fork, kind of like little pencils sticking out of the branch, and every time that Fatty would breath out, his belly would extend onto the points of these little branches, making him quickly breath in and stand up higher. I don't know how long he was standing there when we got home, but he sure was glad to see us. Even happier to see the saw as I cut the branch off.

I guess this was the start of him learning that he could trust me to help him out when he got in trouble. There was another time when Fatty, still a colt, had reared up and, we guess, tried to jump a fence showing off to a mare. He got his front feet over the 4 foot high steel rail at the top of the fence, and then somehow, contrived to get his hind feet over the two-foot-high middle wire of the fence. This is how we found him, stuck again, front feet on the ground, and suspended by his waist from the top rail. Not good for his manhood.

After starting him under saddle, Fatty went on to become a great gelding, always keen to give you his best, willing to try 120% in training at home. In hindsight though, it was probably his willingness to go above and beyond that made it hard to get him shown in competitions. The kind of horse who could end up in the fork of a tree or suspended on a fence showing off for a mare. But beneath that playful exterior was an animal who always struggled with pressure.

At home, Fatty was brilliant. He had a great stop, could change leads with aplomb, would spin like he was on fire. But take him to a competition, and everything changed. The pressure of being in that arena, away from the familiar, triggered something in him that transformed confidence into anxiety.

It was over a decade ago, we entered him in his first cutting competition. I had just started learning about training cutting horses and had no idea of how much he still had to learn. Nor, more importantly, how much I had to learn. But that was okay, we were just entered in the snaffle bit cutting, and we would get through it together, or so I thought.

We arrived the night before the competition, and the next morning he seemed fine as I warmed him up. But when I began to work the flag on him, everything seemed to become too much for him. He would be fine following the flag to the left, but when I asked him to go back the other way, he began to lock up. The more pressure I applied, the worse he got.

He got to where he would rear up in the air, his mind seemed frozen with anxiety or maybe the fear compounding in this situation, full of many unknowns. I don't believe that it was him being disobedient. This was something more like terror.

Over the years, I got smarter, and he got better. We both got more understanding and learnt how to be better prepared. I learnt to handle his peculiarities better. He was a better than average cutting horse, a good camp-draft horse and a great working cow-horse, at home. The last show I took him to, he was fine up until we entered the arena to practice the night before competition.

Then something clicked. Something was triggered in his brain to tell him that this was an important place, an important time, and he was his old nervous, uncertain self again. I kept riding him. Kept talking to him. Kept the touch of my hand on his neck. He slowly calmed down. Through strength of will, his will, by drawing upon my peacefulness, he gradually overcame his insecurity.

As I rode out of the arena after our run, he was puffing a bit. Not as fit as he once was, but he had tried his heart out for me again. I looked down at his legs, I could see a little tremor there, a sign of his inner turmoil. He had done everything I asked him to do, even though he hated being in that situation, even though he hated being under that much pressure. He had drawn every ounce of courage from me that he could.

I realized then that I couldn't keep asking him to do this. There was no point, even though he would have done it for me when I asked. Not because he couldn't do it, he'd just proven he could. Not because I didn't love working with him, I did. But because the cost was too high for what we were gaining.

This is what Peaceful Directedness understands at the pruning level: sometimes the most loving thing you can do is recognize when something must be released, even when you care deeply about it. Especially when you care deeply about it.

Fatty would have kept trying for me. Would have kept drawing on my calm to override his anxiety. Would have kept forcing himself into that arena because I asked him to. But Peaceful Directedness isn't about seeing how much someone will endure for you. It's about recognizing when endurance has become suffering, when challenge has become trauma, when pushing forward serves your ego rather than their wellbeing.

Xenophon wrote that a horse should never be dealt with angrily, and that "nothing forced can ever be beautiful." Fatty performing in that arena wasn't beautiful. It was courage, yes. It was loyalty, absolutely. But it was extracted at a cost that diminished both of us. I was asking him to be something he wasn't meant to be, to live in a way that made him miserable, all because I loved what he could do at home and wanted the world to see it.

That's not leadership. That's selfishness dressed as ambition.

We were blessed that a friend was looking for a forever horse, a trail riding companion. Fatty went to a new home where his intelligence and willingness could shine without the pressure that broke him. Where he could be the character he'd always been without anxiety crushing his spirit. Where his greatest adventures would be exploring trails rather than facing arena crowds.

Peaceful Directedness requires two kinds of wisdom. First, the ability to guide others into difficulty when that difficulty serves growth, the courage to lead them through hard valleys when those valleys lead somewhere worth reaching. Second, the wisdom to recognize when difficulty has stopped serving growth and started causing harm, the compassion to prune paths that lead nowhere good, even when you love what you're pruning.

The shepherd leads sheep through dark valleys, but only valleys that lead somewhere. Not every valley leads to green pastures on the other side. Some are dead ends. Some have wolves waiting in ambush. The wise shepherd knows the difference.

This is direction informed by understanding, powered by courage, but tempered by compassion. This is what emerges when you've refined the Courage and Vision pillar through strategic pruning. And when combined with refined Communication and Service, this contributes to the ultimate harvest of Incorporeal Competence.

What It Looks Like in the Arena

When you bring Peaceful Directedness into your work with horses, several things shift:

1. **Your energy changes.** You stop broadcasting urgency even when you feel it internally. Horses are extraordinarily sensitive to emotional states. When you're anxious about progress, they feel that anxiety and become anxious themselves. When you're frustrated by their lack of understanding, they feel that frustration and shut down or resist.

    Peaceful Directedness requires you to manage your internal state before attempting to direct theirs. This doesn't mean suppressing emotion, suppression creates a different kind of tension that horses read immediately. It means processing your emotions before entering the arena, so you can be present with calm clarity rather than reactive urgency.

2. **You develop comfort with stillness and pause.** Novice trainers often fill every moment with activity, constantly asking for something, unable to let the horse simply be. But horses learn in the quiet moments between requests. They need time to process, to consolidate, to integrate what they're learning. Peaceful Directedness creates space for that processing. You make a request.

    The horse responds. You acknowledge the response, then pause. Let them stand. Let them think. Let understanding develop rather than forcing it. This stillness feels counterproductive initially. You want to keep moving, keep training, use every minute efficiently. But horses don't work on productivity schedules. They work on understanding schedules. And understanding requires pauses.

3. **You learn to distinguish between necessary pressure and excessive pressure.** All training involves some degree of pressure, asking the horse to do something they wouldn't choose to do on their own. The question isn't whether to use pressure, but how much, when, and for what purpose. Peaceful Directedness applies just enough pressure to create change without creating trauma.

    You ask for something slightly uncomfortable but not overwhelming. You hold that request with calm consistency until the horse offers a try, then immediately release the pressure. This creates learning without creating resistance. The key is consistency without rigidity. You maintain clear expectations, this is what I'm asking for, while remaining flexible about the path to meeting those expectations.

The horse might offer ten different responses before finding the one you want. Peaceful Directedness says calmly each time, "Not that, try again," without getting frustrated that they haven't figured it out yet.

4. **You develop the ability to redirect without criticism**. When a horse does something wrong or misunderstands your request, your response matters enormously. React with anger or disappointment, and you teach them that trying is dangerous. Respond with calm redirection, and you teach them that mistakes are simply information leading to better understanding.

   Xenophon wrote extensively about this. He counselled that when a horse refuses something, you should first check whether you've asked clearly. Is the horse confused because your aids were contradictory? Frightened because you pushed too fast? Resistant because they're in pain or exhausted? Only after excluding these possibilities should you treat resistance as disobedience.

   And even then, the correction should be matter of fact, not emotional. "That's not acceptable. Here's what is acceptable. Now let's try again."

5. **You maintain direction without becoming domineering**. There's a crucial difference between being directive and being dictatorial. Peaceful Directedness says, "I'm clear about where we're going and how we'll get there, and I'll guide you consistently toward that destination." Domination says, "You'll do exactly what I say, exactly when I say it, regardless of whether it makes sense to you or whether you're ready."

   The directive leader makes decisions and holds the course. But they also remain aware of how those they're leading are responding. They adjust pacing, modify approaches, provide support when needed. The dominating leader just pushes harder when they meet resistance.

6. **You learn to end sessions at the right moment.** Peaceful Directedness understands that more training isn't always better training. Sometimes the most directive thing you can do is stop for the day when you've achieved one good response, rather than drilling it until the horse is exhausted and resentful.

This requires you to plan sessions with clear goals. What are you trying to achieve today? Once you achieve it, can you end there? Or do you need to repeat it a few times to solidify? The answer depends on the horse, the difficulty of what you're asking, and how much mental and physical energy they have available.

Remember Fatty. He would have kept trying for me. But just because he would doesn't mean he should. Peaceful Directedness knows when to ask and when to release.

What It Looks Like Outside the Arena

The same principles that create Peaceful Directedness with horses create it in all forms of leadership.

In professional settings, Peaceful Directedness manifests as:

1. **Clarity without urgency.** You're clear about objectives, timelines, expectations. But you communicate them with calm confidence rather than stressed intensity. Your team feels directed without feeling driven. They know where they're going and why it matters, but they're not drowning in manufactured urgency that makes everything feel like a crisis.

   This doesn't mean you never move quickly. Sometimes speed is necessary. But Peaceful Directedness distinguishes between actual urgency (this deadline is real and important) and manufactured urgency (I'm anxious so I'm making everyone else anxious too).

2. **Consistency without rigidity.** You maintain clear standards and expectations. People know what excellence looks like because you've defined it clearly and held to those definitions consistently. But you're also flexible about the paths to achieving those standards. Different people will approach the same goal differently.

   Peaceful Directedness provides the framework while allowing for individual expression within it. This is the creative artistry within clear structure. The principles don't change, but the applications adapt to circumstances and individuals.

3. **Direction without micromanagement.** You're clear about the destination and the constraints, then you trust people to navigate within those boundaries. This requires you to actually let go. To resist

the urge to control every detail. To allow people to make mistakes that don't cause catastrophic harm because that's how learning happens.The directive leader says, "Here's what needs to happen and why it's important.

Here are the constraints we're working within. What do you need from me to make this successful?" The micromanaging leader says, "Here's what needs to happen and here's exactly how you're going to do it, step by step, with me checking on you constantly to make sure you're doing it right."

4. **Feedback without criticism.** When something isn't working, Peaceful Directedness addresses it matter-of-factly. "This isn't producing the results we need. Let's talk about why and what we can adjust." Not, "You're failing," but "This approach isn't working, let's find one that does."

   This requires emotional maturity. When someone misses a deadline or makes a mistake, your internal response might be frustration or disappointment. Peaceful Directedness processes those emotions before engaging, so the conversation focuses on solutions rather than blame.

5. **Redirection without rejection.** When people are moving in the wrong direction, Peaceful Directedness redirects them back to the right path without making them feel diminished for having gone astray. "I see where you're going with this. That's not going to work for [specific reasons]. Here's what will work and why."

   The key is explaining the "why" so people develop judgment, not just following orders. Over time, they internalize the principles guiding your decisions and can make similar decisions themselves. This is how you develop leaders, not just followers.

In family and personal relationships, Peaceful Directedness looks like:

1. **Creating structure without control.** Children need guidance, boundaries, clear expectations. But they also need space to develop their own judgment. Peaceful Directedness provides the framework of values and non-negotiables while allowing age-appropriate autonomy within that framework.

"Here's what time dinner is. Here's what behaviour is acceptable at the table. Here's why these things matter." Not, "Do exactly what I say because I said so," but "Here's the structure and here's why it exists."

2. **Maintaining standards without shaming.** When children (or partners, or friends) miss the mark, Peaceful Directedness addresses the behaviour without attacking the person. "That's not how we treat each other in this family. Let's try again." Not, "You're so inconsiderate/thoughtless/selfish."

This distinction matters enormously. Addressing behaviour creates change. Attacking character creates defensiveness and shame.

3. **Guiding without rescuing.** Peaceful Directedness allows people to face natural consequences of their choices while remaining present as a guide. You don't remove all obstacles or solve all problems. You're available for support and counsel, but you let people do the work of navigating their own lives.

This is perhaps the hardest aspect of Peaceful Directedness in personal relationships. Watching someone you love struggle is painful. The urge to step in and fix everything is powerful. But rescuing prevents growth. Peaceful Directedness provides guidance while allowing the struggle that creates capability.

The Development of Peaceful Directedness

So how do you develop this quality? How do you move from reactive urgency to calm direction? How do you become the kind of leader people trust to guide them through dark valleys?

You must develop your own inner peace, and in doing so, you begin pruning away reactive patterns.

You can't project calm you don't possess. This requires dedicated practice of whatever disciplines help you regulate your nervous system and process your emotions effectively.

For some people, that's meditation or prayer. For others, it's physical exercise or time in nature. For still others, it's journaling or talking with a counsellor or trusted friend. The specific method matters less than the commitment to actually doing it.

But here's what's actually happening in these practices: you're pruning urgency, reactive intensity, and fear-based pressure. Each time you sit in meditation and notice frantic thoughts without acting on them, you're cutting away the pattern of urgency. Each time you process emotions through journaling instead of broadcasting them, you're refining reactive intensity. Each time you pray through fear instead of leading from it, you're releasing fear-based pressure.

Xenophon had decades to develop this peace. The march of the Ten Thousand was a crucible that burned away everything unnecessary. Then years at Scillus, where he hunted, wrote, and worked with horses, gave him space to integrate what he'd learned, to prune what the crucible had revealed as excess.

David developed his peace during years alone in the hills with his father's flocks. Solitude. Stillness. Time to think and pray and simply be. Then decades of warfare and political intrigue tested and refined that peace until it became unshakeable. Each test was an opportunity for pruning.

You need your own version of this development. Whatever creates internal stillness for you, make time for it. Prioritize it. Guard it. Because you cannot give others what you don't have yourself. And the practice itself IS the pruning.

You must learn to slow down when everything in you wants to speed up -- and in this learning, you prune impatience and urgency without purpose. This is perhaps the most practical skill in developing Peaceful Directedness. When you feel urgency rising, when you want to force results, when you're tempted to apply more pressure, pause.

Take three slow breaths. Remind yourself of your goal. Ask whether urgency will actually help you reach it, or whether it will create resistance that slows progress even more.

This practice of pausing feels counterproductive initially. You're wasting time when you could be taking action! But the pause isn't wasted time. It's active pruning. Each pause cuts away a bit more of the urgency-without-purpose pattern. Each breath releases a bit more of the reactive intensity.

Over weeks and months of practice, these small prunings accumulate. The urgency that once felt necessary reveals itself as optional. The speed that felt essential shows itself as often counterproductive.

The pause is the pruning shears. Use them often.

You must develop deep understanding of those you're leading, and through this understanding, you prune the need to control outcomes and attachment to specific methods. Peaceful Directedness requires you to see beyond surface behaviours to underlying motivations, fears, capabilities, and needs.

With horses, this means studying equine psychology. Understanding how they process information. Recognizing the difference between confusion, fear, pain, and actual disobedience. Learning to read their body language as fluently as you'd read a book.

With people, it means similar study. What motivates them? What frightens them? What do they need to feel safe enough to take risks? What's their history that shapes how they respond to authority?

This understanding doesn't happen quickly. It requires patient observation, genuine curiosity, and willingness to set aside your assumptions. But it's essential. And here's what happens through this practice: as you learn to truly see others, you naturally release the need to control their path. You discover that each horse, each person, requires slightly different approach, and your attachment to one method dissolves. The pruning happens almost automatically through genuine understanding.

You can't micromanage someone you truly understand. You can't force one method on everyone when you see how differently they process. Understanding itself does the pruning.

You must practice consistency without attachment to specific outcomes in specific timeframes, and this practice prunes both impatience and ego-driven ambition. This is the hardest part for most people. We want results now. We have deadlines, expectations, pressures. Peaceful Directedness requires you to hold your direction clearly while releasing attachment to exactly when results appear.

With any horse you're developing, you must accept that growth takes however long it takes. Could be weeks. Could be months. Your timeline doesn't matter. What matters is maintaining consistent, clear direction until genuine understanding develops.

This doesn't mean you never have deadlines. Sometimes deadlines are real and important. But it means you distinguish between actual deadlines and your preference for faster results. And it means you plan with realistic timeframes rather than optimistic ones.

Each time you choose consistency over quick results, you prune impatience. Each time you maintain direction despite slow progress, you cut away ego's need for immediate validation. The horse that finally understands after the hundredth repetition teaches you that your impatience was never about the horse's limitation, it was about your own. And in seeing that, you can release it.

You must learn to trust the process more than you trust your anxiety, and this gradually prunes fear-based pressure. Your anxiety will tell you that if you're not pushing, forcing, applying more pressure, nothing will happen. Your anxiety will convince you that calm direction is passive inaction.

But Peaceful Directedness isn't passive. It's actively choosing calm clarity over reactive intensity. It's trusting that consistent direction over time produces better results than urgent forcing in the moment.

This trust develops through experience. Every time you choose calm direction and see it work, you build evidence against anxiety's narrative. Every time urgent forcing creates resistance while patient direction creates partnership, you prune a bit more fear-based pressure. Over time, the trust becomes stronger than the anxiety. The pruning becomes easier because you've seen the fruit it produces.

You must become comfortable with other people's discomfort, and this prunes the reactive need to rescue, fix, or solve everything immediately. This is perhaps the most counterintuitive aspect of Peaceful Directedness.

When you're guiding someone through difficulty, whether that's a horse learning something new or a person facing a challenge, they will be uncomfortable. They might be confused, frustrated, uncertain, even temporarily resentful.

Peaceful Directedness doesn't try to remove all discomfort. It creates just enough challenge to facilitate growth while providing enough support to prevent trauma. This requires you to tolerate watching others struggle without rushing in to rescue them from the struggle.

David wrote about walking through valleys of death's shadow. He didn't say the LORD removed the valley. The valley was still there. Still dark. Still dangerous. But the shepherd's presence meant the sheep could walk through it without being overwhelmed by fear.

Your job isn't to remove all valleys from people's paths. Your job is to guide them through the valleys with calm confidence that there's something worth reaching on the other side.

Daily Practice: The Morning Pages

While all the development practices above contribute to Peaceful Directedness, there's one specific daily discipline that accelerates the pruning process more than any other: journaling.

Julia Cameron, in her groundbreaking 1992 book "The Artist's Way: A Spiritual Path to Higher Creativity," introduces what she calls "The Morning Pages." This is the practice she recommends for re-finding your creativity. Each morning, write three pages longhand. Journaling the same way Marcus Aurelius did it all those years ago. Essentially just a brain dump.

Cameron says, "There is no wrong way to do morning pages."

"All that angry, whiny, petty stuff that you write down in the morning stands between you and your creativity. Worrying about the job, the laundry, the funny knock in the car, the weird look in your lover's eye – this stuff eddies through our subconscious and muddies our days. Get it on the page."

This practice is profound pruning work. When you write three pages every morning, several things happen:

- **You externalize what needs to be released.** All the urgency, the reactive intensity, the fear-based pressure, the ego-driven concerns, they live in your head, creating noise that prevents peaceful directedness. Getting them on the page externalizes them. Once externalized, you can see them for what they are: just thoughts, not truth. Just noise, not direction.

- **You create space for what matters.** Cameron is right that all the petty worries stand between you and your creativity. But they also stand between you and your peaceful directedness. Your calm clarity. Your ability to lead from vision rather than anxiety. The Morning Pages clear away the underbrush so the path forward becomes visible.

- **You practice non-attachment.** The rule is simple: write three pages, then don't read them again. You're not journaling to create a record or solve problems. You're journaling to release. This practice of writing without attachment to outcome is itself training in peaceful directedness. You do the work (write the pages) without grasping for results (solving all your problems).

- **You prune automatically.** Each morning that you write, you're identifying and releasing urgency without purpose, reactive intensity, fear-based pressure, and ego-driven concerns. You're not trying to prune them through willpower. You're simply observing them on the page, recognizing them for what they are, and letting them go. Over weeks and months, this daily pruning transforms your baseline state.

Marcus Aurelius practiced this same discipline eighteen centuries before Cameron formalized it. His "Meditations" weren't written for publication. They were his personal morning pages, a place to process his anxieties, remind himself of principles, externalize the concerns that would otherwise cloud his judgment. A place where he could prune away what didn't serve so he could lead from clarity.

"When you wake up in the morning, tell yourself: The people I deal with today will be meddling, ungrateful, arrogant, dishonest, jealous and surly," Marcus wrote. Not because he was cynical, but because acknowledging these realities on the page meant they couldn't blindside him during the day. He'd already processed them. Pruned away the reactive response. Made space for peaceful directedness.

The practice is simple:

1. **First thing in the morning,** before you check email or scroll social media or engage with anyone

2. **Write three pages longhand** (not typed, the physical act matters)

3. **Write whatever comes to mind** without filtering or organizing

4. **Don't reread them** (this isn't about solving problems, it's about releasing them)

5. **Do it every day** (the consistency is what creates the pruning)

You don't need to be a good writer. You don't need to make sense. You don't need to solve anything. You just need to get it on the page.

"Worrying about the job, the laundry, the funny knock in the car", all of this is urgency without purpose and fear-based pressure manifesting in your daily life. Getting it on the page doesn't make the concerns disappear. But it prevents them from controlling your leadership.

When you've externalized your anxieties in the Morning Pages, you can enter the arena (literal or metaphorical) with the peaceful directedness that horses and people need. The worried, anxious, reactive part of you stays on the page. The calm, clear, purposeful part of you leads.

This is the most practical daily practice for developing Peaceful Directedness. More practical than meditation for many people because it's concrete, achievable, and immediately accessible. Three pages. Every morning. Everything that would prevent peaceful directedness, written down and released.

Try it for a week. Then a month. Then three months. You'll notice the pruning happening, not dramatically, but steadily. The things that used to trigger urgency and reactivity will still happen, but they won't control you the same way. Because you've been practicing release every morning. Practicing non-attachment. Practicing peaceful directedness at the level of thought before you ever have to demonstrate it in action.

The Integration: Courage Transformed

Peaceful Directedness represents the culmination of the Courage and Vision pillar. Everything you've developed through Fearless Guidance and Compassionate Ambition comes together here in refined form.

The Fearless Guidance that taught you to step into uncertainty first has matured into the ability to lead others through uncertainty without transmitting your own anxiety. The fear is still there, you're not fearless. But you've learned to act from vision rather than from fear. You've learned that your people don't need you to be unafraid; they need you to maintain direction despite fear.

The Compassionate Ambition that taught you to push forward while honouring wellbeing has matured into the ability to maintain clear direction while remaining responsive to those you're leading. You're not sacrificing ambition for compassion or compassion for ambition. You're holding both in dynamic balance, the clear destination and the care for those travelling toward it.

And now, through consistent practice of both, you've developed Peaceful Directedness. The ability to guide without dominating. To direct without dictating. To maintain clarity without creating anxiety. To hold the course without becoming rigid. To find infinite creative solutions within clear principles.

This is courage transformed. Not the dramatic courage of the initial leap into uncertainty. Not the sustained courage of the long march forward. But the refined courage of calm, consistent direction that others trust enough to follow even when they can't see where they're going.

Think about Xenophon at the head of the Ten Thousand. By the time they reached the Black Sea and shouted "Thalatta! Thalatta!" - The sea! The sea! - those men had followed him through mountains where their comrades froze to death, through ambushes where arrows fell like rain, through river crossings where the current threatened to sweep them away. They'd followed because his direction remained calm and clear even when circumstances were chaotic and terrifying.

Think about David leading Israel. Decades of warfare. Betrayal by his own son. Periods when God seemed distant. But through all of it, maintaining the kind of leadership that kept Israel united and strong enough to become the most powerful kingdom in the region. Not through dramatic displays of power, but through consistent, peaceful guidance informed by deep understanding of both God and sheep.

Think about working with a horse who's confused and frightened. Standing with them in that confusion without becoming confused yourself. Maintaining your certainty about the path forward without becoming harsh when they struggle to find it. Being the calm centre they can orient toward when everything else is uncertain.

That's the effect of Peaceful Directedness pruning the Courage and Vision that has carried you to this point. That's what becomes possible when you've planted seeds of fearless guidance, cultivated them through compassionate ambition, and refined them through consistent practice of Peaceful Directedness.

But here's what's crucial to understand: Peaceful Directedness alone isn't sufficient for the ultimate goal of Incorporeal Competence. It's one-third of the foundation, not the whole structure.

You've developed the ability to guide with courage and vision. You've pruned away urgency without purpose, reactive intensity, the need to control outcomes, impatience with process, attachment to specific methods, ego-driven ambition, and fear-based pressure. You've refined this pillar to its essential form.

The next phase of the journey moves into the Communication pillar. Because it's not enough to know where you're going and to guide others there calmly. You must also learn to communicate with clarity that transcends words, to develop coordination between thought and action, to access centred presence that remains stable regardless of circumstances.

And after that, the Service pillar. Learning to place all your courage, all your communication, all your developed capabilities in genuine service of others' growth. Understanding when to support and when to release. When to build and when to prune.

Only when all three pillars, Courage and Vision, Communication, and Service, have been fully developed through their planting, growing, and pruning stages does Incorporeal Competence emerge. That's the ultimate harvest: the integration of sustainable passion, unshakeable loyalty, and purposeful perseverance that characterizes mastery.

But for now, focus on this: Peaceful Directedness is available to you. Not as an aspiration or theory, but as a practical quality you can develop through consistent practice.

Start today. In your next interaction with a horse or a person who looks to you for guidance, practice calm direction. Slow down when you want to speed up. Soften when you want to force. Trust the process when anxiety urges urgency. Write your Morning Pages tomorrow before you do anything else, externalizing what needs to be pruned so you can lead from clarity.

You're not abandoning decisiveness. You're refining it. You're not becoming passive. You're choosing active calm over reactive intensity. You're becoming the kind of leader whose direction others trust precisely because it doesn't waver with circumstances. Whose guidance through dark valleys is reliable precisely because it remains peaceful regardless of what the valley contains.

That's not theory. That's not wishful thinking. That's Peaceful Directedness, the refined state of Courage and Vision that, when combined with refined Communication and Service, contributes to the ultimate harvest of Incorporeal Competence.

The horse doesn't follow your anxiety. They follow your certainty. And certainty delivered peacefully is the strongest form of leadership there is.

"The groom should have standing orders to take his charge through crowds, and to make him familiar with all sorts of sights and noises; and if the colt shows sign of apprehension at them, he must teach him, not by cruel, but by gentle handling, that they are not really formidable."

- Xenophon, On Horsemanship

CHAPTER 10

CENTRED TRANSCENDENCE

"The Spirit of the LORD will rest on him—the Spirit of wisdom and of understanding, the Spirit of counsel and of might, the Spirit of the knowledge and fear of the LORD."

- Isaiah 11:2

The Breath of Connection

The morning sun had barely cleared the rim of Palo Duro Canyon when Running Wolf led his grandson through the cottonwoods toward the horse herd grazing in the sheltered meadow below. Mist rose from the Prairie Dog Town Fork of the Red River, and somewhere in the distance, a meadowlark sang its cascading song.

It was 1758. The Numunuu (nuh-muh-nuh), the People, had claimed these southern plains as their own for two generations now, ever since the great migration south had brought them to this land of endless grass and buffalo herds that darkened the horizon. But it was not the buffalo that had made them lords of these plains. It was the horse. The "God Dog," as they had first called it when Spanish horses had found their way into Comanche hands.

Seven Arrows was ten summers old, and this morning would mark his formal introduction to the herd. He had ridden since he could walk, of course, all

Comanche children did, learning balance and rhythm before they learned to speak in full sentences. But today was different. Today, Running Wolf would teach him something that went beyond riding.

Today, he would learn about puha (POO-hah).

The old man moved slowly, deliberately, his weathered hand resting on the boy's shoulder. "Watch," he said simply, as they approached the edge of the herd.

Seven Arrows watched.

His grandfather's breathing changed. Became deeper. Slower. The boy could feel the shift even though he couldn't name it, a settling that began in Running Wolf's centre and spread outward like ripples on water. The horses' ears swivelled toward them. Several lifted their heads from grazing. But none moved away.

Running Wolf walked directly toward a young bay gelding, perhaps three summers old. The horse watched him approach, nostrils flaring slightly, reading every signal the old man broadcast. When Running Wolf was close enough, he stopped. Simply stood. Breathing.

The gelding took a step toward him. Then another. Until they stood nose to nose.

Running Wolf breathed out, long and slow, directly into the horse's nostrils. The gelding's eyes softened. His head lowered slightly. When the old man placed his hand on the horse's neck, there was no resistance. No tension. Just partnership.

"You see?" Running Wolf said quietly, not looking at his grandson, maintaining his focus on the horse. "I do not go to him with my mind scattered like leaves in wind. I do not bring yesterday's anger or tomorrow's worry. I come from my centre. From my spirit. And from that centre, I reach out to touch his."

He stepped back, gesturing for Seven Arrows to approach. "Now you."

The boy moved forward eagerly, reaching out his hand…

The gelding wheeled and trotted away.

Seven Arrows looked back at his grandfather, confused and disappointed.

"What was in your mind when you reached for him?" Running Wolf asked.

"I... I wanted to touch him. Like you did."

"Wanting is not being. Reaching is not connecting." The old man settled onto the grass, cross-legged, and gestured for his grandson to sit beside him. "Listen. I will tell you what my grandfather told me, what his grandfather told him. This is old knowledge, from before we had horses, from when we still lived in the mountains with our Shoshone cousins."

Seven Arrows sat, trying to copy his grandfather's stillness.

"Everything has spirit," Running Wolf began. "The rocks. The trees. The buffalo. The horse. And humans. Spirit is what makes things alive, even when they seem still. But spirit alone is not enough. To truly live, to truly be Nʉmʉnʉʉ, you must learn to gather power. We call this puha."

"Like a medicine man has?" Seven Arrows asked.

"Everyone can have puha. Not just puhakatl (poo-hah-KAHT-ul). But yes, like they have, only stronger. Puha comes when you learn to be still inside yourself, even when your body moves. When you learn to reach out from that stillness to touch the spirits around you. When you become..." He paused, searching for the right words. "When you become like the centre pole of our Sun Dance lodge. Still. Strong. But connected to everything around it."

He pointed to the horses grazing peacefully nearby. "That gelding, he felt my puha before I touched him. He knew I came from my centre, not from confusion or fear or wanting. So he could trust me. He could let me touch his spirit with mine."

"How do I learn this?"

"The same way I learned. The same way every warrior learns. Through practice. Through seeking. Through understanding that you are not separate from the world, you are part of it. And from your centre, you can reach to any part of it."

Running Wolf stood smoothly, extending his hand to help his grandson rise. "Come. Try again. But this time, before you move toward the horse, become still inside yourself first. Feel your breath. Feel where your feet touch the earth. Feel where you end and the world begins. And then..." He smiled. "Then understand that you don't end. Your spirit can reach as far as you need it to."

Seven Arrows closed his eyes. He focused on his breathing the way he'd been taught to do during prayer. In. Out. In. Out. He felt the morning sun warm on his face. Heard the river's whisper. Felt the slight breeze moving across the canyon.

And something shifted.

It was subtle. Like the moment just before sleep when thought gives way to something deeper. He was still aware, still present, but differently. His sense of self had expanded somehow, no longer confined to the boundaries of his skin.

"Good," Running Wolf murmured. "Now maintain that. Keep breathing. And walk toward the horse."

Seven Arrows opened his eyes and began walking. The gelding's ears turned toward him, but the horse didn't move away. Step by step, the boy approached, maintaining that strange, expanded awareness, that sense of being centred while somehow being present beyond himself.

When he reached the horse, he did what his grandfather had done. Stopped. Breathed. Let his awareness reach out to touch the horse's awareness.

The gelding stepped closer.

Seven Arrows laughed, a pure sound of delight. The horse startled slightly but didn't flee. The boy steadied himself, returned to that centred place, and carefully extended his hand. The gelding sniffed his palm. Accepted his touch.

"Now," Running Wolf said softly, "breathe into his nostrils. Not to control him. Not to make him yours. But to share your spirit with his. To say, I see you. I honour you. We are connected."

Seven Arrows breathed out gently into the horse's flared nostrils. The gelding breathed back, their breath mingling in the cool morning air. And in that moment, the boy understood what his grandfather meant. He wasn't just touching a horse. He was touching spirit to spirit, centre to centre, creating a connection that would serve them both when they moved together across the endless grasslands.

"This is what makes us different from those who fight us," Running Wolf said. "The Spanish, the Apache, even the Ute, they try to break horses. They try to bend them to human will. But we understand something deeper. When you reach from your centre to touch their centre, when you share spirit rather than imposing will, you don't break them. You become partners. One being with two bodies."

Over the following moons, Seven Arrows learned to maintain that centred awareness not just in stillness, but in motion. He learned to feel a horse's heartbeat through his legs when he rode. To sense which foot was about to step before it moved. To know when a horse was uncertain or confident, frightened or calm, simply by expanding his awareness to include them.

He learned to ride at full gallop across the buffalo plains while maintaining perfect stillness at his core, stillness that allowed him to loose arrow after arrow with deadly accuracy, because his centre remained calm even while his body flowed with the horse's movement.

He learned the techniques that made Comanche warriors legendary: dropping to hang beneath a galloping horse's belly, shielded by the animal's body while shooting under its neck. Picking up objects from the ground at full speed. Transferring from one horse to another without breaking stride. All of it possible only because he had learned to be still at his centre while his awareness expanded to include the horse, the ground, the wind, the target, everything his spirit needed to touch to accomplish what his body was attempting.

By the time he was fifteen, Seven Arrows could ride into a buffalo herd with a dozen other warriors and feel not just his own horse beneath him but the entire herd's movement, anticipating where the buffalo would turn, where the opening would appear, where the perfect shot would present itself. His awareness had expanded to include not just his mount but the entire dance of hunter and hunted.

And when he was eighteen and went on his first war party against the Apache, he rode with the same expanded awareness. He could feel his fellow warriors' positions without looking. Could sense when someone was in trouble and needed help. Could maintain his own centre of calm while reaching out to touch the spirits and intentions of those around him, friend and enemy alike.

This was puha in its highest form. Not power grabbed or stolen or forced. Power that flowed naturally when you learned to be still at your centre while your awareness expanded to touch everything around you. Power that came from understanding that you were not separate from the world, but intimately connected to all of it, reaching out from your centre like the spokes of a wheel reaching from the hub.

When Running Wolf died, old and honoured, surrounded by grandchildren and great-grandchildren, Seven Arrows held his hand and felt the old man's spirit expanding one last time, reaching out to touch everything and everyone he loved before finally releasing into the wind that blew eternally across the plains they had made their own.

And Seven Arrows understood. His grandfather had not left them. He had simply expanded his reach beyond the boundaries of his body, his spirit now part of the wind and grass and horses and buffalo, still present, still connected, still reaching from that unchanging centre that existed beyond the physical world.

This was Centred Transcendence. Not leaving the world behind. But learning to be so still at your centre that your awareness could expand to include all of it, reaching out to guide and touch and influence without losing yourself in the process.

The Third Level

Centred Transcendence is the final level in the Communication Pillar of Incorporeal Competence. The Pruning Level. It inspects everything that's been planted and cultivated through Emotionless Communication and Balanced Coordination, looking for what works and what needs to go.

The progression is essential to understand:

- **Emotionless Communication** planted the seed, learning to communicate without emotional distortion, removing any focus from the static that prevents clear transmission. You learned to recognize your emotional state, to breathe and centre before speaking, to deliver messages that arrive uncoloured by reactivity.

- **Balanced Coordination** was the growing season, when that clear communication matured into embodied congruence. Your words aligned with your actions. Your body language matched your intentions. Mind, body, and emotion moved together in synchronization. You became trustworthy because there was no gap between what you said and what you were.

- **Centred Transcendence** sees the unnecessary, the unproductive, and cuts it away so that communication deepens into something more profound. In 2018 revision of his book, "Developing the Leader Within You 2.0", John C. Maxwell discusses the Pareto Principle which states that 20 percent of our time will create 80 percent of our production. In other words, if we can have the wherewithal to remove some of the 80 percent where we waste our time, we will open ourselves up to being more productive in every way.

You will move from maintaining inner stillness just before you communicate or during coordinated action, to it being a constant state. And from that stillness, your awareness expands outward. You can feel others. Guide them. Touch their spirits with yours. Not through force or manipulation, but through that same quality Seven Arrows learned with the horses: reaching from your centre to touch theirs.

The key distinction between Balanced Coordination and Centred Transcendence lies in the direction of awareness.

In Balanced Coordination, you're primarily focused on integrating yourself, aligning your own thoughts, emotions, body, and actions. The horse or the person you're working with provides feedback that helps you notice when you're out of alignment. The flow of awareness is primarily inward: "Am I congruent? Am I aligned?"

In Centred Transcendence, that internal alignment becomes so consistent that your awareness can expand outward. You're not focused on maintaining your own coordination because it's become automatic. Instead, you're reaching out from your established centre to feel what others are experiencing. The flow of awareness is primarily outward: "What do they need? What are they feeling? How can I guide from here?"

Think about it in terms of riding. When you're learning, you're acutely aware of yourself, your seat, your hands, your legs, your breathing. You're working to coordinate all these elements. That's Balanced Coordination.

But when you've been riding for decades, that coordination becomes unconscious. You don't think about your seat or hands. Instead, your awareness extends downward to feel every footfall of the horse. You sense which leg is about to step. You feel the horse's confidence or uncertainty, their relaxation or tension, their engagement or resistance. Your centre remains still and grounded while your awareness expands to include the horse completely.

That's Centred Transcendence.

The Comanche understood this distinction instinctively. Their horsemanship wasn't about perfecting their own technique, though they did that too. It was about expanding their awareness to include the horse so completely that horse and rider became, as Running Wolf said, "one being with two bodies."

What Gets Pruned

Before we can fully understand Centred Transcendence, we need to recognize what must be cut away to achieve it. The pruning at this level isn't about removing external obstacles. It's about identifying and releasing the internal patterns that prevent your awareness from expanding beyond yourself.

Excessive self-focus gets pruned away. When you're constantly monitoring your own performance, checking whether you're doing it right, worrying about how you look or what others think, your awareness turns inward. It spirals into self-consciousness rather than expanding into presence. Centred Transcendence requires you to release this preoccupation with self. Not to become careless or unconscious, but to become so competent and integrated that you no longer need to monitor yourself constantly.

Think of Seven Arrows learning to ride. Initially, he was acutely aware of his balance, his grip, his position. But as he matured, that self-focus fell away. He didn't stop being aware, he stopped being self-conscious. His competence became automatic, freeing his attention to expand outward to the horse, the herd, the terrain, his fellow warriors.

Scattered attention gets pruned. In our modern world, we're trained to multitask, to keep dozens of concerns active in our minds simultaneously. Email, projects, conversations, worries, plans, all competing for mental space. This fragmentation prevents the kind of focused, expanded awareness that Centred Transcendence requires.

The Pareto Principle reveals the problem: if 80 percent of your mental activity produces only 20 percent of your results, then you're wasting enormous energy on concerns that don't actually matter. Centred Transcendence demands that you prune away that unproductive 80 percent. Not by adding more discipline or effort, but by releasing your grip on what doesn't serve.

This is what Jesus was teaching when he said the Spirit would come only after he left. The disciples' attention was scattered across their concerns about losing him, their anxiety about the future, their attachment to having him physically present. That scattering had to be pruned away before they could access the centred presence that would allow them to feel his guidance from within.

The need to control every detail gets pruned. Micromanagement, whether of yourself or others, stems from the belief that your constant intervention is what holds everything together. This belief keeps you trapped in the weeds, unable to maintain the centred overview that would actually allow you to guide effectively.

The Comanche chief couldn't direct every warrior's action in battle. The centred leader can't approve every decision. The advanced horseman can't cue every step. Trying to control everything doesn't create better outcomes, it just exhausts you and limits what's possible.

Pruning this need for control doesn't mean becoming passive or abdicating responsibility. It means recognizing that your highest value comes from maintaining your centre and extending your awareness, not from managing every detail. When you release the 80 percent of activity that produces minimal results, you free yourself to focus on the 20 percent that actually matters.

The attachment to immediate results gets pruned. When you're desperate to see outcomes now, when you can't tolerate the uncertainty of processes unfolding in their own time, your awareness contracts into anxious monitoring. You become reactive rather than responsive, tense rather than present.

Centred Transcendence requires you to care deeply about outcomes while holding them lightly. To maintain clear intention without desperate attachment. To guide toward destinations without controlling the journey's every step. This pruning of attachment is perhaps the most challenging, because it feels like giving up. But it's actually the opposite, it's becoming free.

Finally, the illusion of separation gets pruned. As long as you believe you're fundamentally separate from the world around you, disconnected from the people you lead and the horses you ride, your awareness can't truly expand. You might extend it outward through effort or technique, but you won't experience the natural flow of centred presence that Seven Arrows discovered.

The deepest pruning happens when you recognize what Running Wolf taught his grandson: "You are not separate from the world, you are part of it. And from your centre, you can reach to any part of it."

This isn't mystical thinking. It's practical recognition that your awareness, your influence, your presence aren't confined to your physical body. From your centre, you can touch far more than you imagine.

This pruning creates space. Space for your awareness to expand. Space for your presence to reach outward. Space for the vital 20 percent of your activity to flourish because it's no longer crowded out by the unproductive 80 percent.

And in that space, Centred Transcendence becomes possible.

The Leader Who Left to Become Omnipresent

Fifteen hundred years before Seven Arrows learned to reach from his centre to touch a horse's spirit, another teacher was trying to explain a similar concept to his followers. But they weren't understanding.

Jesus had been with his disciples for three years. They'd travelled together, eaten together, learned together. They'd watched him heal the sick, teach the crowds, challenge the religious authorities. They'd come to depend on his physical presence, his immediate guidance, his voice answering their questions.

And now he was telling them he was leaving.

"It is for your good that I am going away," he said. "Unless I go away, the Advocate will not come to you; but if I go, I will send him to you."

The disciples must have looked at him like he'd lost his mind. "For our good?" How could his leaving possibly be good? They needed him here. With them. Physically present. How were they supposed to lead this movement without him?

But Jesus understood something they couldn't yet grasp. As long as he remained physically present, he could only be in one place at one time. He could teach one group in one location. Answer questions for the people immediately around him. His influence, powerful as it was, remained limited by the constraints of physical presence.

But if He left, if He returned to the Father, then the Spirit could come. And the Spirit wasn't limited by physical presence. The Spirit could reach into every person who followed him. Could guide from within rather than from without. Could be present in Judea and Samaria and Rome and Alexandria simultaneously.

"But when the Advocate comes, whom I will send to you from the Father, the Spirit of truth who goes out from the Father, he will testify about me," Jesus explained. "And you also must testify, for you have been with me from the beginning."

207

This wasn't abandonment. It was expansion. Jesus was moving from being a local teacher to becoming a universal presence. From external guide to internal compass. From giving direction from beside them to guiding from within them.

"The Advocate, the Holy Spirit, whom the Father will send in my name, will teach you all things and will remind you of everything I have said to you," He told them. "On that day you will realize that I am in my Father, and you are in me, and I am in you."

This is Centred Transcendence in its purest form. Jesus wasn't losing His centre by leaving. He was establishing His centre in the Father, from which His Spirit could reach out to touch every person who would ever follow Him. He was moving from physical limitation to spiritual omnipresence.

The disciples couldn't understand it yet. Not until after the crucifixion, after the resurrection, after the ascension, after Pentecost when the Spirit actually came and they experienced what He'd been trying to tell them. Only then did they realize what He meant.

Peter, who'd relied so heavily on Jesus's physical presence that he'd denied Him three times when that presence was threatened, suddenly found himself preaching with authority to thousands. Not because Jesus was standing beside him telling him what to say. Because the Spirit was within him, reaching out from Peter's centre to touch the hearts of everyone listening.

Paul, who never met Jesus physically, somehow knew Him more intimately than many who had walked with Him for years. Because Paul had learned to access that centred presence within himself, that connection to Christ that wasn't limited by time or space or physical proximity.

The early church scattered across the known world, Jerusalem, Antioch, Ephesus, Corinth, Rome, and in every place, followers experienced the same presence guiding them. Not because Jesus was physically present in each location. Because his Spirit reached from the centre to touch all of them simultaneously.

This is what Jesus meant when He said, "I tell you the truth, anyone who believes in me will do the same works I have done, and even greater works, because I am going to be with the Father." Greater works. Not because his followers were more capable than He was. But because His presence would no longer be limited to one location. Through the Spirit, He could guide and empower people everywhere at once.

The kingdom Jesus established wasn't built on His physical presence micromanaging every decision and directing every action. It was built on His centred presence reaching out through the Spirit to guide everyone who learned to listen for that inner voice, that internal compass, that sense of His presence within them.

He moved from local teacher to universal centre. From external guide to internal presence. From limited reach to infinite connection.

This is the pattern Centred Transcendence always follows: establishing yourself so firmly in your centre that your awareness can expand to reach wherever it needs to reach. Not through force or control. Through connection. Through spirit reaching to spirit. Through centred presence that can touch everything without being diminished or scattered or lost.

Two Ways of Leading

The contrast between these two approaches to leadership couldn't be more stark.

The Micromanager tries to be everywhere by being involved in everything. They make every decision. Approve every action. Check every detail. They move from person to person, place to place, constantly putting out fires and directing traffic and solving problems. They're exhausted. Their team is frustrated. Nothing happens without them, which means everything slows to the pace of their capacity.

This leader hasn't learned to be centred. They try to keep a grip on every aspect; they're spread too thin. They're scattered across a hundred concerns, fragmented by constant demands, unable to rest because they carry every burden themselves. They believe their physical presence and direct intervention are what hold everything together. They hold onto the 80 percent that doesn't really matter, therefore they are not available for the 20 percent that needs them.

The Centred Leader is still. Grounded. Present at their core. From that centre, their awareness extends outward to touch everyone they lead. They can feel when someone is struggling without being told. They sense when a decision point is approaching. They know when to step in and when to trust the process. They guide through influence rather than control. Through vision rather than micromanagement. Through presence rather than proximity.

This leader has learned what Jesus taught: that true leadership isn't about being everywhere physically. It's about being so centred that your influence can reach everywhere spiritually. Your team doesn't need you standing over them because they can feel your guidance from within themselves. Your presence has become internalized.

The Comanche demonstrated this in their band structure. They had chiefs, yes. Leaders who had earned respect through wisdom and courage. But these leaders didn't direct every warrior's action in battle. They couldn't. Comanche warfare was too fluid, too fast, too dependent on individual judgment made in split seconds.

Instead, the chief maintained his centre. Made the overall strategy clear. Shared the vision. And then trusted each warrior to extend that vision into action, reaching from their own centres to make the right decisions in their immediate circumstances.

In a buffalo hunt, the hunt leader might direct the overall approach. But once the hunt began, once warriors rode into the herd at full gallop, there was no time for direction or instruction. Each hunter had to act from his own centre, his awareness expanded to include his horse, the buffalo, his fellow hunters, the terrain, everything at once. The hunt leader's presence remained as a guiding influence, but not as constant instruction.

This is what Centred Transcendence enables: leadership that guides without controlling. Presence that influences without micromanaging. Direction that reaches from centre to periphery without needing physical proximity.

In business terms, it's the difference between the executive who needs to approve every email and the executive whose vision is so clearly communicated, whose presence is so well established, that people across the entire organization make decisions consistent with that vision without needing constant direction.

In military terms, it's the difference between the general who tries to direct every tactical movement and the general whose strategic clarity is so well understood that officers at every level can make appropriate decisions in their immediate context.

In terms of horsemanship, it's the difference between the rider who tries to control every step and the rider whose centred presence allows the horse to carry them both through complex movements that couldn't possibly be directed step by step.

What It Looks Like in the Arena

When you bring Centred Transcendence into your work with horses, everything changes again. Not in the dramatic way it changed when you first learned Emotionless Communication or developed Balanced Coordination. This change is more subtle but deeper.

First, your awareness shifts fundamentally. Instead of focusing primarily on yourself and your cues, your awareness expands to include the horse completely. You feel their footfalls as if they were your own feet touching the ground. You sense their balance, their rhythm, their confidence or uncertainty, their engagement or resistance.

This isn't imagination or projection. It's direct perception that comes from being so centred yourself that your awareness can extend beyond your physical boundaries. You are not trying to control it all, but you are able to feel it all. Horsemen, particularly cutters, talk about developing feel and timing; this is about being able to sense what is about to happen and be in position to help, where and when you need to be.

A Lesson in Letting Go

I remember the first time I experienced this fully. I was working a stallion named Harry on a cow, practicing for the upcoming futurity, again. We'd done this hundreds, if not thousands of times. But on this day, something shifted for me. I stopped being aware of my own body. My focus wasn't on my seat or hands or legs. All of that had become automatic, unconscious.

But let me take you back a step or two in time, before we go on with this moment. We saw Harry born, a brilliant little bay brown colt. What struck everyone that saw him that day were his long legs. So much so that he immediately got the nickname, Harry Highpants.

What I was amazed by though, when I was watching him the night after he was born, was how he fell into this pattern. The perfect pattern he would use when cutting a cow and holding it away from the herd. One moment he was standing there in front of his mother, then he fell into this pattern as she stood there. Run, stop, turn, and again run, stop, turn. Backwards and forwards, again and again in front of his mum.

As he grew, he continued to show his athletic ability, and also as with most colts, his propensity for stupidity and annoying behaviour. On one occasion he showed his willingness to dominate, when we put him in the round-yard with a large rubber ball. He hunted that thing around and across the yard with complete focus and determination, until, in a lather of sweat, he destroyed it.

We were keen to take him to the NCHA Futurity at the end of his three-year-old year, so the world could see how special he was. The leadup to the event was intense, trying to find the parts of his skill set that needed work, trying to build his confidence up without making him overconfident. Hoping that I had done enough to get by with him, wanting more time to train him, but at the same time wanting the event to be on, so we could compete now.

The thing with that show, the biggest cutting event in the nation, is that every horse there is someone's special horse. At the end of the day, that day when the top twenty three-year-olds in the nation compete for the title, when the other hundred or so horses that didn't make it to the final round, fade into the background, the winner is the one with the most skill, ability and luck.

For everyone else, it's a time for reflection, thinking what might have been, thinking how they could have done something better. Planning how they can win the next year. Thinking about what the next year of training will be like, what they can change. What they need to do differently. And every show, every time you compete, it's the same. Review and reflect. Then get back to training.

If the Show pen is where the money is made, whether through winnings or through increase in reputation, the training pen is where the corrections and the connection are made. This is where, the day that I spoke of earlier occurred. The day when something shifted for me. When I stopped being aware of my own body. My focus was no longer on my seat or hands or legs. It all became automatic, unconscious.

Where I could feel the horse. Not just the physical sensations of movement, but something deeper. I felt when he was about to drop into the ground, to stop with the cow before his body began the movement. I was able to sense when he was uncertain about the cow's next move, and more importantly when he was confident that he had it. And then I knew, he knew, he had it. He didn't need my help.

He didn't need my guidance. He was in control. I could sit there and just enjoy the show, from the best seat in the house.

And because I could feel all of this, I could support him. Not with constant cues or corrections. With subtle shifts in my own centre that encouraged him. My centred presence reached down to touch his, supporting without managing.

The result was some of the best work we'd ever done together. Not because I'd become a better rider. But because I'd stopped feeling the need to ride him where I thought he should go, and started simply being present, trusting him. My awareness expanded to include both of us completely.

The Qualities of Centred Presence

Your influence becomes almost invisible. Observers watching can't always tell what you're doing. Your hands barely move. Your legs seem still. Your seat appears quiet. But the horse responds instantly, precisely, to intentions you haven't obviously communicated.

This is what advanced horsemanship always looks like. The great riders make it seem effortless because they're not working. They're being. Their centred presence guides the horse the way Running Wolf's presence guided that young gelding, through spirit touching spirit, not through force or constant direction.

Watch the top showmen in the cutting arena, the way they consistently cut the cow that they want, smoothly, effortlessly. They have no excess movement, no sign that they are obviously controlling their horse better than any other competitor, but they anticipate where they need to be, before they need to be there. They are millimetre perfect in how and where they push the cow they want, where they want it.

They make those precise movements, doing the 20 percent, almost imperceivable to the watcher, placing their horse exactly where they need to be on the cow to push it calmly out of the remainder of the herd, and leave it standing by itself alone in the centre of the arena, "where the money is made". Then they leave it to the horsepower of the team to do their part.

You develop 360-degree awareness. You're not just aware of the beneath you. You're aware of everything around you simultaneously. The arena fences, the judges box. The cattle gathered along the back fence, waiting their turn. The herd holders (riders who keep the cattle bunched together). The turn-back help (riders who push cattle back toward your horse so they try to return to the herd). The wind flapping the flags above. The footing beneath the horse's feet. The music coming through the speakers. All of it is present in your awareness without any taking your presence, your awareness from the cow and the job at hand.

This is essential in cutting competitions. The horse is reading the cow. Working the cow. You're supporting the horse. But you're also reading the cow. Assessing whether you can stay on it for a bit longer, or need to get off it as soon as possible because it is about to "run you over". You are aware of the herd, the turn-back riders, how much time remains. Centred Transcendence allows you to process all of that simultaneously without becoming scattered or overwhelmed.

Your presence becomes calming to the horse regardless of circumstances. When something unexpected happens, a gate bangs, bunting flaps in the wind, a dog barks outside the arena, the herd holder's horse bucks behind you, your centred stability provides an anchor the horse can return to.

The horse learns that no matter what chaos erupts around them, you remain centred. Your awareness doesn't fragment. Your presence doesn't waver. This creates profound trust. They know they can depend on you to remain stable when everything else becomes uncertain.

You learn to guide primarily through intention rather than instruction. You think about where you want to go or what you want to do, and the horse responds. Not because you've become telepathic. Because your centred intention translates into subtle physical cues that happen unconsciously, and the horse, feeling your expanded awareness that includes them, responds to those intentions before they even become explicit cues.

This is what makes advanced riding look magical to observers. The rider appears to do nothing. The horse does everything. But what's actually happening is that the rider's centred presence and clear intention guide the horse through a connection deeper than physical cues.

What It Looks Like Outside the Arena

The same principle that transforms horsemanship transforms all forms of leadership when applied consistently.

In professional settings, Centred Transcendence manifests as:

The ability to sense the emotional temperature of a room without anyone speaking. You walk into a meeting and immediately feel the tension, or the excitement, or the resignation. You don't need to be told. Your expanded awareness picks it up directly.

This isn't mystical. It's attention. The centred leader isn't distracted by their own agenda or anxieties. They're present enough to notice subtle cues, body language, tone shifts, energy changes, that others miss because they're focused on themselves. Doing the 20 percent.

Knowing when people need support before they ask for it. The team member who's struggling. The client who's about to leave. The employee who's burning out. Centred leaders often sense these situations developing before they become crises, because their awareness extends beyond themselves to touch the people they're responsible for. Producing the 80 percent, making the difference to the team.

Making decisions from a place of stillness rather than reactivity. When crisis hits, the centred leader doesn't panic or rush. They return to their centre, expand their awareness to include all relevant factors, and make decisions from that grounded place. Their team takes courage from this stability.

I've worked with executives who embodied this quality. In high-pressure situations where everyone else was frantically scrambling, these leaders remained calm. Not because they didn't care or didn't understand the urgency. Because they'd learned to maintain their centre regardless of circumstances. And from that centre, they could see more clearly, think more strategically, and guide more effectively than they ever could from reactive anxiety.

Creating environments where people feel simultaneously supported and autonomous. The centred leader's presence is felt even when they're not physically present. Their vision is so clear, their values so well communicated, their trust so well established, that people across the organization can make appropriate decisions without constant supervision.

This is what Jesus established. This is what great Comanche chiefs created. This is what transforms management into leadership.

Maintaining clarity and calm in your own mind while holding space for others' emotions. Someone on your team is angry. Frustrated. Fearful. The centred leader can be present with those emotions without being destabilized by them. They don't try to fix the emotions or shut them down. They also don't get swept up in them. They remain centred while their awareness expands to include the other person's experience.

This is profoundly different from either emotional fusion (where you become anxious because someone else is anxious) or emotional distance (where you shut down and become unavailable). Centred presence creates a third option: being with someone in their difficulty without losing yourself in it.

Recognizing patterns and connections others miss. Because your awareness isn't consumed by immediate concerns, you can see larger patterns. How this decision will affect that department. How this person's strength could address that team's weakness. How apparently separate problems might share a common root.

This strategic awareness comes naturally when you're centred. Your mind isn't cluttered with anxiety or distracted by ego concerns. You can simply observe clearly and notice what's actually there.

The Practice of Centred Transcendence

So how do you develop this quality? How do you move from occasional glimpses of expanded awareness to consistent centred presence?

The Comanche had their methods. Their young men would "lie down for power", vision questing in high places, fasting and praying, seeking to connect with spirits. They'd practice breath work with horses. They'd spend long hours alone with animals, learning to expand their awareness to include non-human spirits.

Jesus taught His followers to pray. To seek the Father's presence. To be filled with the Spirit. To remain in Him as branches remain in the vine. All of these were practices designed to help people establish their centre in something beyond themselves and then operate from that centred connection.

For modern practitioners, the path looks similar in principle though different in specifics.

Establish a consistent practice of returning to centre. This might be meditation. Prayer. Qi Gong. Yoga. Breathwork. The specific method matters less than the consistency. You need a practice that trains your nervous system to return to calm, your mind to return to stillness, your awareness to return to presence. You must learn to let go of the 80 percent that you don't need.

Along with prayer, I practice simple breath awareness exercises through Qi Gong each morning. A few minutes of simply working on my breath while controlling my body. This trains my awareness to rest in present-moment experience rather than racing forward into planning or backward into regret.

When I'm consistent with this practice, I notice that my centre becomes more stable throughout the day. When something challenging happens, take a moment, be **silent**. I can return to that centred place more quickly. My awareness doesn't fragment as easily.

Practice maintaining centre during progressively more challenging situations. Start with stillness in a quiet place. Then maintain it while walking. Then while having a conversation. Then while someone is upset with you. Then while you're under deadline pressure. Then while multiple crises demand attention simultaneously. Take a moment, feel the **silence**.

This is how you train the capacity to remain centred regardless of external circumstances. You gradually increase the challenge while maintaining the practice. Take a moment, feel the **silence**.

In the arena, this looks like maintaining your centre first when the horse is standing still. Then when they're walking. Then trotting. Then cantering. Then working cattle. Then in the show ring. Each level adds complexity, but you're training the same fundamental capacity: remaining centred while circumstances become more demanding. Take a moment, feel the **silence**.

Deliberately practice expanding your awareness outward from your centre. When you're centred and calm, intentionally broaden your attention. Notice sounds in the distance. Feel the quality of light. Sense the emotional atmosphere of the space you're in. Let your awareness expand like ripples on water. Take a moment, feel the **silence**.

With horses, this means consciously extending your awareness to include them. Feel their breathing. Notice their weight shifts. Sense their attention. Let your awareness expand until you're not just with the horse but including the horse in your sense of self. Take a moment, feel the **silence**.

With people, practice the same thing. In conversations, instead of being focused entirely on what you're going to say next, expand your awareness to include the other person completely. Notice their breathing. Their body language. The subtle shifts in their energy. Their unspoken concerns. Take a moment, feel the **silence**.

This isn't analysis. It's pure perception. And it becomes possible when you're centred enough that your awareness isn't consumed by self-concern.

Learn to guide from centre rather than from reactivity. When something needs to happen, instead of immediately jumping into action or direction, pause. Return to centre. Let your awareness expand to include the full situation. Then act or speak from that centred, expanded place.

This creates a quality of guidance that others experience as wise rather than impulsive, grounded rather than reactive, clear rather than confused. Your words and actions carry more weight because they're coming from a deeper place.

Practice the art of being present without agenda. This is perhaps the most challenging aspect. We're so accustomed to always wanting something, always trying to accomplish something, always having an outcome we're attached to.

Centred Transcendence requires you to be fully present and engaged while simultaneously holding your agenda lightly. You care about outcomes but you're not attached to them. You guide toward destinations but you're not controlling the journey. You remain focused but not rigid.

The Comanche warrior riding into battle maintained fierce focus on victory while simultaneously accepting death as a possibility. That's not contradiction, it's centred presence. Full engagement without desperate attachment.

Recognize that this is a practice, not a destination. You don't achieve Centred Transcendence and stay there permanently. You practice it. Some days you're more centred than others. Some situations you handle with grace. Others scramble your awareness and pull you to the outer sphere of your influence.

That's fine. That's human. What matters is that you keep practicing, keep returning to centre, keep expanding your awareness, keep learning to guide from that centred place rather than from reactivity or control. Keep learning, and relearning to let go of the 80 percent you don't need.

The Integration: Communication Transformed

Centred Transcendence represents the fulfillment of the entire Communication Pillar. Everything you've developed through Emotionless Communication and Balanced Coordination comes together here in refined form.

The Emotionless Communication that taught you to remove emotional static from your messages has matured into the ability to communicate from such a centred place that your words carry clarity and weight naturally. You're not working to remove emotion. You're operating from a place where reactive emotion doesn't arise in the first place.

The Balanced Coordination that taught you to align body, mind, and emotion has matured into embodied integration so consistent that you're no longer focused on maintaining it. That internal alignment has become automatic, freeing your awareness to extend outward.

And now, through Centred Transcendence, you've developed the ability to remain grounded in your centre while your awareness expands to include everything and everyone you need to guide. You're not scattered, trying to provide solutions across the hundreds of concerns in the outer sphere of your influence. You're centred in one place while reaching out to touch many.

Think about Jesus. His centre was in the Father. From that centre, his Spirit reached out to touch every person who would ever follow him. He wasn't diminished by being dispersed. He was multiplied by going to the centre.

Think about Seven Arrows. His centre was in his connection to puha, to the spirit that animated all things. From that centre, his awareness could expand to include his horse, the buffalo herd, his fellow warriors, the terrain, everything at once. He wasn't overwhelmed by holding all of that in awareness. He was empowered by it.

Think about the moments when you've been most effective as a leader, a parent, a partner, a horseman. Chances are, those were moments when you were deeply centred and simultaneously broadly aware. Present with yourself while being present with others. Grounded while reaching out. Still at your core while engaged fully with what was happening.

That's Centred Transcendence. And it's available through practice.

The Communication Journey Complete

Think about how far this pillar has brought you. You began with Emotionless Communication, learning to remove reactive static from your messages. You grew into Balanced Coordination, aligning body, mind, and emotion into embodied congruence. And now, through Centred Transcendence, you've pruned away everything that prevents your awareness from expanding beyond yourself.

This progression, from clearing interference, to internal integration, to external expansion, represents communication transformed. You've moved from managing your reactions, to coordinating your being, to reaching from your centre to touch others. This is the Communication Pillar ready for harvest.

Moving Forward

But Centred Transcendence, powerful as it is, represents only one-third of the foundation necessary for Incorporeal Competence. You've now developed three levels:

From the Courage and Vision Pillar: Peaceful Directedness, the ability to guide calmly through uncertainty by creating an environment where those you are leading are able to reach back to you with safety and surety, to draw on your certainty and to follow your vision.

From the Communication Pillar: Centred Transcendence, the ability to reach out from stillness to touch others. To have a greater influence in the world around you through your connection to it.

But there's a third pillar still to explore, the Service pillar. Because it's not enough to have Courage and Vision and communication if you're not serving something beyond yourself. It's not enough to be centred and clear if your purpose is selfish. It's not enough to guide with calm and reach with awareness if what you're guiding toward and reaching for serves only your own agenda.

The final pillar will teach you how to place all of this, your vision and courage, your communication, your centred presence, in service of something greater. How to use power gently. How to understand deeply before acting. How to know when structures must be destroyed to enable growth.

Only when all three pillars are fully developed does Incorporeal Competence emerge, that state of sustained passion, unwavering loyalty, and purposeful perseverance that we'll explore in the final chapter. This is where all the planting, growing, and pruning culminates in the harvest.

But for now, practice being centred. Practice expanding your awareness from that centre. Practice maintaining stillness within while remaining fully engaged with everything around you.

Learn what Seven Arrows learned: that you are not separate from the world but intimately connected to all of it. That from your centre, you can touch any part of it even those parts well beyond your reach. That stillness at your core enables movement at your periphery. That centred presence creates influence far beyond physical proximity.

Learn what Jesus taught: that leaving physical location doesn't mean losing presence. That establishing your centre in something transcendent allows your influence to become universal. That the Spirit within can reach further than the body ever could.

And learn what every master horseman discovers: that the horse doesn't follow your hands or legs or seat. The horse follows the presence at your centre. Your spirit reaching out to touch theirs. Your awareness expanded to include them so completely that you move together as one being.

Centred Transcendence is not escaping from the world, but complete engagement with it from a place of unshakeable stillness. Not withdrawal into yourself, but expansion from your centre to touch everything around you.

The Comanche called it puha, power that flows when you learn to be still while your spirit reaches out. Jesus called it the Spirit, we call it the Holy Spirit, the presence of God reaching from the Father through the Son into every heart that opens to receive it.

Whatever you call it, it works the same way: establish your centre, maintain your stillness, expand your awareness, and discover that you can touch far more than you ever imagined possible.

The horse feels it. The team senses it. The people you lead experience it. Not as control or manipulation or force. As guidance. As presence. As the centred stillness from which all wise action flows.

Practice it. Refine it. Trust it. And discover what Running Wolf promised his grandson all those years ago, from his place in the territory of the Southern Great Plains, the plains of Comancheria, that from your centre, you can reach as far as you need to reach.

"Remain in me, as I also remain in you. No branch can bear fruit by itself; it must remain in the vine. Neither can you bear fruit unless you remain in me."

- Jesus, John 15:4

CHAPTER 11

CREATIVE DESTRUCTION

"The greatest conqueror is he who overcomes the enemy without a blow."

- Chinese Proverb

The steppes stretched endlessly in every direction, brown grass rippling like water under the eternal blue sky. fourteen-year-old Temujin (Teh-moo-jin) crouched behind a rocky outcrop, his breath coming in careful, measured draws. His half-brother Begter (Behg-tuhr) stood fifty paces away, silhouetted against the horizon, oblivious to the danger stalking him.

In Temujin's hand, the bow felt heavy. Layers of horn, sinew, bark and wood bound together to create a weapon that could punch through armour at two hundred paces. But this morning, Temujin wasn't hunting armour. He was hunting the past. Hunting everything that had kept his family starving and desperate. Hunting the old structure that no longer served.

Beside him, his full brother Khasar notched his own arrow. They had discussed this through the long night, sitting outside their mother's ger while she slept fitfully inside. Begter had been taking more than his share of the meat. Taking from Temujin's mother Hoelun (Huh-oo-lun or Oo-lun), taking from the younger children, asserting dominance through the old tribal hierarchies that said he, as son of their father's chief wife, deserved more.

Yesterday, Begter had stolen a fish Temujin had caught. A small thing, perhaps. But when you're surviving on marmots and roots. When your father has been poisoned by rival Tatars (Tah-tars) and your own clan has abandoned your family to die on the steppe, a stolen fish isn't small. It's a statement about who has power and who doesn't. It's a declaration that the old order, where birth rank matters more than contribution, where inherited status trumps earned respect, will continue.

Temujin had spent the night wrestling with what needed to happen. The Mongol way, the way his father's generation had done things, said Begter had the right to take what he wanted. He was the son of the chief wife. That mattered. That's how it had always been.

But "how it had always been" had gotten his father killed, his family exiled, his people fragmented into squabbling clans that raided each other for livestock and women while powerful kingdoms surrounded them on every side. "How it had always been" was starvation and shame and weakness.

Temujin rose to his feet. Begter turned, saw his two half-brothers approaching with bows drawn, and understood immediately. He didn't run. He sat down on a rock, cross-legged, and said something that has echoed through history: "Now you are bent on destroying me. But remember, you have no companions but your shadows. If you do this, who will help you take revenge on the Tayichi'ut clan?"

It was a fair question. The Tayichi'ut (Tie-tchoode) had enslaved Temujin just months earlier, locking his head and hands in a wooden board called a cangue. They were the clan that had expelled his family after his father's death. Powerful enemies. Begter was strong. Capable. In the old way of thinking, killing him was foolish.

But the old way of thinking was what Temujin had decided to destroy.

The arrows flew. Begter died sitting upright, refusing to beg or flee, accepting the end with the stoicism of a man who understood the way of the old order, and exactly what was happening.

When they returned to the ger, Hoelun was waiting. Her fury was terrible to witness. "Killers! Destroyers!" she screamed at her sons. "Apart from my shadow, I have no friend. Apart from my tail, I have no whip. And now you have destroyed your own brother, one of the few of us! Who will fight for us now?"

She was right to be furious. By every standard of Mongol tradition, what Temujin had done was unforgivable. He had murdered his own brother. He had violated the sacred bonds of family. He had acted from ambition and calculation rather than from loyalty to the tribe.

But Temujin stood silent, letting his mother's rage wash over him, because he knew something she didn't yet understand. He hadn't destroyed his brother for ambition. He was beginning to destroy a system. He had killed the principle that birth rank determined worth. He had begun to execute the old Mongol way that had led to nothing but weakness and division.

In its place, he would build something new.

The Death of Old Systems

Thirteen hundred years before young Temujin killed his half-brother on the Mongolian steppe, a very different man walked a road toward Damascus with murder in his heart.

Saul of Tarsus was not struggling for survival. He was a Roman citizen, educated, connected to the power structures of his time. He had studied under Gamaliel, one of the most respected rabbis in Jerusalem. He knew scripture, knew law, knew exactly who he was and what his purpose was.

That purpose was to destroy the followers of Jesus. This new sect threatened everything Saul valued. They claimed a crucified criminal was the Messiah. They welcomed Gentiles without requiring full conversion to Judaism. They were dismantling centuries of tradition, disrupting the carefully maintained boundaries between Jew and Gentile, clean and unclean, chosen and unchosen.

Saul had watched, approving, as Stephen was stoned to death for blasphemy. He had gone house to house in Jerusalem, dragging Christians from their homes to be imprisoned. And now he was traveling to Damascus with official letters authorizing him to arrest any followers of "the Way" he found there and bring them back to Jerusalem in chains.

He was certain. Absolutely, completely certain. He was serving God by destroying this heretical movement.

And then, on the Damascus road, a light from heaven blazed around him. Saul fell to the ground, blinded, hearing a voice that asked, "Saul, Saul, why do you persecute me?"

"Who are you, Lord?" Saul asked.

"I am Jesus, whom you are persecuting."

For three days, Saul sat in darkness in Damascus, neither eating nor drinking. Everything he had built his identity on, his education, his certainty, his role as guardian of tradition, lay in ruins. The man who had been so sure he was serving God by destroying Christians now understood that he had been fighting against God himself.

When his sight returned, Saul had become Paul. Not just a change of name, but a complete reconstruction of identity. Everything he had known with such certainty was now revealed as desperately wrong. Every structure he had defended needed to be dismantled. Every boundary he had maintained needed to be torn down.

The man who had persecuted Christians would spend the rest of his life proclaiming Christ to the Gentiles. The man who had defended Jewish law would write that faith, not law, was the path to God. The man who had tried to maintain the old order would become the greatest agent of its creative destruction.

Both Temujin and Saul understood something essential: sometimes the most compassionate thing you can do is destroy what no longer serves. Sometimes service requires you to tear down the old structure so something better can be built.

This is Creative Destruction, the third harvest that grows from the planted seed of Powerful Gentility and the mature fruit of Determined Understanding.

Understanding Creative Destruction

Creative Destruction sits at the culmination of the Service pillar in the Incorporeal Competence framework. It's the harvest that ripens only after you've learned to lead with Powerful Gentility, strength expressed through deliberate softness; and deepened that practice through Determined Understanding, the patient pursuit of truth even when it's uncomfortable.

But there's a paradox here that needs to be addressed immediately: How can destruction be service? How can tearing something down be an act of care?

The answer lies in understanding what we're destroying and why.

Creative Destruction isn't about destruction for its own sake. It's not violence masquerading as progress. It's not the impatient leader who bulldozes resistance, or the insecure one who tears down others' work to make room for their own ego.

Creative Destruction is the gardener's prune. The surgeon's scalpel. The wildfire that clears the forest floor so new growth can emerge. It's the recognition that sometimes the most caring thing you can do is help someone let go of what's holding them back, even when, especially when, that something feels like part of their identity.

Think about Temujin's choice on the steppe. His mother was right to be furious. By every standard of their culture, killing Begter was wrong. But Temujin saw something his mother couldn't yet see: the old tribal structure that elevated birth rank over competence was killing his people slowly. As long as that system remained, the Mongols would stay fractured, weak, preyed upon by more organized kingdoms.

Begter's death wasn't about Begter. It was about destroying a principle. And what Temujin built in its place, a system based on merit, loyalty, and proven capability, would eventually unite the fractured Mongol tribes into the largest contiguous land empire in human history.

Think about Paul on the Damascus road. His entire identity was wrapped up in defending Jewish tradition against this upstart Christian sect. But that identity was preventing him from seeing truth. The destruction of his certainty, three days of blindness and fasting, created space for reconstruction. The man who emerged wasn't damaged by what he'd lost. He was freed by it.

This is what Creative Destruction offers: freedom through strategic release. But only if you understand the timing, the target, and the purpose.

Life on the Mongolian Steppe

But to fully appreciate the significance of what Temujin destroyed that day, and why that act of violence was actually an act of service, we need to understand the world he was born into. To understand what Temujin destroyed when he killed his brother, you need to understand what life was like on the steppes in the late twelfth century.

The Mongolian steppe wasn't a place for the soft or weak. Summers brought scorching heat that cracked the earth. Winters dropped temperatures to forty below zero, with winds that could freeze exposed flesh in minutes. Spring meant floods as the snow melted. Autumn meant racing to prepare for the next brutal winter.

The people who survived there were nomads, constantly moving with their herds of horses, sheep, goats, cattle, yaks, and camels. Everything had to be portable. The ger, a circular dwelling made of felt stretched over a collapsible wooden frame, could be taken down, loaded onto camels or yak-pulled carts, and reassembled at the next camp site in a few hours.

Children learned to ride before they could walk. By age five, both boys and girls were accomplished horsemen. They slept in the saddle during long migrations. They hunted with bows from horseback, learning to loose arrows at full gallop. The saying went: "The nomad is born in the saddle."

Their horses weren't the tall, elegant animals of European cavalry. Mongolian horses stood only about thirteen hands high, barely bigger than ponies. But what they lacked in height they made up in endurance. These horses could travel one hundred and sixty kilometres in a day. They could forage for themselves, surviving on whatever grass they could find under the snow. They would be ridden for three years straight on military campaigns without supply lines.

Everything about steppe life demanded cooperation within the clan. You shared meat with the family. You helped each other move camp. When raiders came, and raiders came often, you fought together. Hospitality was so sacred that it was taken for granted. If a stranger approached your ger, you fed them, gave them kumis (fermented mare's milk) to drink, and offered shelter, no questions asked until morning.

But cooperation within clans often meant competition between them. Raiding other clans for livestock, women, and prisoners was a recognized method of property accumulation. Weak clans got absorbed or destroyed. Strong clans grew stronger. And strength usually came from numbers and from maintaining traditional hierarchies.

When Temujin's father Yesugei died, poisoned by Tatars when Temujin was only nine, their clan made a calculation. Yesugei's family without him was a drain on resources. His widow Hoelun had five young children from her marriage to Yesugei, plus two older sons from Yesugei's other wife. In the harsh economics of steppe survival, that was a liability, not an asset.

So the clan left them. Just packed up the gers, moved to new pastures, and left Hoelun's family to starve.

This was the system. This was how it worked. Birth rank mattered. Tribal affiliation mattered. If you didn't fit into the structure properly, if you were a widow with too many mouths to feed, if you were born to a secondary wife, if your clan deemed you expendable, you died. That's just how it was.

Hoelun kept her children alive through sheer force of will. They dug roots. They caught fish and marmots. They survived. But Begter, as son of Yesugei's chief wife, kept asserting dominance according to the old rules. He deserved more. His status said so.

And Temujin, watching his mother and younger siblings go hungry while Begter took the largest portions, understood that the old rules were going to kill them all.

What Temujin Built

The teenager who killed his half-brother in defence of a new principle didn't become Genghis Khan overnight. It took decades. He was captured and enslaved by the Tayichi'ut clan. He escaped. He built alliances, slowly gathering followers who believed in his vision of a different way.

And the vision he offered was radical: What if competence mattered more than birth rank? What if loyalty and proven ability determined your position, not whose son you were? What if the rigid tribal divisions that kept Mongols fighting each other could be dissolved in favour of a unified identity?

By 1206, when the Kurultai (Koo-rool-tai), the great gathering of Mongol leaders, declared Temujin the "Genghis Khan" (Universal Ruler), he had destroyed the old tribal system and replaced it with something unprecedented.

He organized his forces using a decimal system: units of ten, one hundred, one thousand, and ten thousand warriors. Commanders were chosen based on merit, not aristocratic birth. A common herder who proved himself in battle could rise to command ten thousand men. The son of a powerful chieftain who failed was demoted or removed.

This was creative destruction in its purest form: deliberately dismantling a centuries-old system of inherited privilege and replacing it with meritocracy. And it worked because Genghis Khan understood the timing, his people were ready for change, and the purpose, creating unity and strength from fragmentation and weakness.

But the creative destruction didn't stop with military organization.

When Genghis Khan began conquering beyond Mongolia, he faced a choice. Most conquerors imposed their own culture, religion, and systems on defeated peoples. Force compliance. Extract tribute. Maintain control through fear and dominance. Genghis Khan did something different.

He granted religious freedom to everyone. This wasn't just tolerance, it was official policy backed by law. Religious leaders of all faiths were exempt from taxation. Christians, Muslims, Buddhists, Taoists, Jews, all were free to practice openly. Genghis Khan, who personally followed Tengrism (the shamanistic belief system of the steppes), would organize debates between religious leaders and invite scholars from all traditions to discuss their faiths.

His capital Karakorum hosted twelve Buddhist temples, two mosques, and a Christian church side by side.

This religious tolerance served a practical purpose, happy subjects were less likely to rebel, but it also reflected something deeper. Genghis Khan destroyed the principle that one religion or culture was superior. He dismantled the assumptions that kept people segregated and suspicious. In their place, he built something extraordinary: a multi-faith, multi-ethnic empire where your capability mattered more than your origins.

The same principle extended to governance. In traditional societies, aristocrats ruled by birthright. Genghis Khan destroyed that system. He would execute wealthy elites who had oppressed their people, but he welcomed talented administrators, craftsmen, engineers, and scholars from conquered territories into positions of power.

One of his top generals had shot Genghis Khan with an arrow during the tribal wars. When captured, the man bravely admitted to being the shooter. Instead of executing him, Genghis Khan recruited him to his general staff, giving him the nickname "The Arrow." Later, this man would command armies that conquered kingdoms.

This was the harvest of Powerful Gentility and Determined Understanding: the wisdom to recognize when existing structures served no one, the courage to dismantle them, and the compassion to build something better in their place.

What He Built That Lasted

The infrastructure Genghis Khan and his successors created demonstrated that Creative Destruction isn't just about tearing down, it's about what you build after.

The Yam postal system stretched across the entire empire. Every twenty to thirty miles, a station offered fresh horses, hot food, and lodging. Messages could travel thousands of miles in days instead of months. Merchants received special passports, golden tablets called paiza, that guaranteed them safe passage, accommodations, and exemption from local taxes throughout the empire.

The result was the Pax Mongolia, the Mongol Peace, where trade routes that had been dangerous for centuries became safe. The Silk Road flourished. Goods, ideas, technologies, and people moved freely across Eurasia. Paper money, backed by silk and precious metals, created a standardized currency. Standardized weights and measures facilitated smooth transactions across borders.

This was the first true globalization. Marco Polo's famous journey from Venice to China was possible only because Genghis Khan had destroyed the fractured, hostile kingdoms that had made such travel impossible and replaced them with unified, secure trade routes.

Genghis Khan lowered taxes for everyone and abolished them completely for doctors, teachers, priests, and educational institutions. He insisted that rulers, including himself, were subject to the law, a radical concept in an era when most kings considered themselves above legal restraint. He abolished torture but hunted down bandits and raiders who preyed on travellers.

Kublai Khan, Genghis's grandson, established an Institute of Muslim Astronomy and an Imperial Academy of Medicine that included Indian, Middle Eastern, Muslim, and Chinese physicians working together.

The Mongol Empire facilitated cultural exchange on a scale never seen before. Technologies moved freely: papermaking and printing spread west; gunpowder and the compass spread east. Ideas cross-pollinated. Chinese scholars met Persian philosophers. European craftsmen learned from Indian engineers.

All of this was possible because Genghis Khan had the courage to destroy systems that no longer served and the wisdom to build something better.

The Apostle of Creative Destruction

Paul of Tarsus never conquered an empire. He never commanded armies or built postal systems. But his creative destruction was equally profound and, in some ways, more radical.

For centuries, Judaism had maintained clear boundaries. Jew and Gentile were distinct categories. Clean and unclean were carefully delineated. The covenant was with Israel, the chosen people. To join that covenant, Gentiles had to convert fully, males had to be circumcised, everyone had to follow dietary laws and Sabbath restrictions.

The early Christians, all Jews, mostly assumed these boundaries would remain. Jesus was the Jewish Messiah. His followers would naturally be people who had joined the covenant through traditional means.

Paul destroyed that assumption.

He argued that faith in Christ, not adherence to Jewish law, was what mattered. That Gentiles didn't need to become Jews to become Christians. That the old boundaries between Jew and Gentile, slave and free, male and female, were being dissolved in Christ.

This was intensely controversial. The Jerusalem church, led by Jesus's own brother James, initially opposed Paul's mission to the Gentiles. There were fierce debates about whether Gentile converts needed to be circumcised, whether they had to follow dietary laws, whether they were really part of the covenant or second-class members.

Paul stood firm. "There is neither Jew nor Gentile, neither slave nor free, nor is there male and female, for you are all one in Christ Jesus," he wrote to the Galatians. The old categories didn't just need adjustment, they needed to be destroyed and rebuilt.

This wasn't easy for Paul. These were his categories too. He had been "a Hebrew of Hebrews; in regard to the law, a Pharisee." His entire identity had been built on these distinctions. Letting them go required him to undergo his own creative destruction, the three days of blindness, the complete reconstruction of his understanding of God and covenant and salvation.

But once he had gone through that process himself, Paul could guide others through it. His letters are masterclasses in Creative Destruction: acknowledging the value of what came before while explaining why it needs to be transcended, holding the tension between honouring tradition and embracing transformation, showing people how to let go of identities and structures that no longer serve without losing themselves in the process.

"Forgetting what is behind and straining toward what is ahead, I press on toward the goal," he wrote to the Philippians. Creative destruction in a sentence.

The Christianity that eventually spread throughout the Roman Empire and beyond was possible only because Paul had the courage to destroy the ethnic and legal boundaries of first-century Judaism and rebuild the faith as something universal. That's the power of Creative Destruction as service: you dismantle what limits growth, and you build what enables flourishing.

The Service Paradox

Let me return to the question I raised at the beginning: How can destruction be service? The answer emerged clearly when I was working with a mare named Harley during the 2025 show season.

Harley is a fantastic young mare, electric on a cow, so fast she epitomized greased lightning. I had shown her at the Futurity earlier in the year. She did well enough, though I made a couple of pilot errors that kept us out of the finals. But watching the videos of her runs, I could see problems developing in the way she worked. Small issues that could become huge issues if left unaddressed.

We made a decision. We wouldn't show her for the rest of the year. Instead, we'd work on fixing those issues, even though fixing them would mean temporarily making her worse.

One thing I was happy about was the level of confidence Harley carried into the show. That confidence was crucial. Any horse that steps into that competition arena needs to believe in their ability to perform, and in your ability to help them perform their best.

But I was going to have to tear holes in that confidence to fix the underlying problems.

Her "enthusiasm" had reached a level where our conversations had become one-sided. I would start to ask her to do something, and she would interrupt my request: "Yep, this is it! Here's your answer... Okay, let's move on."

She was confident in the knowledge that "This is what you want." She would power through exercises without really understanding how much input I wanted from her, what exactly I was asking for, or when I wanted it done.

Enthusiasm is important. But the ability to moderate that enthusiasm is equally important. She didn't understand that I was going to ask her to do something requiring more finesse than she expected.

What did her enthusiasm look like? She would trot around with her head held high, as if looking to see who might be lucky enough to watch her perform. When I asked her to give to the bit, she would go into little half-rearing jumps mixed with a stomping fit. The more I asked her to yield to pressure, the more intensely she would argue.

One morning's session took so long to get her listening that we never got to the actual training goal I had planned. But that was all right. The important thing was recognizing the situation and being willing to pivot.

If I had not insisted on asking her to give her head that little bit more, if I had let her carry her head where she was comfortable and just gone on to work the flag, she would have had that "knowledge" more deeply ingrained. And each time she would have been more insistent that she was right. Each time her fight escalating a little more.

This kind of communication breakdown is what gets riders hurt. Not because the horse is trying to be mean, but because it's a small misunderstanding left unaddressed. The rider either doesn't see it as an issue or hopes it will resolve itself.

But it won't. It doesn't. Left alone, the problem metastasizes. What starts as a mare carrying her head too high can become a mare who rears seriously and at the worst possible moment. What begins as enthusiasm can become dangerous rebellion.

I had to destroy Harley's confidence that she already knew what I wanted. I had to dismantle her certainty. I had to create confusion and doubt where there had been cocky assurance.

This felt terrible. Watching her confusion and frustration as I kept asking for something different than what she expected. Seeing her try her usual responses and finding they weren't working. Feeling her resentment build as she realized I wasn't going to let her do things her way.

But this was service. I was serving her development, her safety, and our long-term partnership. The confidence I was destroying was false confidence, confidence built on misunderstanding. The confusion I was creating was necessary confusion, the kind that precedes genuine learning.

Creative Destruction in service means being willing to dismantle something that looks like it's working because you can see that it's actually stopping what needs to happen.

Weeks later, after we had rebuilt her understanding about the correct response, Harley showed me something different. She was still enthusiastic. But now she was listening. She would start an answer and then pause, checking: "Is this what you want? Or is there more?"

That pause, that responding without overcommitting, was what we had built in the space created by destroying her old patterns.

The Seven C's of Service Through Destruction

The Seven C's framework outlines seven levels of competence and commitment that transform someone from novice to leader. Understanding these helps clarify how Creative Destruction functions as service.

1. *Conform*   Learning to do what is asked

2. *Comply*   Learning to do it when it is asked

3. *Correct*   Learning to do it without mistakes

4. *Confidence*   Doing it with enthusiasm

5. *Cheerfully*   Doing it with good humor

6. *Consistently*   Doing it with accuracy and dependability

7. *Cause*   Understanding the Why

Harley had rushed to Confidence (level 4) without fully mastering Conform, Comply, and Correct (levels 1-3). She was enthusiastic about doing what she thought I wanted, but she hadn't fully learned what I was actually asking or when I was asking it.

Creative Destruction meant taking her back to level 1. Destroying the confidence that we had built so we could rebuild solid foundations. It looked like regression. It felt like failure. But it was actually service, serving her development by insisting on proper sequencing.

This is what Creative Destruction is all about: the willingness to go backward temporarily to move forward sustainably.

In military basic training, this process is formalized. New recruits spend six months learning to Conform, Comply, and do things Correctly. Only then do they join their units where they develop Confidence, learn to do their jobs Cheerfully and Consistently, and finally understand their Cause deeply enough to become leaders who teach others.

The system works because it recognizes that you can't build genuine competence on shaky foundations. Sometimes you have to destroy what someone thinks they know so they can learn what they actually need to know.

What It Looks Like in the Arena

When you bring Creative Destruction into your work with horses, several things change:

1. **You develop the ability to distinguish between problems that need adjustment and problems that need complete reconstruction.** Many training issues are the result of unintended oversight and slight modifications to the program can fix this. But some issues, like Harley's false confidence or a horse who has learned to fear the bit because of harsh hands, require you to dismantle the entire pattern and start fresh.

   This discernment is crucial. Creative Destruction isn't about starting over every time something isn't perfect. It's about recognizing when the foundation itself is flawed and having the courage to rebuild from the ground up when you need to.

2. **You become comfortable with the temporary confusion and regression that comes with dismantling old patterns.** When you start asking a horse to do something differently than they've been doing it, they will be confused. They will try their old responses. They will resist the change. This is normal and necessary. The horse needs to shown the inadequacy of their old pattern before they can be open to learning a new one.

   The trainer's job during this phase is to stay calm, stay consistent, and stay committed to the reconstruction, even when it feels like you're making things worse. Because you are making things worse, temporarily, in the service of making them fundamentally better.

3. **You learn to support the horse through the deconstruction without abandoning them to it**. Creative Destruction requires exquisite timing and emotional attunement. You're creating instability deliberately, which means the horse needs to trust that you'll be their

stable point while everything else shifts. This is where all the previous principles come together. Humble Strength gives you the presence to remain steady.

Emotionless Communication keeps you from broadcasting anxiety. Fearless Guidance lets you lead into the uncertainty. Powerful Gentility ensures you're creating just enough discomfort to facilitate learning without so much that you traumatize. Determined Understanding helps you read whether the horse is processing productively or shutting down.

4. **You develop patience for the rebuilding process.** Destruction is often quick. Construction takes time. After you've dismantled a problematic pattern, expect to spend weeks or months rebuilding properly. The horse needs to learn new responses, practice them until they become automatic, and develop confidence in the new way of moving or responding.

   Rush this phase and you'll end up with either a return to old patterns or a horse who never fully trusts the new ones.

5. **You learn to recognize when deconstruction is complete and when it's time to start building again.** There's a moment when the old pattern has been sufficiently dismantled and continued pressure would just be destructive without being creative. You have to sense that shift and transition from "we're undoing what doesn't work" to "we're building what does."

What It Looks Like Outside the Arena

The same principles apply when working with people, though the stakes are often higher and the relationships more complex.

In professional settings, Creative Destruction might mean:

Dismantling a team structure that has stopped serving its purpose. Maybe you have silos that prevent collaboration. Maybe you have hierarchies that stifle innovation. Maybe you have processes that made sense five years ago but now just create unnecessary friction.

Identifying these structures is Determined Understanding. Having the courage to dismantle them is Creative Destruction.

But here's the critical part: you can't just blow things up and hope something better emerges. You need to understand:

- what you're destroying and why,

- communicate clearly about the purpose,

- support people through the transition, and

- actively build the new structure while the old one is being phased out.

In the army and in the corporate world, I've seen leaders who were good at destruction but bad at reconstruction. They identified dysfunctional systems and courageously dismantled them. But then they left people in chaos, assuming they'd figure out the new way on their own. The result was confusion, resentment, and often a reversion to the old patterns or the emergence of even worse ones.

Creative Destruction as service means you're present through the entire cycle. You're there when things are being torn down, you're there in the uncomfortable middle when nothing is settled, and you're there actively building and reinforcing the new patterns.

Challenging someone's limiting beliefs is another form of Creative Destruction. Maybe a team member believes they're not creative, or not good at public speaking, or not capable of leadership. These beliefs, true or not, function as structures that limit their development. Your job might be to destroy those beliefs, gently but firmly. Show them evidence that contradicts their self-assessment.

Create situations where they have to do the thing they think they can't do. Be willing to let them experience the discomfort of having their identity challenged. But you also have to support them through it. You can't just say "you're wrong about yourself" and walk away. You have to be there for the confusion and frustration and fear that comes up when someone's self-concept is being deconstructed. You have to help them build a new, more accurate self-understanding.

In personal growth work, and in therapy, Creative Destruction often involves dismantling defensive patterns, outdated coping mechanisms, or trauma-based responses that once served a purpose but now prevent healing. This is delicate work. These patterns exist for reasons. They protected someone at a time when protection was needed.

You can't just rip them away. You have to honour what they provided, while helping the person see how they're now limiting rather than liberating. You have to create enough safety that the person can let go of old protections without feeling exposed and vulnerable. You have to be present for the grief that often comes when someone releases patterns that have been part of their identity for decades.

After difficult conversations, intense emotional work, or periods of significant change, you have to ensure rest and integration. Creative Destruction is exhausting. The person who has had their certainties challenged, their patterns disrupted, their identity deconstructed, needs time to consolidate what's emerging before the next wave of change.

This is where compassion and wisdom meet. You know more change is coming. You know the reconstruction isn't complete. But you also know that pushing too hard, too fast, without rest, will result in collapse rather than transformation.

The Danger of Incomplete Destruction

One of the most important lessons Creative Destruction teaches is the danger of stopping halfway through.

Partial destruction is often worse than no destruction at all. If you dismantle someone's confidence or certainty but don't help them rebuild something more solid, you've just created a lost, confused person. If you tear down a team structure but don't build a better one, you've just created chaos. If you challenge someone's beliefs but don't help them find new ground to stand on, you've just created a cynic.

Genghis Khan understood this. He didn't just destroy the tribal system, he built meritocracy. He didn't just tear down ethnic and religious barriers, he built policies that protected diversity. He didn't just eliminate aristocratic privilege, he created systems where talent could rise.

Paul understood this. He didn't just deconstruct Jewish law, he constructed the theology of grace. He didn't just eliminate ethnic boundaries, he built a vision of universal humanity in Christ. He didn't just challenge existing religious structures, he planted churches that would become new communities of belonging.

The pattern is to identify what needs to be dismantled, have the courage to dismantle it, and then dedicate yourself to building something better in its place.

This is why Creative Destruction is the third harvest, not the first planting. You can't do this work effectively without first developing Powerful Gentility (the ability to be strong and soft simultaneously) and Determined Understanding (the patience to seek truth thoroughly before acting).

Without Powerful Gentility, destruction becomes cruelty. You hurt people without the softness to support them through the transition. Without Determined Understanding, destruction becomes reckless. You tear things down without fully understanding what you're destroying or why.

But when Creative Destruction grows from those roots, when it emerges as the natural harvest of service matured through practice, it becomes something extraordinary: the wisdom to know when renewal requires release, the courage to facilitate that release, and the compassion to guide people through to what emerges on the other side.

The Integration: Toward Incorporeal Competence

Creative Destruction is the final harvest of the Service pillar, but it's not the end of the journey. It's preparation for the ultimate integration: Incorporeal Competence.

Incorporeal Competence is what emerges when all three pillars, Courage, Communication, and Service, have been planted, cultivated, pruned, and harvested. It's passion that has been through fire and emerged stronger. It's loyalty that has been tested and proven genuine. It's enthusiasm that has survived discouragement and deepened into committed purpose.

Creative Destruction prepares the ground for Incorporeal Competence in specific ways:

- It teaches you that temporary loss serves long-term gain. The confidence Harley lost during our training was false confidence. Losing it hurt, but what grew in its place was real. Incorporeal Competence requires the same pattern: being willing to let go of shallow excitement for deep commitment.

- It shows you that identity isn't fixed. Temujin became Genghis Khan. Saul became Paul. The mare who was cocky and argumentative became the mare who listens and partners. Incorporeal Competence requires this fluidity, the ability to evolve while maintaining core purpose.

- It demonstrates that service sometimes means doing difficult things. Not because you're harsh or uncaring, but because you care enough to do what's actually needed rather than what's comfortable. Incorporeal Competence maintains passion precisely because it has learned to serve what matters more than serve immediate gratification.

Most importantly, Creative Destruction teaches you that renewal is possible. Patterns can change. Systems can be rebuilt. People can transform. This knowledge, this lived experience of watching old structures fall away and better ones emerge, becomes the foundation for maintaining enthusiasm through decades of practice.

When you've seen Creative Destruction work, when you've guided horses or people through the full cycle from dismantling to reconstruction, you develop faith in the process itself. You learn to trust that confusion leads to clarity, that loss creates space for gain, that death precedes resurrection.

This faith sustains enthusiasm. You can remain passionate about the work because you've seen that the work produces transformation. You've watched the painful middle phase where nothing seems to be working give way to breakthrough. You've experienced the moment when new patterns suddenly click into place and the horse or person reaches a level of capability they couldn't access before.

That experience, repeated over years of practice, creates Incorporeal Competence. Not naive optimism, but seasoned confidence. Not blind passion, but eyes-wide-open commitment. Not enthusiasm that depends on constant success, but enthusiasm rooted in understanding that even failure and frustration serve the larger process of growth.

The Legacy

When Genghis Khan died in 1227, he had destroyed the old tribal system that had kept Mongols weak and divided for centuries. He had built in its place an empire that stretched from the Pacific Ocean to Eastern Europe, the largest contiguous land empire in human history.

But his legacy wasn't the territory. Territory can be lost, and indeed much of it was lost within a few generations. His legacy was the systems he built: meritocracy over aristocracy, religious tolerance over forced conversion, rule of law over arbitrary rule, infrastructure that enabled connection over barriers that enforced separation.

The Pax Mongolica, the Mongol Peace, facilitated the first true globalization. Ideas and technologies that had been trapped in isolated regions spread throughout Eurasia. The exchange of knowledge during this period laid foundations for the Renaissance, for the Scientific Revolution, for the eventual emergence of the modern world.

None of this would have been possible if a teenaged boy on the Mongolian steppe hadn't had the courage to destroy what no longer served.

When Paul died, probably executed in Rome around 67 AD, Christianity was still a small sect, persecuted by both Jewish and Roman authorities. But he had destroyed the ethnic and legal boundaries that would have kept it confined to Judaism. He had built a theological framework that made Christianity accessible to anyone, anywhere.

Within three centuries, Christianity had spread throughout the Roman Empire and beyond. It became the dominant religion of Europe and eventually the most widespread religion in human history. None of this would have been possible if Saul hadn't experienced his own creative destruction on the Damascus road and then dedicated his life to facilitating that same transformation in others.

The mare named Harley will probably never know that her story is being used to teach leadership principles. But the partnership we're building, where she listens before responding, where her enthusiasm is channelled rather than chaotic, where we can work together with precision and trust, is possible only because we were willing to destroy her false confidence to rebuild genuine understanding in its place.

That's the pattern. That's the legacy. That's what Creative Destruction offers when practiced as service: the courage to let go of what limits, the wisdom to build what liberates, and the compassion to guide others through the transformation.

Every day in the arena, we have opportunities to practice this. Every time a horse offers a dysfunctional pattern, we can choose: accept it, try to modify it slightly, or dismantle it completely and rebuild from better foundations.

Every day in our work with people, we face similar choices. When we see someone trapped in limiting beliefs, or teams stuck in obsolete structures, or organizations perpetuating systems that no longer serve, we can choose: accept it, try to adjust it, or facilitate genuine transformation.

Creative Destruction asks more of us than the other options. It requires us to tolerate discomfort, both our own and others'. It demands that we see beyond the immediate reaction to the long-term result. It insists that we remain present through confusion and stay committed through resistance.

But when practiced with Humble Strength as foundation, Powerful Gentility as approach, and Determined Understanding as guide, Creative Destruction becomes what it's meant to be: not violence or loss, but renewal. Not destruction for its own sake, but space-making for what wants to emerge.

The horse who has been through this process trusts you more, not less. They know you'll guide them through difficulty toward capability. The person who has experienced this kind of transformation becomes capable of facilitating it for others. They understand that temporary disorientation serves lasting development.

This is the wisdom that ripens as the third harvest of the Service pillar. This is the fruit that grows when compassion matures into the courage to do what's difficult because it's what's needed.

The walls of old systems fall. The certainties that limited growth dissolve. The patterns that no longer serve are released. And in the space created by that strategic destruction, something better has room to grow.

That's not theory. That's not metaphor. That's the lived reality of everyone who's ever transformed, every system that's ever evolved, every partnership that's ever deepened.

The young boy who killed his brother, destroying a principle in the process, became the leader who created the framework for global trade and cultural exchange. The zealot who persecuted Christians became the apostle who wrote that "if anyone is in Christ, the new creation has come: The old has gone, the new is here!"

The mare who was cocky and resistant becomes the partner who listens and responds.

And you, reading this, recognizing patterns in your own work and relationships that no longer serve, having the courage to name what needs to change, you are practicing Creative Destruction.

The question isn't whether destruction will happen. Patterns break down. Systems become obsolete. Identities evolve. The question is whether the destruction will be creative, whether it will serve something beyond itself, whether it will create space for genuine growth, whether it will be done with enough wisdom and compassion to guide people through to what emerges on the other side.

That's the work. That's the harvest. That's Creative Destruction as service.

"The greatest conqueror is he who overcomes the enemy without a blow, but sometimes the greatest service is destroying what prevents the conquest from even beginning."

- The Horseman's Way

PART V

THE HARVEST

CHAPTER 12

INCORPOREAL COMPETENCE

"Strong men can always afford to be gentle. Only the weak are intent on 'giving as good as they get'"

- Elbert Hubbard

The Boy Who Felt Everything

Northeastern Oregon, 1914. The ranch house near Enterprise sat in remote country where the nearest neighbour was measured in miles, not minutes. Inside, a mother worried over her sixth child, a boy so small at birth they didn't think he would survive.

Tom Dorrance's sole occupation in those early years, as his nephew would later recount, was to eat and take naps. But it was during those naps, out on the porch when the weather was nice, that something extraordinary began to develop.

The boy would sleep with his hand resting on the dog's head. And if he had his hand on that dog's head when a fly landed on the dog's tail, he could feel it. Through fur and muscle and bone, across the entire length of that dog's body, the small boy could feel the disturbance of a single fly.

Where others saw weakness, a sickly child who needed constant rest, something else was growing. An ability to feel. To sense. To read the smallest changes in another living creature. The disadvantage that kept him from the rough work his older brothers could do was quietly becoming an extraordinary gift.

The Brothers' Journey

Tom was one of eight children born to Church and Minnie Dorrance at the turn of the 20th century. Their father built the homestead with a team in the 1880s, keeping up to 150 head of horses for ranch work and sale. In a time and place where horses were necessity, not luxury, all the Dorrance children learned to work with them. But they learned in the old way, the way that had been passed down for generations.

Bill Dorrance, born in 1906, four years before Tom, would later recall those early methods with a mixture of honesty and regret. Once, showing a visitor his tack room and telling stories, he mentioned a horse they'd thrown down and tied. He paused, looked seriously at his guest, and said: "I know that sounds rough. But that's the way we did it before Tom got us straightened out."

This admission reveals something profound. Bill wasn't a cruel man, far from it. He would become known throughout California as one of the most skilled horsemen and rawhide braiders of his generation. But he, like almost everyone else working with horses in that era, had inherited methods based on domination. Force. Making the horse submit through superior strength and determination.

Tom saw something different. Perhaps because he couldn't rely on physical strength, standing just 5'6" and never weighing more than 150 pounds, he was forced to find another way. Or perhaps that early sensitivity, developed during those naps with his hand on the dog, opened a channel of perception that others simply didn't have access to.

The Gift That Changed Everything

People who worked with Tom often described his abilities in mystical terms, much to his discomfort. They said he could see what a horse was thinking before the horse thought it. That he could "get life" from any part of the horse's body, the stifle, hip, shoulder, pastern, wherever he needed it. That he could become the horse in an important sense, seeing out their eyes and feeling with their feet.

Tom would deflect this kind of talk. "Everything I learned, I learned from the horse," he would say quietly. It was true, but not in the way people might think. He hadn't learned techniques or methods from horses. He'd learned to listen to them. To feel them. To understand them in a way that went beyond the physical and mental, into territory he struggled to articulate.

He wrestled with that word, Spirit. It was the closest he could come to describing what he felt was most important, but he knew it didn't capture the full meaning. "For lack of a better word, I've taken to calling this the horse's spirit," he admitted. "The older I get, the more I have come to believe that this aspect of the horse is the most important and the most overlooked."

The Quiet Revolution

In the mid-1950s, Tom was president of the Wallowa County Stockgrowers. He had a local radio show. He was a 4-H leader. Word was spreading about this quiet man who worked with horses differently, who seemed to help horses with their people problems rather than fixing problem horses.

It was radical, this touchy-feely stuff, as sceptics called it. But it worked. So well that when Tom sold his Oregon ranch in 1960 and set out to travel in a trailer to see the country, people were already referring to him as "the horse's lawyer."

Bill, meanwhile, had moved to California years earlier, establishing himself at Mt. Toro Ranch near Salinas. He became legendary for his work with a reata, a rawhide rope he braided himself with such precision that he could spot a single turned strand across 90 feet of rope in ten seconds. Over his career, he braided 67 reatas, 122 pairs of hobbles, 103 hackamores, 35 bosals, and hundreds of hondas. His hands were so skilled at 92 years old that he could out rope men a third his age.

But Bill's greatest contribution wasn't his technical skill with rawhide or rope. It was his willingness to keep learning. If he was successful with something with a horse one day, the next day he was thinking about how he might make it easier or better for the horse. He was constantly searching, constantly questioning, constantly refining.

The Meeting That Changed Natural Horsemanship

Around 1960, at a fair in Elko, Nevada, a young cowboy named Ray Hunt was having trouble with a difficult horse. The horse's name was Hondo, and Ray had tried everything he knew to get along with him. Nothing was working.

Ray asked his friend Bill Dorrance for advice. Bill's response was simple: "You should talk to my brother Tom. He's pretty good with horses."

When Ray finally met Tom, it changed his life. "Until I met Tom, I wasn't working from the horse's needs," Ray would later say. "I was working from my own needs. Tom's whole emphasis was helping and supporting the horse."

What Tom showed Ray, and what Ray would spend the next forty years teaching in clinics around the world, wasn't a method or a technique. It was a way of being with horses. Tom told the horse's side of the story. He knew what the horse was going to do before the horse knew it. And he showed Ray how to work from where the horse is, rather than from where the rider wants the horse to be.

Ray became the evangelist. Where Tom was shy, preferring to stay out of the spotlight, Ray travelled extensively, sharing what he'd learned. "I'm here for the horse," Ray would say at the start of every clinic, "to help him get a better deal."

Through Ray, and later through Ray's students like Buck Brannaman, the Dorrance philosophy spread worldwide. Every clinician working in what came to be called "natural horsemanship" can trace their approach back to Tom. The revolution that began with a small, sickly boy who could feel a fly land on a dog's tail eventually transformed how millions of people work with horses.

The Final Years

In his later years, Tom moved to California to live at Bill's ranch. The two brothers, both in their 90s, would work together with horses and students. Each would deflect praise to the other. If you complimented Bill's horsemanship, he'd tell you Tom was better. If you praised Tom, he'd say the same about Bill.

Bill Dorrance's son Steve and his wife Leslie tell a memorable story because it captures several Dorrance principles in miniature. Once, when Tom and Bill were braiding rawhide in Bill's workshop, they heard a loud "splat" from the barnyard. Without looking up, Bill said calmly with no drama, no blame, no panic, "Sounds like Margaret's come off her horse."

Margaret was Tom's wife, and they found her on the ground in pain. Tom arrived on his golf cart and asked if her horse had gotten out from under her. As always, understanding events without moralising them and assuming that the horse was not at fault.

Margaret, shaken by the fall was indignant. "No! You get Tom…", she said, not realizing Tom was already there. the humour and awkwardness of the moment underline a deeper truth. A good horseman doesn't rush to defend ego, human or equine, but seeks to understand the feel that was lost.

This was characteristic of both brothers. The calm competence in the face of trouble, this non-adversarial approach to everything, and incredible compassion for both horses and people.

Humbling Failure

Tom Dorrance could feel a fly land on a dog's tail through his hand resting on the dog's head. I thought I understood that kind of feel. I thought I had it with Harry. For three years, I was wrong.

For three years I showed him, confident each time before the show that he was right, this time. This time those watching would see him do what I knew he could do. This time he would work for me the way he does in the practice pen. Three years in a row we took him to the futurity, the big show, where dreams come true or are dashed on the rocks of reality.

Three years of the same result.

After the third year, I vowed never to bring him back again to that show. I just couldn't seem to get him to show with the style that the judges wanted to see. Every time I competed on him, my team and I would review the video of his run. Normally this would give us an understanding of what we needed to fix for the next competition, any little mistakes we were making.

But looking at the video, time after time I could see him showing the same style costing us dearly. He would move across the arena, head high with quick jerky movements. When the judges are scoring on eye appeal, it doesn't matter that he never lost a cow because he never looked relaxed doing it. I thought, "We just can't afford to keep showing him to the world this way."

Ten hours of interstate traffic. Two fruitless weeks. Thousands of dollars gone. I turned into the dark gravel driveway, hands aching from gripping the steering wheel, throat tight with frustration I couldn't swallow down.

"No more." I said it out loud to the empty truck. "No more showing and hoping things will be better next time. No more wasting money on dreams."

"What am I doing wrong?"

The question woke me at 3 AM. It followed me through morning feeds. It sat beside me at dinner. For a week, it was the only thought that mattered.

Then other questions started creeping in. "How can I make him better?" I'd tried everything the other trainers were doing. "Is there something you haven't tried yet?"

That's when it hit me. I'd been asking the wrong questions. The problem wasn't what I was doing. The problem was "make."

The whole time I had been trying to "make" him do the things that all of the top horses were doing. I wanted to force him to be like the other horses. I could see that I had been trying to force him into the frame of the horse that I thought he should be, to train him the way I thought he had to be to win.

What could I do differently? Is there something that I can do to help him relax? What is it like for him when we compete? Does he draw on my tension? How can we change that?

I walked into his yard and took off his rug. I ran my fingers along his neck. The muscles were taut as wire rope, running from wither to poll. I pushed deeper into his hindquarters, finding pockets of tension buried in the muscle.

He was ready to go, ready to compete. He had nowhere to go but he wouldn't relax. Always wanting to do his best whenever I asked it. By taking the time to step back and actually look at the horse that I had made him into, I could see why he couldn't be competitive. I could feel why he acted the way he did.

I stood there with my hand on his tense neck, and the truth hit me like a gut punch. I hadn't been training Harry. I'd been breaking him. Not his body, he was sound. Not his mind, he knew the job. His spirit. I'd been breaking his spirit by trying to force him into a shape he couldn't take.

The horse standing in front of me, anxious, tense, self-protective, wasn't the horse I'd set out to create. He was the horse my methods had created. The horse my force had shaped.

I could see the horse he had become, the intensity that had become one with his spirit. I'd wanted confidence; he'd learned anxiety. I'd wanted trust; he'd developed concern. I'd wanted selflessness; he'd embraced self-preservation. Where I'd imagined feel and horizontal flow and smoothness, he'd learned flight and fear and that vertical, jerky action the judges couldn't reward.

If I was going to be successful with Harry, I was going to have to rebuild his whole psyche. Teach him to relax. To trust. To believe his spirit was safe with me.

This was going to take time. And it was going to require something I'd always thought I had but clearly didn't, the ability to work from feel instead of force. From invitation instead of demand. From spirit instead of technique.

It was going to require Incorporeal Competence.

The Third Factor: Spirit in Horse and Human

Tom Dorrance struggled for years to articulate what he meant by the horse's spirit. It wasn't the physical body, though it affected how the horse moved. It wasn't the mind, though it influenced how the horse thought. It was something deeper, something he could feel but couldn't quite capture in words.

"I've been trying for some time to think of words to get this third factor to where it comes to light," he wrote. "The rider needs to recognize the horse's need for self-preservation in Mind, Body and the third factor, Spirit."

He knew the word "spirit" wasn't quite right, but it was the closest he could come. What he was describing was the horse's innermost self, the part that could be broken or preserved, crushed or honoured, violated or respected. The essence of who that particular horse was, beyond training and conditioning and learned behaviours.

And here's what Tom understood, perhaps better than anyone before him: you couldn't reach true unity with a horse, couldn't achieve that willing communication he spent his life pursuing, unless you honoured this third factor. You could train the body through repetition. You could shape the mind through conditioning. But the spirit? The spirit could only be invited, never coerced.

What Tom didn't often say explicitly, but what becomes clear when you study his work long enough, is this: humans have the same third factor. The same innermost self that can be broken or preserved. The same spirit that responds to invitation but resists coercion.

And everything he learned about working with the horse's spirit applies, with remarkable precision, to working with the human spirit.

Self-Preservation: The Core Need

When Tom talked about the horse's need for self-preservation in mind, body, and spirit, he was describing something fundamental to all living beings. A horse whose sense of safety has been violated, whether physically through harsh handling, mentally through confusion and inconsistency, or spiritually through domination that crushed their essential nature, becomes defensive, shut down, or explosive.

We see this same pattern in people.

The person whose body has been harmed learns to flinch before the blow comes. The person whose mind has been manipulated learns to trust no one's words. And the person whose spirit has been crushed, who has been made to feel that their innermost self is wrong, shameful, or worthless, learns to hide that self away where no one can reach it.

We call these people "difficult." We say they have "trust issues" or "walls up" or "resistance to authority." We diagnose and label and strategize about how to change them.

Tom would have asked a different question: "What happened, before what happened happened?"

What happened to that person's sense of self-preservation before they built those walls? When did they learn that the world wasn't safe for their spirit? Who taught them that protecting their innermost self required shutting down, lashing out, or disappearing?

And more importantly: how do we create conditions where that person can maintain their self-preservation, can keep their spirit safe, while still responding to what we're asking of them?

This was Tom's genius. He didn't try to override the horse's need for self-preservation. He didn't try to convince the horse that their instincts were wrong or that they should just trust him despite all evidence to the contrary. Instead, he created an atmosphere where the horse could feel their self-preservation was honoured, respected, protected, and then, from that place of safety, they chose to participate.

The Spirit Can Be Broken

Bill Dorrance once admitted to a visitor, "We used to throw them down and tie them. I know that sounds rough. But that's the way we did it before Tom got us straightened out."

He wasn't confessing to exceptional cruelty. He was describing standard practice, the accepted method of his time for "breaking" horses. The language itself tells you everything: breaking. You took a creature with its own will, its own spirit, its own sense of self, and you broke it. You forced submission through superior strength until the horse learned that resistance was futile.

It worked, in a sense. The horse learned to obey. The body responded to cues. The mind learned the patterns. But something essential had been damaged. That third factor, the spirit, had been crushed. You got compliance, but you never got true partnership. You got a tool, but you lost the relationship.

We do the same thing to people.

We break them through shame when they don't meet our standards. We break them through contempt when they fail to understand what we want. We break them through manipulation when they won't willingly give us what we demand. We break them through isolation when they question our authority.

And like those broken horses, these broken people learn to comply. They perform the required behaviours. They say the expected words. They produce the demanded results.

But their spirit is gone. That innermost self, that third factor, has learned to hide so deep that sometimes they forget it's even there. They become, in the most tragic sense, functional. Useful. Productive.

And utterly diminished from what they could have been.

Working From Where They Are

"I like to work from where the horse is," Tom would say, "to get him to be able to operate wherever and whenever I need him."

This simple statement contains profound wisdom about working with any living being that has a spirit.

Most of us work from where we want someone to be. We see what they should do, who they should be, how they should respond. We get frustrated when they're not there yet. We try to pull them, push them, cajole them, shame them into being the person or horse we need them to be.

Tom did the opposite. He started by observing where the horse actually was. What were they feeling in this moment? What were they capable of understanding right now? What would they need to feel safe enough to try the next small step?

He met them there. Not where they'd been yesterday. Not where they should be tomorrow. Where they were right now, in this present moment, with all their fears and confusions and limitations and possibilities.

And from that meeting place, he built something real.

This is perhaps the most challenging aspect of Incorporeal Competence to develop: the ability to see past what someone should be and connect with who they actually are. To resist the temptation to fix, correct, or improve, and instead to simply be present with another spirit, acknowledging its reality without requiring it to be different before you'll engage with it.

The alcoholic who needs to admit they're an alcoholic before you'll help them. The employee who needs to demonstrate motivation before you'll invest in them. The family member who needs to apologize before you'll forgive them. The horse who needs to stop being afraid before you'll work with them patiently.

All of these represent working from where we want someone to be, not where they are.

Tom's approach required something harder: accepting the current reality of another being's spirit fully, without demanding they change before you'll honor their existence. Only from that place of acceptance could real transformation begin.

The Innermost Self

Tom often spoke about working with what was happening "right in the horse's innards", a slightly awkward phrase that nonetheless captures something important. He wasn't talking about the stomach or intestines, obviously. He was talking about that deep inner place where the horse's essential being lived. The place where their spirit resided.

"What brings on trouble," he explained, "is disturbance, both mental and physical, being brought to the inside of the horse, right in his innards."

External disturbances, a scary object, a confusing cue, a painful experience, didn't just affect the horse's body or mind. They reached all the way down into that innermost place, creating turmoil in the spirit itself. And unless you addressed the disturbance at that deepest level, you could never really resolve it. You might suppress the symptoms, but the trouble would remain, waiting to surface again.

Humans work exactly the same way.

We can be disturbed at the surface level, annoyed by an inconvenience, frustrated by a setback, stressed by deadlines. But these surface disturbances don't usually damage our spirit. They're uncomfortable, but they don't reach our innermost self.

The disturbances that cause real trouble are the ones that penetrate deeper. The betrayal that makes us question whether anyone can be trusted. The failure that makes us doubt our essential worth. The cruelty that makes us wonder if we deserve to be treated as fully human. The judgment that makes us feel our innermost self is fundamentally unacceptable.

These disturbances reach our spirit. They create turmoil "right in our innards." And unless they're addressed at that deepest level, we can't fully heal. We might manage the symptoms, develop coping mechanisms, override our feelings, present a functional exterior, but the trouble remains.

Tom understood this with horses. He knew that if a horse's spirit had been disturbed, if something had reached down into their innermost self and created fear or confusion or pain, you had to address it at that level. Surface training wouldn't fix it. Repetition wouldn't cure it. Only patient, careful work that reached down to where the actual disturbance lived could bring genuine resolution.

The same principle applies to working with people. Surface solutions don't heal spirit-level wounds. Behaviour modification doesn't address innermost disturbances. You have to be willing to work at the level where the actual trouble lives, which requires the courage to acknowledge that such a level exists, and the humility to approach it with the respect it deserves.

Good and Evil: The Spirit's Capacity

Here's where the parallel between horse and human becomes both clear and complex.

A horse's spirit is largely innocent. Yes, horses can be aggressive, defensive, or difficult. But these behaviours typically arise from pain, fear, confusion, or violated self-preservation. Address the root cause, and the behaviour changes. A horse doesn't usually choose to be malicious. They don't plot revenge or harbor resentment or deliberately hurt others for the pleasure of causing pain.

Human spirits are different. We have capacities horses lack.

We can choose cruelty when kindness would serve us better. We can harbor grudges that poison us more than their object. We can deliberately violate another person's spirit out of our own wounded rage. We can sacrifice others' wellbeing for our gain, fully aware of what we're doing.

We can also do the opposite. We can choose compassion when revenge would be easier. We can forgive the unforgivable. We can sacrifice our own comfort to honour another's spirit. We can create beauty where ugliness reigned.

Tom's question, "What happened, before what happened happened?", becomes more complicated with humans because sometimes the answer is: "They chose to do evil." Not because they were wounded, though woundedness might have been part of it. Not because they didn't understand, though understanding might have been limited. But because some part of their spirit, in that moment, chose to cause harm.

This doesn't invalidate Tom's approach. If anything, it makes it more necessary.

When you encounter a human being whose spirit has chosen evil, or is capable of choosing evil, which describes all of us, you have several options. You can respond with domination, trying to force better behaviour through superior power. You can respond with abandonment, writing them off as irredeemable. Or you can respond the way Tom responded to difficult horses: with a clear-eyed acknowledgment of reality, firm boundaries about what's acceptable, and an unwavering belief that transformation is possible.

Not guaranteed. Not easy. Not quick. But possible.

This is perhaps the most challenging application of Incorporeal Competence: maintaining both boundaries and hope when dealing with the human capacity for evil. Refusing to be naive about what people are capable of while also refusing to give up on what they might become.

True Unity: Spirit Touching Spirit

"True unity and willing communication between horse and human." This was Tom's life goal, the north star he oriented everything toward. Not mere obedience. Not simple compliance. But unity, a coming together of two separate beings into willing partnership.

You couldn't achieve this unity through coercion. You couldn't force willing communication. The very phrase is almost paradoxical: willing communication can't be compelled. It can only be invited, encouraged, made possible through creating the right conditions.

This required Tom to bring his whole self, body, mind, and spirit, into alignment. The horse could sense incongruence instantly. If his hands said one thing while his body said another, the horse believed the body. If his actions said one thing while his spirit said another, the horse believed the spirit.

Tom had to become congruent. Integrated. Authentic. His innermost self had to align with his outward actions. Only then could he invite the horse's spirit into genuine connection.

The same principle governs all deep human relationships.

You cannot achieve true unity with another person, whether in marriage, friendship, business partnership, or any other significant connection, unless you bring your authentic spirit into the relationship. If you're performing a role, playing a part, presenting a false self, the other person's spirit will sense it. They might not consciously know what's wrong, but they'll feel the incongruence. Trust won't fully form. Unity will remain elusive.

And you cannot invite another person's spirit into genuine connection with you unless you're willing to honour their spirit as fully real, fully valid, fully deserving of respect, even when it differs from yours. Even when it frustrates you. Even when it disappoints you.

This is what Tom meant by working with the horse rather than on the horse. The preposition matters. When you work on someone, you're treating them as an object to be shaped. When you work with someone, you're acknowledging them as a subject, another centre of consciousness, another spirit whose reality is as valid as your own.

True unity requires two spirits choosing to come together in willing communication. It cannot be unilateral. It cannot be forced. It can only emerge when both parties bring their authentic selves and choose, freely, to create something together.

The Harvest: Incorporeal Competence

Everything in the previous eleven chapters has been preparing you for this understanding:

- **Humble Strength** taught you to possess power while refusing to wield it carelessly; essential for working with any spirit, including your own.

- **Fearless Guidance** showed you how to step into uncertainty first; necessary because working at the level of spirit always involves risk and requires courage.

- **Emotionless Communication** developed your ability to convey truth without emotional distortion; critical because spirits are exquisitely sensitive to incongruence.

- **Powerful Gentility** integrated strength and softness; the balance required to honour another's spirit while maintaining clear boundaries.

- **Compassionate Ambition** matured your drive into something that acknowledges impact on others; understanding that pushing for results at the expense of someone's spirit defeats the purpose.

- **Balanced Coordination** synchronized your mind, body, and emotions; the integration necessary for your own spirit to be authentic and trustworthy.

- **Determined Understanding** built your capacity to stay with complexity; required because spirit-level work is never simple or quick.

- **Peaceful Directedness** refined your ability to give direction without aggression; maintaining clarity while respecting another's spiritual autonomy.

- **Centred Transcendence** anchored your presence in something deeper than circumstances; accessing your own spirit consistently so you can recognize it in others.

- **Creative Destruction** developed your wisdom about strategic release; knowing when protecting someone's spirit requires dismantling what's damaging it.

All of these have been building toward this harvest: **Incorporeal Competence.** The ability to work at the level of spirit, your own and others', with the same skill, sensitivity, and wisdom that Tom Dorrance brought to working with horses.

This is mastery that transcends physical technique and mental strategy. It operates from that third factor, from the innermost place, from the part of you that recognizes and honours the same part in others.

It's competence that isn't limited by the body's strength or the mind's cleverness, because it draws on something deeper. The Latin root "incorporeal" means "without body", not in the sense of being ghostly or insubstantial, but in the sense of not being limited to the physical and mental realms.

This is the competence that allows you to:

- Sense what's happening in another person's spirit before it manifests in their behaviour

- Create conditions where people feel safe enough to bring their authentic selves

- Maintain your own spiritual centre regardless of external pressures

- Invite transformation without demanding it

- Hold boundaries without crushing spirits

- Build true partnerships rather than mere compliance

- Recognize when spirit-level damage has occurred and address it at that depth

- Remain grounded in hope without being naive about human capacity for harm

Tom and Bill Dorrance spent ninety-three years each developing this competence with horses. They demonstrated that it's real, that it can be learned, and that it transforms everything it touches.

Their gift to us isn't a method or a technique. It's an invitation to develop the same competence in every area of life. To recognize that spirit, in ourselves and in every person we encounter, and to learn to work with it the way they learned to work with horses.

With patience. With respect. With humility. With an unwavering commitment to creating unity rather than forcing compliance.

This is the harvest. This is what all the planting, growing, and pruning has been working toward. The development of mastery that operates from the deepest level of who you are, engaging with the deepest level of who others are, creating partnerships and possibilities that purely physical or mental approaches could never achieve.

It's what Tom called "true unity and willing communication." Not just between horse and human, but between spirit and spirit, in the arena and far beyond it.

I don't know what Harry and I will win together into the future. That's not the point anymore. What I know is this: the door to Incorporeal Competence, once opened, changes everything. Not just how I work with Harry, but how I work with every horse, every person, every challenge.

Tom and Bill spent ninety-three years developing this competence. I'm just beginning. But even at the beginning, I can feel the difference between force and invitation, between breaking and building, between working on a spirit and working with one.

This is where I am going in my journey in the arena. Where can you see yourself going if you incorporate this new understanding with your work with your horse? With your family? With your employees? Or with your business?

"Physical Strength can never permanently withstand the impact of Spiritual Force."

- Franklin D. Roosevelt

APPENDIX

BIBLIOGRAPHY

Chapter 1: Antiquated Intelligence

Historical Figures & Horsemen:

- **Ray Hunt** (1929–2009). American horseman and clinician who revolutionized natural horsemanship through his work with Tom Dorrance. Known for the phrase "The horse is a mirror to your soul."

- **Tom Dorrance** (1910–2003). American horseman, author of 'True Unity: Willing Communication Between Horse and Human' (1987). Mentor to Ray Hunt and foundational figure in natural horsemanship.

Quotations:

- **Emerson, Ralph Waldo**. 'Journals', 1831. "To the dull mind all nature is leaden. To the illumined mind the whole world burns and sparkles with light."

- **Emerson, Ralph Waldo** 'The Conduct of Life', 1860. "A great part of courage is the courage of having done the thing before."

Biblical References:

- **Moses**. 'Book of Exodus', Old Testament. The narrative of Moses from Egyptian prince to shepherd to deliverer of the Hebrews.

Chapter 2: Humble Strength

Biblical References:

- 'Matthew 23:12', New Testament. "For those who exalt themselves will be humbled, and those who humble themselves will be exalted."

- **Moses**. 'Book of Exodus', Old Testament. Extended narrative of Moses's transformation in the wilderness.

Academic Sources:

- **Peterson, Christopher, and Martin E. P. Seligman**. 'Character Strengths and Virtues: A Handbook and Classification'. Oxford University Press, 2004. (Reference to the 24 character strengths: Judgment, Bravery, Perseverance, Kindness, Fairness, and Self-Regulation)

Quotations:

- **Morneau, Robert F.** "Humility is that habitual quality whereby we live in the truth of things." (Source: 'Humility: 31 Reflections on Christian Virtue', 1997)

- **Morneau, Robert F.** "I think I saw it, once or twice, this lowly thing called humility." (Source unknown - attributed)

Chapter 3: Fearless Guidance

Historical Sources:

- **Alexander the Great** (356–323 BCE). Ancient Macedonian king. Story of taming Bucephalus, sourced from Plutarch's 'Life of Alexander'.

- **Plutarch** (c. 46–120 CE). 'Parallel Lives: Life of Alexander'. Ancient Greek historian's account of Alexander the Great, including the Bucephalus episode.

Biblical References:

- **Joshua**. 'Book of Joshua', Old Testament. Narrative of Joshua leading Israel across the Jordan River and into the Promised Land.

Academic Sources:

- **Maxwell, John C**. 'Developing the Leader Within You 2.0'. Harper Collins, 2018.

Quotations:

- **Alexander the Great**. "Through every generation of the human race there has been a constant war, a war with fear. Those who have the courage to conquer it are made free and those who are conquered by it are made to suffer until they have the courage to defeat it, or death takes them." (Source: attributed)

- **Alexander the Great**. "I am not afraid of an army of lions led by a sheep; I am afraid of an army of sheep led by a lion." (Source: attributed)

Chapter 4: Emotionless Communication

Historical & Philosophical Sources:

- **Marcus Aurelius** (121–180 CE). Roman Emperor and Stoic philosopher. 'Meditations' (written c. 170–180 CE). Multiple quotations including:

  - "You have power over your mind — not outside events. Realize this, and you will find strength."

  - "The nearer a man comes to a calm mind, the closer he is to strength."

  - "When you wake up in the morning, tell yourself: The people I deal with today will be meddling, ungrateful, arrogant, dishonest, jealous and surly..."

Biblical References:

- **Jesus of Nazareth**. New Testament Gospels. References to Jesus weeping at Lazarus's tomb (John 11) and teaching his disciples.

Chapter 5: Powerful Gentility

Quotations:

- **Chinese Proverb.** "The greatest conqueror is he who overcomes the enemy without a blow."

Historical Figures:

- **Prince Rupert of the Rhine** (1619–1682). Royalist cavalry commander during the English Civil War. Historical accounts of the Battle of Edgehill (1642) and his horsemanship.

Biblical References:

- **Jesus of Nazareth**. New Testament Gospels. References to Jesus blessing children and his teachings on gentleness and strength.

Quotations:

- The Horseman's Way. "In true partnership, power is shared, not hoarded. Gentleness is offered, not withheld. And strength reveals itself not through dominance, but through the confidence to invite rather than demand."

Chapter 6: Compassionate Ambition

Biblical References:

- 'Genesis 50:20', Old Testament. Joseph's words to his brothers: "You intended to harm me, but God intended it for good to accomplish what is now being done, the saving of many lives."

- **Joseph**. 'Book of Genesis', Old Testament. Extended narrative of Joseph from pit to prison to palace in Egypt.

Historical Sources:

- **Ulysses S. Grant** (1822–1885). 18th President of the United States and Union general. Historical accounts include:

  - West Point graduation (1843) and the high-jump record with York

  - Appomattox Court House surrender (April 9, 1865)

  - Generous surrender terms to General Robert E. Lee

- **National Museum of American History**. Description of Appomattox surrender: "The terms of surrender, however, would be a simple gentlemen's agreement."

Literary Sources:

- **Middleton, Ant** 'Military Mindset: Lessons from the Battlefield'. Hodder & Stoughton, 2024.

- **Clear, James** 'Atomic Habits: An Easy & Proven Way to Build Good Habits & Break Bad Ones'. Avery Publishing, 2018.

Chapter 7: Balanced Coordination

Quotations:

- **Brannaman, Buck.** "The horse is a mirror to your soul, and sometimes you might not like what you see in the mirror." (Horseman, clinician, subject of documentary 'Buck', 2011)

- **Hunt, Ray.** (1929–2009). The horse will teach you, if you'll listen."

Historical Figures:

- **Lis Hartel** (1921–2009). Danish dressage rider who competed in the 1952 Helsinki Olympics despite paralysis from polio, winning the silver medal. Historical Olympic records.

Biblical References:

- **Daniel**. 'Book of Daniel', Old Testament. Narrative of Daniel's faith and prayer practice in Babylonian exile, including the lions' den account (Daniel 6).

Chapter 8: Determined Understanding

Quotations:

- **Einstein, Albert.** "The measure of intelligence is the ability to change." (Attributed)

Historical Figures:

- **Harry Chauvel** (1865–1945). Australian general. Historical military records include:

  - Gallipoli Campaign (1915), including Quinn's Post

- Desert Mounted Corps campaigns in Sinai and Palestine

- Battle of Romani

- Battle of Beersheba (1917) and the famous cavalry charge

Biblical References:

- **Job**. 'Book of Job', Old Testament. Narrative of Job's suffering and his friends' counsel.

Academic Sources:

- **Leaf, Dr. Caroline**. 'Cleaning Up Your Mental Mess: 5 Simple, Scientifically Proven Steps to Reduce Anxiety, Stress, and Toxic Thinking'. Baker Books, 2021.

  - The Neurocycle method (5 steps: Gather, Reflect, Write, Recheck, Active Reach)

  - Personal account of her son's attack in Rome (pp. 237–240)

  - Application of the Neurocycle to traumatic events (pp. 229–233)

Quotations:

- **The Horseman's Way**. "What will it be for you? What purpose is worthy of your strength? What relationship deserves your gentleness? What vision requires your service?"

Chapter 9: Peaceful Directedness

Classical Sources:

- **Xenophon** (c. 430–354 BCE). Ancient Greek historian, soldier, and horseman.

  - 'Anabasis' (The March of the Ten Thousand). Historical account of the Greek mercenaries' retreat from Persia.

  - 'On Horsemanship' (c. 350 BCE). Ancient treatise on horse training. Quotations include:

- "For what the horse does under compulsion... is done without understanding; and there is no beauty in it either, any more than one should whip and spur a dancer."

- "The groom should have standing orders to take his charge through crowds, and to make him familiar with all sorts of sights and noises..."

Historical Reference:

- **The Ten Thousand**. Greek mercenary force (401–399 BCE). Historical account of their service to Cyrus the Younger and subsequent retreat through Persian Empire.

- Battle of Cunaxa (401 BCE). Where Cyrus the Younger was killed.

- Tissaphernes. Persian satrap involved in the betrayal of Greek generals.

Biblical References:

- **David**. Old Testament, 'Books of Samuel' and 'Kings'. References to David as shepherd, warrior, and king of Israel.

Creative & Practical Sources:

- **Cameron, Julia**. 'The Artist's Way: A Course in Discovering and Recovering your Creative Self'. Pan Books, 1994. (Morning Pages practice: three pages of longhand writing every morning)

Chapter 10: Centred Transcendence

Biblical References:

- 'Isaiah 11:2', Old Testament. "The Spirit of the LORD will rest on him—the Spirit of wisdom and of understanding, the Spirit of counsel and of might, the Spirit of the knowledge and fear of the LORD."

- 'John 15:4', New Testament. Jesus speaking: "Remain in me, as I also remain in you. No branch can bear fruit by itself; it must remain in the vine. Neither can you bear fruit unless you remain in me."

Historical & Cultural Sources:

- **Comanche Nation** (Nʉmʉnʉʉ). Indigenous people of the Southern Great Plains (18th–19th centuries). Cultural concepts referenced:

  - 'Puha' (spiritual power)

  - Traditional horsemanship practices

  - Spiritual connection with horses ("God Dogs")

  - Historical context: Comancheria territory, circa 1758

Note: The narrative of Running Wolf and Seven Arrows is a composite representation of Comanche horsemanship traditions, not a documented historical account.

Academic Sources:

- **Maxwell, John C.** 'Developing the Leader Within You 2.0'. Harper Collins, 2018.

Chapter 11: Creative Destruction

Quotations:

- **Chinese Proverb.** "The greatest conqueror is he who overcomes the enemy without a blow."

Historical Figures:

- **Genghis Khan** (Temujin) (c. 1162–1227). Founder of the Mongol Empire. Historical references include:

  - Childhood and family dynamics (killing of half-brother Begter)

  - Unification of Mongol tribes

  - Establishment of the Pax Mongolica

  - Merit-based system replacing aristocratic hierarchy

Biblical References:

- **Saul of Tarsus / Paul the Apostle**. New Testament, 'Acts of the Apostles'. References include:

  - Education under Gamaliel

  - Persecution of early Christians

  - Stephen's martyrdom (Acts 7)

  - Damascus Road conversion (Acts 9)

  - Missionary journeys and letters

Quotations:

- **Paul the Apostle**. '2 Corinthians 5:17'. "If anyone is in Christ, the new creation has come: The old has gone, the new is here!"

- The Horseman's Way. "The greatest conqueror is he who overcomes the enemy without a blow, but sometimes the greatest service is destroying what prevents the conquest from even beginning."

Chapter 12: Incorporeal Competence

Quotations:

- **Hubbard, Elbert** (1856–1915). "Strong men can always afford to be gentle. Only the weak are intent on 'giving as good as they get.'" (American writer, publisher, artist)

- **Roosevelt, Franklin D**. (1882–1945). "Physical Strength can never permanently withstand the impact of Spiritual Force." (32nd President of the United States)

Horsemen & Natural Horsemanship:

- **Tom Dorrance** (1910–2003). American horseman, author of 'True Unity: Willing Communication Between Horse and Human' (1987). Known for the concept of "feel" and "true unity and willing communication." Developer of "Spirit-based" horsemanship.

- **Bill Dorrance** (1906–1999). Tom's older brother, master horseman and rawhide braider based at Mt. Toro Ranch, California. Known for continuous refinement and "making things better for the horse."

- **Ray Hunt** (1929–2009). Student of Tom Dorrance, traveling clinician who spread Dorrance philosophy worldwide. Author of 'Think Harmony with Horses' (1978). Known for the phrase "I'm here for the horse, to help him get a better deal."

- **Buck Brannaman** (1962–). Student of Ray Hunt and Tom Dorrance, clinician and subject of the documentary 'Buck' (2011). Continues the Dorrance/Hunt tradition.

Historical References:

- Dorrance family homestead, Enterprise, Oregon (1880s–early 1900s)

- Natural horsemanship movement (1960s–present)

- Elko, Nevada fair (c. 1960) where Ray Hunt met Tom Dorrance

General References

Conceptual Framework:

- **Golden, Dr. Myron**. Business consultant and speaker. "Be, Do, Do, Do, Have" framework referenced in Preface. (Specific publication source unknown)

The Horseman's Way:

- Original quotations and synthesis throughout the book attributed to "The Horseman's Way" represent the author's integration of horsemanship principles with leadership and personal development.

Biblical Translations

All Biblical quotations are drawn from commonly available English translations (primarily NIV - New International Version) unless otherwise noted. Biblical narratives represent interpretations of scriptural accounts for illustrative purposes.

Note on Sources

Every effort has been made to accurately attribute quotations and historical references. Some historical accounts, particularly of ancient figures like Alexander the Great, Moses, and Xenophon, are drawn from traditional historical sources that may contain legendary or interpretive elements. Where quotations are widely attributed but original sources are uncertain, they are marked as "attributed" or "source unknown."